Urban Access for the 21st

CW00521074

This book sets out a road map for the provision of urban access for all. For most of the last century cities have followed a path of dependency on car dominated urban transport favouring the middle classes. *Urban Access for the 21st Century* seeks to change this. Policies need to be more inclusive of the accessibility needs of the urban poor. Change requires redesigning the existing public finance systems that support urban mobility. The aim is to diminish their embedded biases towards automobile-based travel.

Through a series of chapters from international contributors, the book brings together expertise from different fields. It shows how small changes can incentivize large positive developments in urban transport and create truly accessible cities.

Elliott D. Sclar is Director of the Center for Sustainable Urban Development (CSUD) at Columbia University's Earth Institute. He is also Professor of Urban Planning in Columbia's Graduate School of Architecture, Planning and Preservation, an economist and an urban planner.

Måns Lönnroth is a member of the VREF, Volvo Research and Educational Foundations and the International Institute for Sustainable Development, Winnipeg, Manitoba, Canada.

Christian Wolmar is an author and journalist based in London, specializing in transport. He contributes regularly to national newspapers such as *The Times* and *The Guardian* as well as to specialist magazines.

Urban Access for the 21st Century

Finance and governance models for transport infrastructure

Edited by Elliott D. Sclar, Måns Lönnroth and Christian Wolmar

Routledge
Taylor & Francis Group

LONDON AND NEW YORK

earthscan
from Routledge

First published 2014
by Routledge
2 Park Square, Milton Park, Abingdon, Oxon, OX14 4RN

and by Routledge
711 Third Avenue, New York, NY 10017

Routledge is an imprint of the Taylor & Francis Group, an informa business

© Selection and editorial material, Elliott D. Sclar, Måns Lönnroth and Christian Wolmar; individual chapters, the contributors

British Library Cataloguing in Publication Data
A catalogue record for this book is available from the British Library

Library of Congress Cataloging-in-Publication Data
Urban access for the 21st century : finance and governance models for transport infrastructure / edited by Elliott D. Sclar, Måns Lönnroth and Christian Wolmar.
pages cm
Includes bibliographical references and index.
1. Urban transportation. 2. Urban transportation—Finance. 3. Urban transportation—Economic aspects. 4. Urban transportation policy—Developing countries. 5. Urbanization. I. Sclar, Elliott, editor of compilation. II. Lönnroth, Måns, editor of compilation. III. Wolmar, Christian, editor of compilation.
HE305.U673 2014
388.4'042—dc23
2013026288

ISBN13: 978-0-415-72047-2 (hbk)
ISBN13: 978-0-415-72049-6 (pbk)
ISBN13: 978-1-315-85749-7 (ebk)

Typeset in Sabon
by FiSH Books Ltd, Enfield

Printed and bound by CPI Group (UK) Ltd, Croydon, CR0 4YY

Contents

List of illustrations

Figures

Tables

List of contributors

Jonas Eliasson is Professor of Transport Systems Analysis at the Royal Institute of Technology (KTH) and director of the Centre for Transport Studies at KTH. His research interests include transport appraisal and cost-benefit analysis, transport demand modeling, transport pricing (in particular congestion pricing) and valuation of non-market goods (especially valuation of travel time and reliability).

Sylvie Fol is a Professor of Urban Planning at the University of Paris 1 Panthéon-Sorbonne and a member of Géographie-Cités, a Research Centre specialized in Geography and Urban Planning. Author of the book "La mobilité des pauvres" and several articles dealing with the mobility of low-income people and mobility inequalities, her research work deals also with the sociospatial effects of urban shrinkage and includes an analysis of the selective process of residential mobility that results from economic and social decline.

Caroline Gallez is researcher at the French Institute of science and technology for transport, development and networks (IFSTTAR), in the City Mobility and Transport Laboratory (LVMT). Particularly interested in the question of the policy change, in connection with changes in ideas, doctrines of action and the power relations between the public actors at the different territorial levels, she recently co-directed with Pr. Vincent Kaufmann (EPFL) a collective book devoted to the representations and practices of transport and urban planning coordination in four Swiss and French urban areas.

Måns Lönnroth, trained in applied mathematics with a graduate degree from KTH, has research interests located in the meeting point between politics, policy and science. He has been managing director of Mistra, a Swedish endowed foundation for strategic environment research, and the international vice chairman of the China Council for International Cooperation on Environment and Development. He has also been a political advisor at the Prime Minister's Office between 1985 and 1991, organizing the Swedish government's commission on HIV/AIDS, and was a state secretary at the Swedish ministry of environment during the 90s.

Rosário Macário is Professor of Transportation at the Department of Civil Engineering, Architecture and Georesources at Instituto Superior Técnico (IST) Lisbon Technical University and member of the Scientific Council of several Master and PhD courses at IST and frequent guest professor at the Faculty of Applied Economics of the University of Antwerp in Belgium. Simultaneously with her academic and corporate activity she occupies the following international positions: Vice-President of the Scientific Council of WCTRS (World Conference on Transportation Research Society), co-founder and member of the Executive Council of the PANAMSTR – Panamerican Society for Research in Transportation and Deputy Chair of the Council of the European Association of Transport (AET).

Robert E. Paaswell is a Distinguished Professor of Civil Engineering (CCNY), Director of the City University Institute for Urban Systems and Director Emeritus of the University Transportation Research Center. Paaswell is active in Public Transportation Issues and has reported on governance structures for US Transit organizations, Public–Private issues in New York and Chicago, Labor Union/Management issues, and training for new technologies.

Fred Salvucci is a Senior Lecturer and Research Associate in the Department of Civil and Environmental Engineering at the Massachusetts Institute of Technology, teaching graduate subjects on Urban Transportation Planning, and Transportation Policy and Environmental Limits. He has been a key participant in urban transportation and city planning projects in Boston, USA, and abroad, and also a leading investigator in several MIT research projects with transportation agencies, currently in London, San Sebastian (Spain), and in Boston with the Massachusetts Department of Transportation.

Elliott D. Sclar is the director of the Center for Sustainable Urban Development (CSUD) at Columbia University's Earth Institute and a professor of urban planning in Columbia's Graduate School of Architecture, Planning and Preservation. Sclar was a co-coordinator of the Task force on Improving the Lives of Slum Dwellers, one of ten task forces set up by the UN Millennium Project to aid in the implementation of the United Nation's Millennium Development Goals.

Eduardo A. Vasconcellos is a civil engineer and a sociologist who received a PhD in public policy (transport policy) from the University of Sao Paulo, Brazil. Currently technical advisor for the Brazilian Public Transport Association (ANTP), coordinator for CAF (Banco de

Desarrollo de América Latina) of the Latin American urban mobility databank and director of the Instituto Movimento in São Paulo, he is also a collaborator for the Volvo BRT Centre (Santiago) and a member of the board of the Volvo African Centre (ACET).

José M. Viegas is Full Professor of Transportation at the Civil Engineering and Architecture Department of the Instituto Superior Técnico, Technical University of Lisbon. He has invented and applied the concept of the Intermittent Bus Lane, was responsible for the 2005 Mobility Study for Lisbon, and for an OECD study on Organization and Financing of Urban Public Transport, and has been actively involved in many UITP initiatives. Since the initial presentation of his contribution to this book, he has joined the International Transport Forum (at the OECD) as Secretary General.

Christian Wolmar is an author and journalist based in London, specializing in transport. He is a frequent speaker at conferences both in Britain and abroad, and has written a series of books on railway history, including *The Subterranean Railway* (the London Underground), *Fire and Steam* (Railways in Britain) and *Blood, Iron and Gold* (the influence of railways across the world).

Acknowledgements

No volume is the singular effort of the editors and authors. That is especially true in the present case. Therefore we, the editors, want to acknowledge people who were especially critical to the completion of this effort.

The idea of looking at transport finance as a more complex input into shaping both the goal of urban transport as well as the choice of modes in shaping the ways that metropolitan life has evolved owes much to the critical thinking of the Volvo Research and Education Foundations' (VREF) first Chairman, Arne Wittlöv, now Chairman Emeritus. It was his prodding that led Måns Lönnroth and Elliott Sclar to began outlining the ideas and topics that led to the current effort. We are grateful for his intellectual leadership in this endeavor.

Ideas only move from paper to action when there are resources. For that we are grateful to the current VREF Chairman, Anders Brannstrom. It was not only his strong support for this project but also his willingness to continue support for this project and his active interest in our research and writing that matter so greatly to us. We especially thank him for his active and enthusiastic participation in our initial workshop.

We were also fortunate that VREF's Director, Henrik Nolmark, was also willing to be both an administrative support and an important intellectual contributor in shaping this endeavor. Fabienne Niklasson, the Secretary of the Foundation, ensured that all the complications that must be addressed to move such a large international project along were professionally and smoothly addressed.

At a critical moment the Rockefeller Foundation stepped in to help by generously offering us the use of their amazing Bellagio Italy conference center for that all-important initial convening of the authors and commentators. We especially thank Rockefeller Foundation Managing Director Robert Garris for guiding us through the process of using this amazing meeting space.

We are especially grateful to the distinguished group of invited commentators who greatly aided our understanding of the full depth of the challenge. These were George Banjo, Jit Bajpai, Margaret Greico-Kanbar, Shreekant Gupta, Gunnar Johansson, Eva Lerner-Lam, Ronald McQuaid and Corrine Mulley.

At the Bellagio conference where the papers that became the chapters were first vetted and discussed, we were supported by a strong team of rapporteurs from Columbia University. We thank Professor David King for leading this effort and doctoral students Danielle Petretta, Andrea Rizvi and Alexis Perrotta who ensured that our deliberations were thoughtfully monitored, reported and carefully considered. What made this team especially helpful was the fact that all of them came with professional experience in the field of urban transport.

After the work of the conference was completed, Lauren Ames Fischer, another Columbia University doctoral student, stepped in as the editorial coordinator. She took up the task of assisting us in completing the transformation of what was a set of individual background conference papers into the chapters of this volume that build upon one another.

We were also fortunate to have the support of the highly professional team at Routledge, our publisher. We are grateful that Nicki Dennis, Commissioning Editor, saw the value in this project and supported us from the beginning. Alice Aldous, Senior Editorial Assistant, has been there for us at each step along the way. Lastly, as we moved from manuscript to book, Ruth Bourne, freelance editor, stepped in to turn this into a highly polished professional product. Anyone who has ever produced a book will understand just how much we appreciate the professionalism of our publishing team.

Elliott Sclar
Måns Lönnroth
Christian Wolmar
(Editors)

Preface

This is the first time in the history of the human race that more people live in cities than rural areas. By mid century at least two out of every three people will live in urban places. If this global urbanization is to produce a better life for all, the ways in which urban transport satisfies urban needs for access is going to be absolutely critical.

Since 2000 the Volvo Research and Educational Foundations (VREF) has supported a worldwide program to address that challenge. We call it Future Urban Transport (FUT). FUT emerged from the realization that rapid urbanization and the simultaneous increase in motorization that accompanies it were on a collision course with each other. VREF asked: How could transport and urbanization be reconciled in environmentally sustainable and socially equitable ways? The technical outlines for potential solutions are often reasonably clear and easily understood. What is not well understood is how the world can go about effectively implementing the solutions. It was out of this realization that efforts such as this volume were born.

FUT-financed research and education efforts are distinctive in the ways they cross boundaries of academic disciplines and professional boundaries within the domains of government and industry. We believe that successful responses to the challenges of the 21st century require addressing the problems comprehensively in terms of their technical, social, political and historic context. We realized that we had to create forums that would bring these diverse stakeholder communities together. Within the academic sphere we sought out the usual transport scholars, typically found in engineering, economics and urban planning, along with scholars from less usually consulted disciplines. That meant seeking out sociologists, anthropologists, historians and others who investigate human behavior in the context of an urbanizing world, although not necessarily directly in transport matters. In the political domain that means finding the political decision makers and agency actors concerned with these questions. In the industrial domain that means finding the corporate executives, entrepreneurs and investors who also grapple with these questions in more applied ways.

The papers in this volume were initially produced for a workshop organized by Måns Lönnroth, a member of the VREF Board, and Elliott Sclar of Columbia University. VREF sponsored that workshop in cooperation with the Rockefeller Foundation at their Bellagio Italy conference centre in the spring of 2012. Sclar, Lönnroth and Christian Wolmar then edited the papers into the chapters of the present volume.

The purpose of the workshop was to bring together a distinguished group of international experts to assist VREF in making decisions about launching a new global initiative into the complex challenges of financing urban access. Urban access is only partly a question of urban mobility. Access in cities can also be achieved through land use, walking and bicycling. If access is the true goal and mobility merely one means, how could we reorient the financial models through which land use and transport connect with one another? The chapter writers in this volume took their mission as exploring that question from a range of vantage points. As VREF moves ahead on our consideration of financing access, we expect that we will delve more deeply into the details and encourage more interaction between practitioners and academics. We intend to disseminate the findings in publications such as this one and FUT conferences. Our goal with the publication of this volume is not to definitively answer the question. Rather it is to start a broader dialogue on ways to align the mobility needs of cities with the equally pressing needs for social equality in access and environmental sustainability.

Anders Brannstrom
Chairman of the VREF Foundations

Chapter 1

An introduction to the challenge of financing urban access

Elliott D. Sclar and Måns Lönnroth

The basic assumption behind this volume is straightforward: *Cities are about people meeting and interacting with one another*. The greater the number of meetings, the more diverse the participants and the richer the quality of the interactions, the more vibrant and productive is the city.

Ease of access is the urban quality that facilitates all the interactions and the ensuing business and personal transactions. Cities create easy access partly through crowding people together and partly through the ways they permit them to move from one place to another. Put slightly differently, the quality of urban access is determined by how well cities are able to co-locate a range of diverse activities in close proximity to one another and through the ways that their urban transport systems bring people together and then allow them to disperse in an orderly, safe and dependable fashion.

However, and this is a big however, the obvious complementarity between co-location and movement experienced by urban people is not necessarily matched by the organisational structures that determine land uses and transport options. The organisational complexity of delivering urban access has increased exponentially in recent decades as the institutions responsible for land use policy and thus location, and the institutions that govern the size and shape of transport systems, and thus mobility, have become increasingly divorced from one another. More importantly as their effective missions have diverged, they have become increasingly entrenched in single-minded pursuit of their respective aims even as these have narrowed. The result has been a fragmentation in the governance of urban access. What to the citizen should appear as a seamless whole is instead, when seen through the multi-focused lens of the several competing organizational governors, a complicated and fragmented system. The aim of this book is to start the discussion about how to overcome this fragmentation. We approach this task from the perspective of creating a better appreciation of the crucial role of finance in the governance of these critical urban institutions.

Few dispute the fact that the goal of expanding urban transport is to facilitate improved urban access. Yet growing worldwide experience demonstrates that the agencies charged with delivering urban transport increasingly tend to see the continual expansion of mobility as their sole mission. The result is the spread out and socially segregated metropolitan regions that increasingly characterize so much of the urban world. These spatially segregated regions hinder access for the urban population as a whole.

Much of today's expansion in transport infrastructure is occurring in rapidly urbanizing low- and middle-income countries. While there is a clear need for mobility enhanced access in these places, the reality is that much of what is being created is detrimental to comprehensive access. This is because much of the current growth in urban transport infrastructure is being undertaken to meet the land consuming needs of a small but admittedly growing car owning middle class, rather than the needs of the whole population. The situation has now degenerated to the point where, in many places, expanding automobile use is actually impairing the quality of the access even for this middle class – as well as inevitably for the non-car-owning social classes. The evidence can be seen in the traffic jams in places as diverse as Beijing, Nairobi, and Los Angeles.

Ease of access is what economists call a "public good", from which it is difficult to exclude anyone and the use of which by an individual does not diminish its value to others. A person's use of the city is, not only, not diminished, but is actually enhanced by ease of access to the city. Obviously there are limits but within the realm of most alternatives, the more people that have easy access the better it is for everyone else. While public goods are highly valued, they are almost invariably under-produced by private markets. One of the dilemmas associated with urban mobility is that while its ultimate product is: ease of access is a public good; the trip to bring this about has all the essential characteristics of a private good. Travel can be bought and sold in private markets. The confusion between the "access ends" and the "mobility means" for different social classes has to be confronted. If left only to the vagaries of the private market, access will be under produced especially for those with less income. The chapters of this book, written by a range of international experts, take on the various aspects of this complex dilemma. In the final analysis this is a challenge that can only be resolved as a matter of public policy and planning.

This book is the beginning of a dialogue intended to disentangle and redesign the institutional arrangements that shape urban access. This challenge can be framed in terms of politics, history, economics or culture. But there is one consistent thread that cuts across all of these and that is finance. Ultimately it is the ways in which the incentives and disincentives are built into the systems of finance for land use and transport development that determine how policies and plans evolve. Finance is at the sharp end of institutional arrangements. A greater understanding of the mechanisms of finance and a more judicious use of finance arrangements could open up possibilities for a better integration between the policies of location and mobility. But policies do not exist in a vacuum separate from the institutions that carry them out. Integration of the fragmented governance and financial structures requires first integration among the different transport modes within any single place, and, at the same time integration across the spheres that govern land use and mobility in isolation from each other. The starting point for effective change requires that we address not just policy in the abstract, but on the ground within the institutions at the same time.

In principle, the social and economic value of urban access may be well understood. In practice supporting high quality access consistently and ubiquitously has proved to be problematic. While there are always many locally-based reasons for this state of affairs, the two most important are, in the terminology of social science, demography and path dependence.

In terms of demography, most of the world's cities are under enormous population pressure. They are in the midst of an unprecedented and rapid global urban population expansion that began just after World War II. In 1950 the global population was approximately 2.5 billion people. The urban population at that time constituted about 750 million or 30 per cent. UN forecasts for 2050 place the world population in the range of 10 billion and the urban population at 7 billion or 70 per cent. Put slightly differently, while the world's total population is expected to have expanded 300 per cent, the urban portion of that population is expected to have exploded, increasing over 800 per cent in that same 100 years. The main loci of this expanding urbanization are in the world's low- and middle-income countries. The cities in sub-Saharan Africa and Southeast Asia are growing the fastest. Here, the principal story is that population growth is running well ahead of the development of all forms of urban infrastructure, including transport, needed to support the expanded number of people living at high densities. All the promise of urban access will not be realised if these spatial and physical conditions are not ameliorated.

The rapidly growing cities in Asia and Africa are repeating the same pattern of response to urban growth that cities in other parts of the world followed decades ago. Urbanization has by and large run its course in OECD countries and Latin America, giving city authorities some breathing space to catch up and strike a reasonable balance between the needs for access of different social classes. The mobility concerns in those cities are now within the existing urban populations rather than meeting the needs of a large influx from rural areas. Many large cities – from New York City to Stockholm – continue to attract people at rates that hover around population replacement rates (deaths minus births). Other, smaller cities may in fact stagnate. Many cities experience gentrification in the center, pushing low-income households out to the low-access periphery where housing costs are less but transport costs accordingly higher. In high-income cities, an overreliance on automobile-based mobility contributes significantly to traffic congestion, pollution and climate change as well as increased segregation between social classes leading to the gradual erosion of social and even economic stability.

While demographic shifts have established the basis of the present state of thinking about urban mobility and access, it is the nature of path dependency that is the biggest obstacle to a paradigm shift. Path dependence means that today's choices are constrained by those made in the past. The path taken constrains the future by closing out alternative options. For much of the twentieth century the main path has been determined by the ingrained financial arrangements whose effect – intended or unintended – has been to subsidize greater reliance on automobile-based urban mobility. The promise of individual freedom to come and go unconstrained by travel schedules or public transport routes was a powerful attraction for the emerging middle classes after the Second World War in Europe, North America and Oceania. However, with the benefit of 20/20 hindsight, it is obvious that the increased freedom for one social group led to decreased freedom for another group. As automobile-based mobility increased, the ridership of public transport decreased, services were cut back, prices increased and the less well-off became even poorer due to the loss of cheap, accessible transport.

Moreover, the expanding road networks to accommodate this expanding middle class of auto users tended to be built right through the areas that were home to the relatively deprived classes, where land prices were lower and political opposition to displacement less articulated. Once societies embarked on this path, highway agencies and finance models to sustain it soon followed and became embedded in the institutional arrangements that came to define transport development. Institutional re-arrangement is therefore key in designing a new path. It is never easy for society to move from one path to another. But that does not mean it is impossible. Even small changes in the way that agencies responsible for land use and transport are incentivized can have major cumulative impacts over time. Indeed history is replete with examples of small changes in one place that quickly led to larger ones everywhere else. Consider the ways in which small software companies quickly revolutionized the larger field of information technology. While path change in the private economy can be random and serendipitous, path change in terms of public policy is always deliberate. A powerful belief motivating the production of this book is that we now know enough about urban development to understand that a less mobility-based and especially a less automobility-based policy is a precondition for the improvement of urban life.

The path dependence of the high-income countries is now tragically being replicated in the rapidly urbanizing lower income nations of Asia and sub Saharan Africa where the vast majority of urban residents neither own nor drive cars. The emphasis on accommodating the cars of the more affluent few results in constraining access for the less affluent majority, to say nothing of the harmful environmental impacts.

Moving to a new path that systematically improves access for all has to start with the recognition that the present trend is embedded and manifest in the financial models that underwrite the institutions that govern contemporary urban land use and transport.

These various institutions are public as well as private. They include those that control the housing markets for different social groups, those which govern the development of different types of commercial property and which determine the different modes of urban transport.

A great deal is known about the types of land use patterns, urban designs and transport options that can address the concerns raised by the need for better accessibility such as how to develop great metros, sound bus rapid transit systems, safe non-motorized transport and attractive walkable cities. Much is understood about how these modal options and land use choices can help create a more environmentally sustainable and socially equitable urban region. The major obstacle to bringing about this transformation results less from a question of what to do and more from a question of how to get it done and in particular the challenge of overcoming current path dependence.

The path through which our cities have evolved is to a large degree shaped by a series of organizational and political silos. "Organizational and political silos" is a metaphorical reference to describe administrative units or political institutions that act in ways counter to creating more accessible cities. This dysfunction typically takes the form of agencies and organizations working in the same traditional way expected by their political masters even as the needs of the larger social mission require them to change. To a very large extent the presence of organizational and political silos characterizes the way in which urban transport and land use regulation functions in cities around the world.

How can policy and planning alter the current trajectory? Once it is recognized that access is a public good, it is changes to the political-economics and finance structures that are needed. We recognize that to speak knowledgeably of political economy and finance requires that we address the broad panoply of social concerns that define modern urban life, and that is the goal of this volume. We seek to put the broader social and environmental challenges into a political economic context from which it is possible to draw effective policy and planning options. "Effective" here means workable solutions as distinct from theoretically elegant ones that would have little hope of political viability.

The confusion between access as a public good and transport as a private good lies at the heart of managing this context. Two situations illustrate this.

First, the methods commonly used in appraising additional transport capacity do not distinguish between different social groups. It is common in trip generation models to take land use as "given" and individual trips are then seen as market responses to costs and opportunities. The travel time saved by a person with the freedom to choose where to live has the same weight as the travel time saved by the person with much more constrained choice of where to live, despite the fact that the economic opportunities opened up by travel time savings by the latter may be greater. If the emphasis were to be put on access to economic opportunities rather than simply travel time saved, the low-income households would carry a heavier weight in the overall appraisal.

Second, the principles of financing public transport also illustrate the fallacy of looking at transport as a market for private services, which leads to the assumption that it is only natural to state that each traveler should pay for his or her trip and that each mode should cover its costs. Thus, the corollary of this type of thinking is that public transport should essentially be paid for through the fare box and only as a last resort be subsidized by taxes. The result of such thinking can be seen in the badly congested streets and roads of the rapidly urbanizing cities of sub-Saharan Africa and Southeast Asia. In these places informal public transport providers compete fiercely with one another for scarce street space and passengers, resulting in a situation where everyone can only move very slowly or not at all.

When urban access is seen as a public good, however, the principles of financing public transport change. First, the services provided have to be of sufficient quality to ensure that travelers with choices opt for the public mode.

A public transport system of this quality also has benefits for agents other than the travelers that ought to be included in the raising of revenues for infrastructure investment and service provision. It will certainly influence property values, and therefore it is logical to raise parts of the revenues from the property market. It will also influence the access for people who do not travel by public transport, since the road congestion would be reduced making it logical to raise revenues from these beneficiaries.

These two situations demonstrate the powerful ways that the financial system that supports urban access needs to better recognize the multiplicity of ways that it adds value to urban life. Mobility and co-location have to be seen as an interdependent and intermodal whole. The reality that has to be addressed is that urban transport is financed through modal-based silos. It is also important to understand the financial impact of the divorce between the regulation of urban land use and the structure of choices for urban mobility, the everyday reality faced by every metropolitan area in the world. Ultimately it is the locational value of access created by urban mobility that must be enlisted to sustain the transport systems that make it possible.

Each of the chapters in this book leads the reader through our proposal for restructuring the ways in which urban transport and urban land use are financed.

Chapter 2: Towards a political-economics of finance for urban access

This chapter sets out the complex political-economic and planning context in which the challenge of creating an innovative approach to financing urban access is taking place. It points out that any successful resolution needs to addresses issues of equity, efficiency and environmental sustainability simultaneously. As a result of the long-established and mistaken conflation of mobility with access that characterized the closing decades of the twentieth century, the alternatives of co-location, including pedestrian access and non-motorized transport options, were reduced to, at best, a minor supporting role in the urban planning and urban policy process. What emerged as the twentieth century drew to a close was a range of urban spatial plans and policies in which the solution to urban access problems was reduced to ever more strident calls for more largely automobile-based urban mobility. A hopeful sign that things are now reversing has been a renewed interest in public transport-based mobility in recent years. Nonetheless to the extent that the vision of policy makers has not fully shifted to embrace the complete range of options for enhancing access, we still have some distance to go (a rather unfortunate simile).

Chapter 3: Social inequalities in urban access: better ways of assessing transport improvements

In the field of transport studies, research on urban access generally deals with this notion in a narrow sense. Most of the time the issue of access is analysed in terms of transportation network performance, using economic models that were designed to assess infrastructure efficiency. This chapter argues that the social characteristics of space and of individuals, along with the provision of urban amenities in a given urban environment, are also essential elements in the complex notion of urban access. Therefore, urban access should be analysed not only in terms of transportation networks but also from the perspectives of spaces and individuals. By rejecting a narrow definition of urban access, this chapter seeks to broaden thinking on measuring social access inequalities and their implications for public policy. The chapter then proceeds to examine policies implemented to improve accessibility, focusing on those policies that emphasize the social dimension of urban access, and offering a critical review of the models and indicators used to assess transportation investments and policies.

Chapter 4: Access as a social good and as an economic good: is there a need for a paradigm shift?

From an economic perspective accessibility has been mostly measured on the basis of direct costs from the users' and suppliers' perspective, and total costs (including indirect and non-market costs) from society's perspective. On the benefit side the key concept has been travel timesaving, which is quantified and valued for the purpose of social appraisal. This has contributed to the shift of transport policy away from the concept of access, the main purpose of transport, to provide access solely to desired destinations. This chapter argues that the economic valuation of accessibility, in the light of public and private provision of goods and services, should be considered as an implicit funding and financing mechanism of urban mobility systems. The goal should be to reposition transport as an urban utility, just like electricity, water and sewage. Furthermore the chapter suggests ways to transform this strategic formulation into the tactical and operational levels necessary to make the accessibility concept effective in the political analysis of the benefits of investment in access.

Chapter 5: Opportunities for transport financing through new technologies: state of the art and research needs

This chapter explores the potential for technological developments to increase funding opportunities for urban transport systems, without distorting the services they provide to users. Efficient transport pricing is difficult for a variety of reasons, many of which are caused by the technical difficulties of differentiating transport prices with respect to time, place or quality of service. The chapter summarizes technical developments and discusses how these could enable more efficient forms of transport pricing and financing to be created.

Chapter 6: Assessing the diversity of schemes for financing urban access and mobility in preparation for a comparative study

The need for a solid and stable financing framework of urban mobility is critical at this time; a time in which the growth of cities and the increasing levels of car ownership require a brave response from public transport providers to increase market share, especially as an ageing population means there is competition for public funds that would traditionally have been available for public transport. This chapter seeks to provide a framework for the analysis of the options and is the preparation for the launch of a comparative study of schemes of financing of urban mobility across the world.

Chapter 7: Public transport: the challenge of formal and informal systems[1]

This chapter provides a background to the discussion of proposals to better organize and finance public transport in developing countries. It is based on the fact that current conditions are often inadequate, with unreliable, uncomfortable, expensive and unsafe services. The problem is becoming worse with the recent rapid increase in private motorization with motorcycles and, later, cars. One key aspect considered in the chapter is the transition from an informal system to a more formalized one. An important related question is how efficiency and effectiveness of public transport systems could be improved through public policy.

Chapter 8: Reflections on the usefulness of accessibility as a lens through which to consider the evaluation of transportation and land use policies and projects

This chapter discusses the institutional context, particularly within the United States, for developing accessibility concepts as a lens through which to evaluate transportation and land use. It argues that economy, equity and environmental crises all require both institutional changes and major and sustained investment, particularly in transit infrastructure and services over the next decades in order to achieve outcomes consistent with triple bottom line sustainability. It proposes that research on accessibility measurement is needed to choose the most convincing approaches to support the case for this policy and institutional change and investment program, and to support decision making with appropriate evaluation techniques in order to stay on course. While the focus is on the US institutional context, it suggests that a similar approach of analysing existing context and hypothesizing a new policy and institutional structure together with very significant and sustained investment will likely be appropriate to support achieving triple bottom line sustainable transportation and land use in Europe and the rapidly-developing countries in Asia, Latin America, and Africa.

Chapter 9: Accessibility and transportation funding

This chapter explores the idea of using value capture techniques to support transport investment, and suggests there may be dangers with an over reliance on this technique, arguing that the most important characteristic of a funding mechanism is its adequacy and stability. It briefly discusses the most frequently suggested mechanisms, and recommends in particular consideration of parking access fees and carbon taxes on petroleum excise taxes that are designed to impact the companies' windfall profits, rather than the transportation users. It also recommends the exploration of an institutional structure similar to the old electric utility model, subject to public oversight.

10   Elliott D. Sclar and Måns Lönnroth

Chapter 10: Technology and information technology: living with and paying for sustainable access

How does modern information technology (IT) impact on urban access? We are in the very early stages of an IT revolution, the ramifications of which will profoundly reshape the spatial relations between mobility and co-location. In so doing they will reshape the meaning of urban access. In this chapter the implications of this change for urban access are explored.

The ramifications of the IT revolution include a powerful impact on urban spatial form given that urban transportation is always a technologically determined service. What has been a greater technological shift in the transport paradigm than the advent of mass production of the automobile? The chapter explores the importance of IT to the quality of urban access. Its value stems from its ability to provide real time data instantly to transport suppliers and travelers. The availability of smartphones and tablets has also created a cultural shift in how users see and achieve activities. Much of this shift is generational – age dependent – and is having an emerging, but powerful influence on how transportation is supplied as well as how urban areas look and function.

Chapter 11: Conclusions: the end of the paradigm

Note

1   Several concepts of this text were taken from Vasconcellos, 2001, *Urban Transport, Environment and Equity: the case for developing countries,* Earthscan.

Chapter 2

Towards a political-economics of finance for urban access

Elliott D. Sclar

2.1 Introduction

2.1.1 Jacobs and Moses: a tale of two urbanisms

The 1960s civic battles between Robert Moses and Jane Jacobs that in part shaped New York City's current spatial landscape have become the stuff of legend. In the literature that followed (Alexiou, 2006, Flint, 2009) the general story line is cast as a vulnerable David (Jacobs) felling an invincible Goliath (Moses). The *pièce de résistance* about their decade long clashes is the battle over the proposed Lower Manhattan Expressway, a ten-lane elevated highway across Manhattan Island. Moses staunchly championed its construction and Jacobs as staunchly opposed it. Had Moses prevailed, the nation's interstate highway system would have cut a swathe through the heart of New York City's central business district destroying SoHo and most likely Tribeca, the "global city" neighborhoods of modern New York. The accounting of this epic battle endures in part because of the timelessness of its David vs. Goliath theme; a fight between a band of politically weak community activists defending their home turf from a politically powerful city planner's bulldozer. Moses saw his mission as one of transforming an older industrial city that grew up around railroads and ports into a new one prepared for the challenges that post World War II automobile based urbanization would pose (Ballon and Jackson, 2007).

Because the protagonists were also exceptionally articulate and prolific advocates for their points-of-view (see for example Jacobs, 1961 and Moses, 1970) the documentation of that story is both rich and well preserved. But it also endures for a reason beyond this eternal theme; it is a clear exemplar of the competing visions of modern urban life. For Jacobs, the important value to be defended was the social benefit of density. For Moses the challenge was overcoming the high social costs of the crowded slums and traffic congestion that this density created.

So framed, the clash becomes, as a matter of transport policy, a case study of the costs and benefits of creating urban access through co-location or through expanded urban mobility. The former implies higher density, mixed use neighborhoods and compact urban forms, while the latter envisions a spatially broader metropolitan region with lower living densities and more specialized and segregated land use patterns. In the rapidly expanding metropolises that characterize contemporary global urbanization the practical challenge that local officials and residents face is the same one that Jacobs and Moses confronted: how to enhance the value of urban life? Its value derives directly from its ability to create access through the density of co-location and yet mitigate the human and vehicular congestion that is the inevitable by-product of rising density via the deployment of mobility options to connect to a larger region.

The solution to the Moses–Jacobs dichotomy is rooted in better understanding the complex ways that the social and political institutions that govern land uses and organize urban mobility are divorced from one another and are, themselves, internally fragmented. The solutions that ultimately emerge will not be the either/or types that the protagonists whose names are attached to this dichotomy envisioned. The reality of urban life as it has evolved in the half-century since then is that to produce the enhanced access that is both socially equitable and environmentally sustainable requires a complex blend of both more co-location and more mobility. Specific solutions, borne of local needs and constraints will vary greatly. The generic problem that confronts all of the world's cities concerns the role of public and private finance in structuring positive solutions to the co-location–mobility challenge. But finance is neither an isolated nor purely technical issue. Rather the ways in which it operates reflect deeply embedded values in the institutions that govern land use and urban mobility.

As we face the issue of improving access through a better balance of co-location and mobility, we find ourselves in a tough situation, trapped by our past choices. The existing structure of financial incentives within which we must work to effect change is rooted in an older set of urban values and sensibilities. We are, in effect, confronting twenty-first century urban challenges, including climate change and rising energy costs, with tools rooted in the values and beliefs that extend back as far as the first industrial cities of the nineteenth century. If we are to be effective in creating meaningful improvement we must better understand the strengths and limits of the policy tools with which we work. Any attempt to address the environmental and social challenges of twenty-first century urban life has to first address the embedded institutional and financial incentives and disincentives that constrain our present options. This is not a simple task because these options are physically embedded in both the existing spatial character of the world's cities as well as in the institutions of governance as they have evolved.

2.1.2 The quality of urban access and the evolution of urban transport policy

As a tangible geographic quality, urban access is the ease (how fast, inexpensive, and comfortable) with which the friction of distance is overcome for individuals seeking to engage in necessary or desired activities (Couclelis, 2000). A city is a set of physical locational arrangements intended to minimize distance among diverse activities. It is thus a solution to the geographic problem of access. For many authors it is precisely this geographic quality that has made possible all the innovations in production and distribution that have raised living standards wherever urbanization has occurred (Glaeser, 2011, Schaeffer and Sclar, 1980, Jacobs, 1969).

Urban access, because it enhances physical proximity among people from all social walks of life, is an important catalytic element in a globalized world. Diverse populations living within the confines of urbanized regions develop modes of social interaction and tolerance across divisions of race, ethnicity, class, gender and age. This diversity in turn is the source of the continual innovation that we associate with urban life (Sennett, 1970). Conversely urban settlements unable to achieve a successful social *modus vivendi* tend to stagnate and shrink. Put slightly differently, a vibrant culture of urbanism is a critical factor in the success of a global economy and it is a product of good urban access.

Despite the fact that the social and economic value of urban access has long been accepted as a valid proposition in the academic literature (Hansen, 1959), it has not significantly shaped the practical approach to urban transport policy as it has evolved over the last half century. Instead over the course of the late twentieth century, urban access became ever more tied to the singular policy aim of expanding mobility options. While co-location was always accepted as valuable, the mission of improving urban access became ever more singularly focused on options for expanded mobility. For all intents and policy purposes mobility and access became conflated.

This conflation was not irrational in the initial phases of modern urbanization when population densities in tightly packed slums and comparatively small city centers were reaching intolerable numbers. An important response to this was technological; the development of rail-based and mechanically powered trams and, later, metros. Those rail-based modes provided real options for more healthful living in easy commuting distance of the urban employment locations in the older city centers (Warner, 1962, Schaeffer and Sclar, 1980). One result of this positive initial experience was that every transport enhancement that promised even more improvements in terms of travel speed in overcoming geographic distance came to be seen as desirable as less time spent in transit would mean more time for both work and leisure. The problems with this formulation only became apparent as the automobile came to dominate rail-based transit modes. That transformation, which began in the 1920s, was virtually complete by mid century. From 1950 onwards, for all intents and purposes, automobile-based travel was assumed to be the way in which urban development was to proceed.

As a technical matter this presumption of the superiority of expanded automobile travel as the way to sustain urban access became a presumption of transport planning. It became enshrined in the cost–benefit analyses used to justify large, road-based infrastructure projects. A recent study reported that over 80 percent of the "benefits" used to justify more mobility was timesaving (Metz, 2008). From a dynamic and evolutionary vantage point this approach was effectively applied static analysis. That is to say the approach ignores or heavily discounts the longer-term, second order impacts of the decision, specifically the subsequent and induced impacts of expanded mobility options on urban spatial form, urban trip generation and the physical environment. In technical terms, this policy decision-making process is one that is effectively organized around maximizing the discounted present value of travel time saved, assuming all else remains equal.

As a result of this grand conflation the alternatives of co-location including pedestrian access and non-motorized transport options were reduced to, at best, a minor supporting role. What emerged as the twentieth century drew to a close was a range of urban spatial plans and policies in which the solution to urban access problems was reduced to ever more strident calls for more largely automobile based urban mobility. In the 1960s, Jane Jacobs and a few others saw the implications of this, but they were a handful against a larger, conventional wisdom held by the many that automobiles were the future of urban life. As the century drew to a close, the full social and economic costs of this grand conflation became apparent to an ever-widening circle of experts and citizens. A hopeful sign that things are now reversing has been a renewed interest in public transport-based mobility in recent years. Nonetheless to the extent that the vision of policy makers has not fully shifted to embrace the complete range of options for enhancing access, we still have some distance to go.

2.1.3 Auto dependence and the challenge of access

The challenge we face as the urban age of the automobile enters its second century can be characterized as too much of a good thing. The current almost universal adoption of the automobile as a primary mode of urban transport is a classic instance of path dependency[1]. However, it is becoming clear that as we move from a planet of approximately 7 billion people to one that around mid century will be inhabited by between 9 or 10 billion people, the projected path forward needs to be significantly modified. For starters we need to disentangle the too-frequent conflation of automobile-based mobility with urban access. It is not only environmentally unsustainable, but even in terms of its initial goal, enhanced urban access, it is leading to a situation, as a result of traffic congestion alone, of diminution of access.

As a matter of path dependency it is easy to understand how we arrived at the present situation. Consider the case of Robert Moses and New York once more. Moses' work in the decades before World War II, when he created parks, beach access and parkways via improved automobile access, greatly enhanced the quality of urban life in the dense city where he served as chief planner. It was only in the decades after 1960, through his desire to further retrofit the city to the spatial needs of even more automobiles, that the costs of this path dependency became readily apparent.

Jacobs was initially something of a lone voice in opposition to this notion. It was only when the accumulation of motor vehicles in cities began to require conurbations to begin physically consuming their land areas to accommodate the voracious spatial needs of cars that the pressure to change course became broadly self-evident in cities everywhere. This need to change became more urgent as time went on because changes in the global macro economy and physical environment further rendered an urbanism based on sprawl even less tenable. In terms of macroeconomics, the energy demands of newly industrializing nations have ended the era of inexpensive energy. We can no longer support urban spatial forms around the assumption that there is a plentiful supply of low-cost power to sustain low-density patterns of metropolitan sprawl. The good news on this score is that this altered energy cost calculus is creating incentives to find alternative solutions that are more efficient in the use of energy.

In terms of the physical environment, sustainability is now a watchword across a range of urban policies. The environment can no longer absorb all the waste products of today's urban lifestyle. Transport is a particular focus of sustainability concerns because it is a major source of greenhouse gas emissions. The constraints of these new economic and environmental realities combined with a concern over rising numbers of traffic injuries and deaths explain much of the current renewed interest in the writings of Jacobs, Glaeser and others on the importance of urban co-location in the creation of urban access.

The challenge then is to begin weaning an urbanizing world off of its dependence on automobile-based mobility as a prime approach to the creation of urban access in an increasingly globalized world. In a world where automobile ownership is the privilege of a comparative minority, removing urban land from other uses to create space consuming metropolitan locational patterns suited to automobile-based travel inevitably exacerbates social inequality.

Despite this accumulating evidence, the power of a path dependence

characterized by automobile-based expansion abides. If this situation does
not change, the outlook for the future is not promising. Data on the relationship between rising income levels and rising rates of automobile
ownership suggest a strong positive correlation. A recent World Bank report
estimated that for every 1 per cent increase in average disposable income,
automobile ownership in Chinese cities is expected to increase by 1.8 per
cent (see Table 2.1).

Figure 2.1 illustrates the same relationship globally by comparing the per
capita income and the number of registered vehicles in 166 countries.
Looked at alone it suggests a weak relationship between income levels and
auto ownership. Most important however is the fact that at the low end of
the income scale the relationship is strong. At higher income levels it weakens significantly because equal sums of money take on different social
meanings at different income levels. To understand this, consider Figure 2.2.

Figure 2.2 uses data similar to that in Figure 2.1, though not with the
exact set of countries. It suggests a far stronger relationship between rising
global incomes and auto ownership. By casting the relationship in logarith-
mic rather than absolute terms, we are able to look at the same relationship
proportionally. To understand what this shows, consider that a $1000
increase in income in high income countries would have little to no impact
on auto ownership rates, but a $1000 in a low income nation would be
proportionately far greater. As with the World Bank data on Chinese cities
(Table 2.1), the data in Figure 2.2 for the world as a whole demonstrates a
similar, strong relationship between income growth and auto ownership
expansion. While in China a 1 per cent rise in income is associated with an
almost 2 per cent increase in auto ownership, globally the relationship is
somewhat weaker: for every 1 per cent rise in GNI per capita, there is a

Table 2.1 Income elasticity of automobile ownership, selected Chinese cities

City	Year	Income elasticity
Weihai	2001–2006	2.7
Zhengzhou	2005–2006	2.4
Shanghai	2005–2006	2.2
Urumqi	2001–2006	1.9
Xi'an	2002–2006	1.8
Jinan	2002–2006	1.6
Guangzhou	2003–2006	1.5
Luoyang	2001–2005	1.5
Beijing	2003–2006	0.7
Simple average		1.8

Note: Based on average disposable income.
Source: Darido and Mehndiratta, 2009

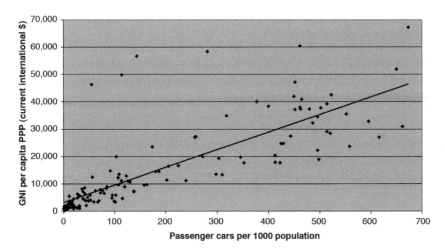

Figure 2.1 Automobile ownership as a function of national income (2006–2008)

Notes: Latest available data (2006–2008) for 141 countries (accounting for 91.7 per cent of the world's population). GNI PPP = gross national income at purchasing power parities.

Source: Based on World Bank data, http://data.worldbank.org/, accessed 27 October 2011

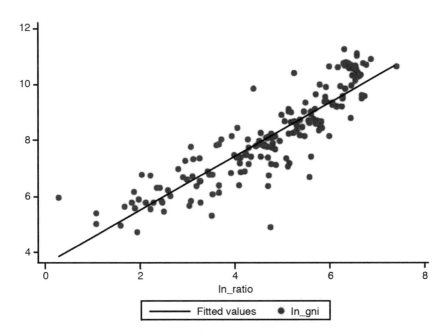

Figure 2.2 Log–log regression of GNI and auto registrations 2009[2]

corresponding 0.8 per cent rise in the ratio of vehicles to population. The regression model that produced the straight line has an R-squared of 0.7834. This means that approximately 80 per cent of the increase in automobile ownership is "explained" by increases in per capita national income. A simulation I performed on the lowest income countries in that data set using that 0.8 per cent estimate revealed that if we assumed population growth of 3 per cent (not unreasonable) and real income growth of 1 per cent (conservative estimate) and ran the data out 10 years, we would find that population had grown 36 per cent, income just over 10 per cent and auto ownership would have expanded by 46 per cent. To look at it another way, the increase in auto ownership would have outpaced the increase in population by almost 28 per cent. Thus even in the world's lowest income countries, if policies remain unchanged, motor vehicle usage would outstrip both population growth and income growth. The proviso here is the assumption that nothing else changed.

Without active efforts to improve both the quality and quantity of public transport, the world's cities will find themselves under ever-greater pressure to accommodate automobile-centered urban transport with its insatiable demand for increasing amounts of road and parking space. One simple explanation for this is that given the contemporary state of urban public transport in the world's low- and middle-income countries, private automobile use is almost universally considered to be the superior alternative whenever people can afford the choice. Only when the travel times of public transport equal to or less than those of private cars do people opt for it (See Crozet, 2006). Where both are poor, as is the case in most cities in developing countries, automobile travel is preferred as it is seen as a far more comfortable and safer way to wait out congested travel times. On the other hand, in parts of Europe and high-income cities in Asia such as Hong Kong (Cervero and Murakami, 2008) and Singapore, high quality public transport outperforms automobile travel for routine activities.

2.2 The access-finance nexus

The experience of cities such as Hong Kong and Singapore suggests the obvious direction of change. In both cases the underlying financial models capture a portion of the access value transit creates to support the high quality service that it generates. More specifically, in both of these cases, the models capture part of the increase in social value via the portion reflected in the real estate profits generated by transit access. These revenues in turn are used to financially support the public transport system. Without such seamless financing mechanisms, it is difficult to create environmentally and socially sustainable urban transport networks because transport services are forced to compete for funds with other governmental priorities. Sometimes these services do well but too often they fare poorly when weighed against other pressing needs for public money. Relying on appropriations from general public revenue sources is not a sufficiently sustainable foundation for a public good as vital to modern urban life as transport. This is in part the case because its full value is not widely recognized.

Although public transport must be a principal focus of any successful financial scheme to support urban access, it is important to bear in mind that access is a multifaceted phenomenon. Any successful system must be designed to recognize and appreciate the complex interconnections among all modes of urban transport and patterns of urban land use. Transport infrastructure is networked, and, with the exception of segregated rail-based systems, is shared by other modes. Hence we need to move away from present financial models rooted in modally specific forms of organization and support. To succeed in this challenge it is necessary to understand and appreciate the current system with all its differentials in support among modes. These differentials, reflective as they are of past values and choices, are visible in the current imbalances in travel patterns and modal splits. To recognize that significant differentials exist is not to imply that future expenditures across modal options should strive for equality. Rather an understanding of the extent of these helps to make clear the nature and extent of the local challenges we face in designing new integrative institutional and financial models for improved urban access.

Whether by active decision or passive default, investment choices will be made given the population pressures that so many of the world's cities find themselves under. These choices will inevitably favor one mode over another. The challenge in terms of enhanced access is to create a financial system that addresses the need for a comprehensive urban transportation system that underpins efficiently accessible urban development patterns. In many cases this means supporting transport options that compliment mixed use and higher density land use patterns. The key to success requires designing an investment decision-making process that addresses the organizational and individual behavioral incentives and disincentives built into the existing finance system. Only when the operation of the existing system is well understood will it be possible to contextualize the ways that the various modes can be integrated within a "seamless" new financing system based on prioritizing access.

It is useful to think of modal choices in hierarchical terms according to sustainability. Public transport occupies the mid point on this scale between co-location and pedestrian travel and non-motorized travel on one side and private automobile use on the other. Starting from public transport as a fulcrum, it becomes possible to grasp the broader implications for land use and trip generation and all modal options. That means setting a series of investments in motion that favour public transport over the private car. Such a prioritization will also need to privilege "walkable" and "bikeable" urban spaces over ones that are more dependent on motorized transport.

To assess the options for sustainable financial economics, it is necessary to appreciate the role of transport in the functioning of an urban economy. The next step is to develop an understanding of the system of incentives and disincentives built into current finance methods. From there it becomes possible to propose policies and plans that permit urban transport to contribute to the realization of socially and environmentally sustainable cities.

Although there is a certain intuitive attractiveness to this, past experience suggests that achieving success on this score is hard. Success requires that there be an alignment between the urban transport planning models we use and finance models intended to support the new system. Yet as Martin Wachs observed in passing, over a decade ago, we "ignore the significance of financing in bringing about the desired behavior, the desired effect on urban form. We concentrate solely on building the system, on its physical characteristics."[3] In this chapter I seek to examine the issues that need to be addressed in order to better align the mechanisms of transport finance with system planning aimed at enhanced access.

2.3 The dual nature of urban transport: a public and private good

The first step in aligning finance and physical characteristics is understanding and disentangling the fundamentally dualistic nature of the product itself, urban transport. As an economic good it is simultaneously a private and a public good.[4] This dualistic nature is the source of some of the policy confusions that lead to the disjuncture between finance and physical planning. Its private good characteristics, called excludability and rivalrous consumption by economists,[5] are constantly on display in the daily market transactions for urban transportation services. There is a vast array of buyers seeking to be transported and willing to pay for the service. At the same time there are numerous public and private sellers of urban mobility services prepared to meet the demand. In that sense urban transport can be conceived as an ordinary private good that responds to the laws of supply and demand as described in every introductory economics textbook. However, unlike the typical goods that these textbook writers have in mind, more time spent in travel does not increase buyer satisfaction the way say two beers might make one happier than one. The problem lies in the nature of the product itself. Travelers rarely, if ever, value the purchased ride as a desired end. Economists label the demand for mobility a "derived demand", a demand that originates in the desire for something else. In the present case the desired good is access. Unlike a refreshing glass of beer, most travelers would prefer less rather than more time to be spent in transit.

The nature of the derived demand for transport is further complicated by the fact that the benefits it creates affect not only the traveler who bears the cost in both money and time, but also to those whom the traveler interacts with during the journey. Economists label these added benefits as "external benefits". They are external in the sense that they are not accounted for in the transaction for the transport service. Because these benefits relate to physical access they become manifest in differential prices for goods and services exchanged at locations where, as a result of some combination of mixed land use and the intersection of transport routes, a significant density of people, businesses and residencies accumulates. It is the physical aggregation of these external benefits in urban places that transforms these external benefits into public goods. The more people and activities that can be reached at a given location, the more valuable is access to that location for any given individual interchange, up to some point of overwhelming congestion of course. Unlike private goods, the value of which are enhanced by exclusion, the value of the public good access is improved by its opposite, inclusion. The more people and activity that can access a given urban location the more desirable it becomes. In that sense locational value meets the public goods test of non-rivalrous[6] consumption. Further because it is by definition a public space, it is by and large non-excludable, a major facet of its attractiveness.

The agglomerative value of access that derives from urban transport is an important public good because it is greater than the sum of the individual value that it creates merely for the travelers. This "scalable" quality results from collective and multi-purpose interactions permitted by the ease of access created for people and activity in such urban places. Hence from a policy standpoint, as we attempt to align the mechanisms of transport finance with system planning in furtherance of enhanced access, the public goods aspect of urban transport must be our primary concern and its private goods aspect secondary.

To understand the importance of approaching urban transport policy as principally a public good, consider the alternative: treating its private goods characteristics as principal. In that case the policy goal would be the promotion of market competitiveness among transport suppliers and consequently the removal of all barriers to entry into the market for services. To the extent that such competitive markets are presumed to be self-regulating and guided by price and efficiency, our ultimate policy goal would be *laissez faire*. We would seek to have the suppliers competing head-to-head with one another to satisfy the travel demands of their customers. Given the practical problems of limited street space and production costs in relation to market prices, studies consistently demonstrate that the result of this approach is almost invariably poor quality services for the majority of urban residents with heavy traffic congestion and long travel times, and even systems regulated by organized criminals, high rates of pedestrian and vehicular fatalities, and air pollution around streets and highways. Taken together these results create the very opposite of enhanced and improved urban access. The proper approach therefore must be to make the public goods aspect of the service primary but to the extent possible the private market aspects should be leveraged to promote the larger end. Nonetheless policy making in this area has demonstrated an ongoing ambivalence in which policy makers move back and forth between a private goods first/public goods first approach to the challenge.

The experience of the World Bank in recent years is illustrative of the problems that this ambivalence can create. In 1986 the Bank produced a major strategy paper simply titled "Urban Transport". It typified the private good approach to transport reflective of that era's neo-liberal conventional wisdom. The report opposed operating subsidies and questioned the wisdom of infrastructure projects that could not recover costs through user charges. This was especially the case for projects targeted at aiding poor people. Its preferred solution for the problems of operating deficits was strong competition and minimal public regulation. If the services failed in the market, they were clearly not needed. By the turn of the century, the internal World Bank fervor for neo-liberalism had abated somewhat. The Bank modestly acknowledged "the context has changed in some significant respects since 1986".[7] The notion that urban transport is primarily a public good is increasingly accepted as the starting point for policy recommendations, though this has not yet been taken into meaningful discussions about the detail of service organizations that are needed for this to be effective. Instead policy remains stuck at a more abstract level concerned with the "proper" balance between private market suppliers and public sector regulators or suppliers in creating "efficient" public goods.

While the World Bank has, commendably, begun to change its policy, it is but one actor. Revenue-starved national, regional and local governments almost automatically continue to push hard for urban transport policies rooted in the belief that it is mainly a private good and that it is possible to attain something close to full cost recovery via user charges. This is an example of the triumph of an ideological faith over actual experience as the result is almost invariably the same: attempts to raise fares to cover costs result in lost ridership and revenues. Lost in this narrow casting of the issue is the complex nature of urban transport. Urban transport is not a unified systemic whole. Instead it is a series of organizational silos defined by local modal systems. Rises in the cost of one mode have repercussions on the others as well as on patterns of land use. The lesson here is that we need to approach this issue via systems thinking that goes beyond simple supply and demand, partial-equilibrium analysis of the microeconomics of individual travel modes. Instead we need to deploy a dynamic model of urban development that takes into account the interactive and longer-term land use and environmental impacts. Urban regions are not tending towards "equilibrium", in the sense that economists use this term. Urban regions are ever changing spaces that require understanding in the context of analytic models that fully account for the dynamics between spatial form and transport modes over time.

Taking the issue up a notch, we need to model the relationship between enhanced urban access, increased GDP, and greater availability of resources to sustain investment in improved access. In theory at least improved access leads to increased GDP that in turn should lead to the availability of more resources for investment in access. To the extent that this is correct, the problem, as we shall see below, is one of designing comprehensive systems of finance that permit localities to capture a portion of the enhanced value of improved urban access to continue supporting the system in an ongoing way.

2.4 Towards a financial model of urban access

2.4.1 The problem

To create a transport finance model that creates incentives to prioritize the public good aspect of urban transport over its private good quality requires a practical parsing of the two concepts. A useful first approximation is to conceive of "access" as the public good aspect of transport and "mobility" as the private good or market quality. Using this dichotomy as a guide, we seek to design financial models that incentivize the former, and not merely promote more of the latter. Further we seek to develop models in which the revenue flows that support the production of access are tied as explicitly as possible to the economic value that it creates, to the extent that these can be monetized.

Because urban mobility encompasses a range of guises: walking, non-motorized transport and various public forms, the clear identification of access as distinct from mobility is never going to be an easy job. Most importantly in terms of our concerns, it requires that we identify instances when more mobility creates better access and when it merely leads to more congestion. Depending on time and place, all means of conveyance can contribute or be an impediment to accessibility. To devise finance systems that reward the former and penalize the latter requires understanding the ways that conveyance modes complement and compete with one another as well as the institutional structures that shape the way these alternatives are organized.

If mobility alone were the policy goal, issues of complementarity and competition could be treated as secondary concerns. It would be possible to analyse issues of cost generation and recovery in a simpler mode-by-mode manner using conventional business models. Such models place the internal cost and revenue structure of the individual provider at the centre of analysis and treat issues of complementarity and competition as matters of secondary "market conditions and risks". However, once the financial context is framed around the unified production of access, considerations of the comparative issues of cost generation and recovery become central to policy analysis and, by extension, to the design of financial models.

If urban transport, in all modal forms, could be supported entirely through charges on direct users (user-based cost recovery), the public–private goods dichotomy would still remain theoretically interesting but not pressing as a policy concern. If travelers were willing and able to pay the full production cost of the specific transport services they used, much of the access problem would cease to be a public policy issue apart from questions surrounding the externalities created by providing transportation in high-density urban spaces. There are few instances where user charges are able to represent full cost recovery. These exceptions, such as the previously cited cases of Singapore and Hong Kong, typically take the form of rail segregated public transport systems located in cities where populations are highly concentrated and where there is tolled infrastructure such as bridges, tunnels and roads. They work well as a result of the specific political-economic context in which they are embedded. For our present purposes it is the underlying principle illustrated in these cases that is of general interest, not the exact replication of the specific institutional practices that sustain them. We will consider this in more detail in a subsequent section for its broader policy lessons.

From a market-based (mobility) point of view, the general cost recovery problem is one of under-pricing (costs exceed user generated revenues). There are two reasons for this: instances of conscious public policy and limits on general affordability. Typically situations contain elements of both. In terms of conscious under-pricing, the prime example is urban automobile use. There have been many studies that consistently demonstrate that urban automobile users do not pay charges that cover the full cost of the streets and roads they use for driving and parking or the damage they do to the environment (Breithaupt, 2004).

Limited affordability is the major source of under-pricing, especially for public transport. It reflects an almost universal phenomenon inherent in the basic cost economics of urban transport: the full costs of adequate urban transport are unaffordable at prices that much of the actual and potential riding public could pay. Because of the critical contribution mobility makes to access via the externalities its use generates, it is also an almost universal phenomenon that governments find ways to close the revenue–cost gap. In the following sections we consider the elements that drive the cost of urban transport.

2.4.2 Infrastructure construction and maintenance

A transportation service requires high-cost, networked infrastructure, such as streets, roads and rail beds. Costs include acquiring rights-of-way and infrastructure construction. Given the high value of urban locations both these costs are higher than for comparable infrastructure in rural places. Once the infrastructure is in place there are on-going costs for its maintenance. Although these costs are most obvious when we consider rail-based public transport, the cost of roads or exclusive lanes for bus rapid transit are also significant but less visible as a result of the way investments in services and financing are often fragmented across governmental agencies and the way they are subsequently accounted for. Additionally roads are usually competitively shared among modes, accommodating freight, taxis, private automobiles and public transport. Within modes there is even further complication as minivan and taxi providers compete with one another in pursuit of fares in an overlapping market. The time and money costs caused by congestion from crowding and competition must also be accounted for in evaluating the contribution of mobility to access.

2.4.3 Operational costs

The direct operating costs for service delivery include the labour, maintenance and fuel for the operation of the service plus the expense of acquiring and maintaining the vehicles or rolling stock needed to deliver the service. The direct service provider typically needs to account for these costs if its operations are to remain economically viable. However, for our purposes we would also want to account for the public costs of regulation and law enforcement as well as emergency services in the event of accidents or breakdowns. These provide important value added and must be considered in a comprehensive finance model.

2.4.4 Costs, prices and modal incentives

Financial models that seek to prioritize more efficient access modes need built-in parameters to incentivize the desired behaviours. For example in the context of crowded street infrastructure high capacity buses and bus rapid transport (BRT) routes might be encouraged because their carrying volumes add more value to access than an expansion in automobile-based traffic, especially single occupancy vehicles. Complicating matters further is the fact that if travelers are to be dissuaded from automobile use, the quality of the public transport option in terms of speed, safety, and reliability must be of sufficient quality to induce them to leave their automobiles at home.

Taking all of these factors into account, it is easy to understand the elements that drive urban transport costs above the "ability-to-pay" of a significant share of urban households.

2.4.5 Impediments to unified transport infrastructure finance

The costs of constructing and maintaining transport infrastructure comprise a major portion of total urban mobility cost. They involve the pouring of tons of concrete, the paving of hundreds and thousands of kilometres of road surface, the construction of drainage and control systems. Because the infrastructure is networked, the challenges of financing its construction and maintenance are like those faced by other networked urban infrastructures such as power, water, sanitation and communications. All require significant capital investments in the construction of physical facilities and face similar long-term maintenance concerns. All therefore fit easily in the economist's category of "natural monopoly". Natural monopolies occur when high capital costs and a long project lifespan make it inefficient to duplicate the required facility in the hope of creating a competitive market among suppliers. Given the typically large volume service capacity of such infrastructure, competition would prove inefficient. The market would develop significant excess capacity as these large-scale competitive infrastructure suppliers sought to attract market share away from one another. Indeed because of the large absorptive capacity of roads, power grids and the like, these facilities tend to generate economies of scale with average cost per user falling as the number of users expands.

The typical policy solution to situations of natural monopoly takes one of two forms: tightly, publicly regulated private operation with governments having rate setting powers or direct government ownership and operation. Because other forms of networked infrastructure use variants of these two structures, it is sometimes suggested they could be adapted to address the urban access financing issue. Despite similarities in the economic characteristics of the physical assets, there are significant differences in the nature of the actual service and the organization of its production that make an easy adaptation of such approaches far more problematic to implement. The critical differences originate in the more diverse and disbursed nature of the stakeholders involved in transport service production and the diverse nature and motives of the service users.

Power, water and sanitation are undifferentiated products and are delivered through a unitary network that physically permanently ties the producer to the user. Electric power,[8] piped water and sanitation create use value as a result of the networks of wires and pipes that move power and water in and waste out of fixed locations throughout a city or region. The rigid connections between producers and user locations make the regulatory approach of public authority or ownership easier to administer and set user prices in a measured and fair manner. This is not the case with mobility. Although the networked infrastructure is similar in macroscopic ways, the services it produces are diverse owing to the range of modal forms that urban transportation takes. Moreover, while it is possible to pinpoint the exact physical locations where power, water and sanitation services are used, mobility consumers are, by definition, not so easily connected. Hence a pricing scheme that can levy a charge for infrastructure use and charge for use intensity is not possible. Furthermore because the public good, access, is the more valued output, there might be good reasons to under price the use of the infrastructure by travelers.

There are other specific problems with developing a regulatory or rate setting scheme to finance urban transport infrastructure. An obvious problem is the disconnect between the public agencies responsible for building and maintaining highways and streets and the mobility suppliers or automobile users who use the infrastructure. The breakdown between agents responsible for the infrastructure and agents responsible for operation takes its most obvious form in the case of highways and cars. The highways are public infrastructure, with use determined by public directive; the use of the rolling stock, cars and buses, is a private decision. By way of contrast, in the case of electric power, users pay a single and unavoidable charge divided between a fee for the fixed costs of the infrastructure and a charge that reflects the level of use. The move towards imposing congestion charges on auto use in central business districts or to vary charges for kerb side parking with the time of day reflect efforts to alter this state of affairs.

In terms of rail-based travel, some of the cost for infrastructure can be built into fares. But at present, congestion and parking charging not withstanding, it is a difficult challenge in urban areas where highways, rail lines and streets complement one another and intersect at many points. Additionally the multiplicity of vehicles and purposes that comprise daily traffic make the challenge of charging for use value and intensity even more complex. In the case of public transport, the extent that fares must be made affordable for people with limited incomes means that the goal of cost recovery must be balanced against the need to keep the public service within reach of the majority of the urban population. If the costs were too high the access gains of such transport would be lost as the volume of use declined.

The second structural source of institutional fragmentation that could impede a unified regulatory rate setting system relates directly to the first: transport infrastructure finance is often undertaken by public sector agents separated from those making decisions about pricing. Further complication ensues because the usefulness of specific elements of transport infrastructure such as a limited access highway is not independent from the context of streets and roads with which it connects. The quality and quantity of these are critical to the value created by the element of highway infrastructure. These roads require free access for a variety of comings and goings, as that is inherent in the nature of urban life. Given the divorce between the governance of these complimentary goods, the pricing of the use of the infrastructure is usually undertaken without consideration of its impact on the network of streets and roads that support it and that in turn are supported by it. The social cost accounting for the two is almost always entirely separate.

From an economic perspective, transport infrastructure finance has two characteristics: high upfront capital requirements to launch the project and comparatively low marginal operating costs to maintain it. Together, they often operate at cross purposes and effectively hinder efforts to enhance urban access. High upfront capital costs require governments to turn to capital markets to fund projects as the amounts needed are usually significantly more than can be generated from taxes and other income sources. These latter funds are used to support ongoing service requirements. Bonds to support transport infrastructure typically carry a stipulated fixed rate of interest payment and both principal and interest are backed up by the faith and credit of the state issuing the bonds. This mechanism is seen most clearly in the case of funds used to construct local roads. Because of the need for free access, there is no revenue stream attached to their direct use.[9] It is only through the full faith and credit of the government issuing the bonds that this infrastructure is financed and built.

In the case of specific isolated units of transport infrastructure such as a bridge, tunnel or highway where the potential for direct project revenue-backed bonding is possible, the finance conundrum clearly emerges. In such cases it is always tempting to finance the infrastructure element through user tolls designed to repay the principal and interest over the life of the bonds as well as the maintenance. From a market-based mobility point of view this makes a great deal of sense, as users pay its full costs. But from a public goods access viewpoint, this approach is often counter-productive. Once the capital has been invested in the creation of the facility, from a social point of view, it is a sunk investment. On a forward basis the construction has been fully paid for and the only real costs are for its operation. Given that reality, from a public goods perspective it makes eminent sense to encourage the use of the capital good by as many people as possible through low or zero tolls. But because bonds issued to build it are backed by a pledge of the revenue stream from its use, tolls that cover the full costs are required which effectively discourage maximal use. This contradiction becomes most apparent in the case of public-private partnerships (PPPs) devised to create elements of transport infrastructure. In these cases the private partner enters into the venture to attain an attractive rate of return on capital via building and maintaining the facility. But as economic theory makes clear, a monopolist maximizes income by restricting use to those willing to pay the highest prices. The experience as revealed by many PPPs has been perverse from both a mobility and access point of view. The high tolls, as predicted by economic theory, discouraged use. The result is that it diverts travelers to pursue their journeys using the highly congested "free" streets and roads that the facility was meant to relieve. The loss of volume on the facility in turn leads to disappointing investor returns and often defaults on the bonds.

The third source of complexity in transport infrastructure finance relates directly to its multimodal nature. Every city has a diversity of transport modes, paid for in different ways by the user and provided by numerous suppliers. These range from formal rail-based systems down to informal motorcycle taxis. Each mode has its own way of setting and collecting fares. Together it is the totality that comprises the urban transportation system of a city region. To devise a system of prices and financial models for this inter-dependent whole is a daunting task. By way of contrast, an electric grid, a water supply or sewer system carries a single product through a uniform network of conduits.

Taken together these factors make the challenge of devising financing models for urban transport that align with goals for enhanced access far more difficult than for other networked infrastructures. It is important however to remember that difficulty is not necessarily impossibility. The urban transport system is both a network- and time-fragmented collection of modal elements responding to the needs of their individual organiza-tional forms and the variegated land uses that these serve. Yet it is clear that if urban transport as a total network is to add to access value, each element has to contribute to the public mission of creating access and at the same time cover the costs of its existence. These ways can include cross-subsidies such as using congestion charges and parking revenue to underwrite the costs of public transport, analysed below.

2.5 The unique problems of cost recovery in public transport

There is a global chronic cost recovery problem for urban public transport. This relates largely to the lack of clarity about its importance as a public good versus its manifestation as a private one. This lack of clarity reinforces the politics of funding silos for specific transport modes that characterize virtually every city-region in the world. To the extent that the private good vision prevails, the net result is continuous pressure on governments to off load responsibility for public transport and to underfund it. The result is that quality deteriorates and users flee to alternatives, few of which are good for the access quality of urban life. This is especially the case in devel-oping countries where public funding is scarce and individual private motorized transport is increasingly within reach of a larger segment of the urban population initially in the form of motorcycles, and later low-cost imported used vehicles and then cheap locally produced cars.

In general, fare box recovery sufficient to support the public transport system is rare. It can only be found in places where use density is high, public transport operates on exclusive rights-of-way, and where affluent users eschew their private cars. Two types of situation fit this scenario: Certain Asian cities and fast rail lines connecting major airports to city centres. In the first category are cities such as Hong Kong, Tokyo, Osaka and Taipei.[10] The fare box recovery ratio in Hong Kong in 2007 was 149 per cent,[11] compared with the best performing European and North American cities where typically the fare box recovery rate is between 30 per cent and 50 per cent.[12] However, in the lower density North American cities the rates go down to as little as 9 per cent as is the case in Austin Texas.[13] In the second category, successful airport connectors include the London Heathrow Express, Arlanda – Stockholm, Brussels, and Amsterdam – Schipol. But these latter examples of cost recovery work through models of monopoly pricing in which they are able to charge unusually high fares to a small, high-income social stratum of travelers who are able to bear these costs. The London Heathrow Express for example, charges a fare of £24 (though £18 if bought before boarding), more than a £1 per mile. In both cases, it is the ability of rail-segregated modes to outperform highway-based automobile transport in terms of time and convenience that gives them the advantage.

The comparison of rail-segregated modes with road-based modes raises another important consideration. While transport infrastructure in general is a form of natural monopoly, competition for use of the system of highways, streets, roads, bridges and tunnels can be fierce between different modal-based users. This reality contributes to a great deal of the street and highway congestion that is becoming commonplace in the world's city-regions. Ownership of a motorized vehicle is a comparatively low entry barrier into the space competition for urban travel. Obviously, this is not the case with rail-based modes which can be the most thoroughly monopolistic of natural monopolies because of their ability to restrict infrastructure access to selected service providers. As a result, rail-based systems tend to display the clearest outcomes in terms of increasing returns to scale. A passenger rail train requires about the same amount of staff and operating costs whether it is one-quarter, half or completely full. The marginal costs of capacity are low so the net effect is that as use increases, unit costs per trip fall. That in part explains why rail fares can cover so much of the cost of lines in high-density cities where, especially in Europe and Asia, it is often the case that significant portions of the residential population elect not to own automobiles or not to use them for their daily commute. It is also often the case in these places that a high percentage of the population resides within 300 to 500 metres of a metro station.

When we move along the public transport spectrum from the rarefied cases of high density fixed rail characteristic of the best systems in the wealthiest locations in the world to the informal and mini-bus based services that characterize public transport in the poorest cities, the situation changes significantly. Here, the linkage between infrastructure and operation is virtually non-existent as these informal systems depend heavily on free unlimited access to existing public rights of way. From a fiscal perspective, the situation changes in two ways: the large infrastructure-based capital and maintenance costs for roads are almost completely divorced from the capital and operating costs of the service suppliers for whom the principal capital cost is the rolling stock, typically older mini-vans and second-hand buses, and the operating costs are vehicle maintenance, fuel and labour. To the extent that the fare box, supported by a low-income clientele, is expected to cover these costs, the result is a system of unsafe and poorly maintained vehicles driven dangerously through congested and poorly maintained roads. Urban public transport services created for the poor and maintained by the purchasing power of the poor are unsurprisingly poor quality. If the goal is enhanced access for all, these systems need to be funded by revenue streams that tap into the value of the access they create for non-users of the system as well as users. But for that to occur, as a matter of political expediency they need to operate at a standard that can attract a middle class clientele.

2.6 Financing access as social policy

It is not possible to appreciate fully the economic dimensions of urban access finance without understanding the ways in which urban transport systems are powerfully interconnected with the social dimensions of urban life. A successful financial model for urban access has to incentivize shared use across social classes. Transport is always a class-based endeavour in a society organized on the basis of social classes. But the essence of good urban transport provision, enhanced access for all, is the antithesis of such class-based distinctions. Good transportation systems aim to overcome distinctions of class in the movement of urban populations. Urban transport aimed at the affluent, such as the aforementioned airport access systems, has little impact on the lives of the larger mass of the urban population or the spatial shape of the metropolis. On the other hand, if urban transport is essentially a residual and informal service aimed solely at meeting the most basic mobility needs of deprived social groups, as we have seen, it will be a poor and marginal service. Its impact is most obviously manifest in the massive slums in walking distance of employment and services that are used by the poor that characterize the rapidly urbanizing cities of the world. In reaction to this urban chaos, gated communities in the outer reaches of urban areas for the rich and upper middle classes accessible only by private automobile begin to appear. Without the mediation of a good urban public transport system between walking and the private automobile, anyone who can afford a motorcycle or car buys one. The result is continually accumulating congestion of the streets and roads by an assortment of motorized vehicles with all the negative social and environmental costs that this entails. This congestion in turn creates significant political pressure for the expansion of infrastructure and spatial development patterns catering to the car regardless of the social and environmental costs. Only an urban public transport system aimed squarely at the needs of the broad middle class, which is of sufficiently high quality, is capable of reversing this political dynamic. Although services must be primarily aimed at the middle class, urban mass transport will only realize its full potential if it serves the needs of the rich and poor as well.

The best urban public transport systems such as those of London, Moscow, Zurich, Stockholm, Paris and New York share this social equality: they are widely and comfortably used by the middle classes regardless of other differences in their social systems. In each instance the public sector, however organized, invests sufficiently in the quality of these systems to entice middle class users to see it as a travel alternative. In the final analysis the only way to diminish the global tendency towards the unwelcome over-reliance on automobile-based travel is to ensure that as the cities of the South expand, they do so around good quality public transportation systems that support the aspirations of the emerging middle classes and accommodate the poor.

2.7 Towards a methodology of valuing access

2.7.1 A matter of time

There are many reasons why present urban transport policy focuses on mobility rather than access. A principal one is that the methods and metrics for measuring mobility are deeply rooted in contemporary planning methodology. This is a result of the way that the conceptualization of the general urban transportation problem evolved. In the context of post World War II Europe and North America, when massive construction and reconstruction began after two decades of depression and war, it was not unreasonable for policymakers and planners to assume that pre-war experiences of city growth would determine post-war patterns. The policy makers had all come of age in an urban world dominated by rail-based mobility. For those people born around the turn of the twentieth century, the lesson of those early decades was that rail-based transport contributed to solving the overcrowding of urban slums around city centers. Like Robert Moses, his contemporaries saw the promotion of mobility as, *prima facie*, the promotion of urban access, regardless of modal option.

By the time the massive post-war construction was getting underway the automobile had eclipsed rail-based modes as the preferred means of motorized urban transport. It made perfect sense in terms of the conventional wisdom of that era to presume that more motorways would mean better urban access just as metros and trams had meant that in an earlier time. Hence the promotion of auto-mobility was seen as the equivalent to the promotion of urban access.

The congested modern urban motorway is the fundamental example of the way in which the concepts of mobility and access began to pull in different directions. The mere fact of the constraint of valuable urban physical space means that more motorized mobility often leads to less access.

Figure 2.3 Mobility is not access, Beijing

As Figure 2.3 above, drawn from contemporary Beijing, makes power-fully clear, it is possible to have an enormous amount of auto-mobility and yet inadequate access. That was a lesson that experience needed to teach. History, or in the language of modern social science, path dependency always exerts a powerful hold on our mindsets.

In terms of planning methodology, if it were the case that mobility enhancement promoted improved urban access, then measuring the cost and quality of mobility would provide a good proximate estimate of the enhance-ment in the ultimate end product, access. Further, as we will see below, mobility far more than access lends itself easily to tangible measurement.

Once the ethos of the post war era became embedded in the methods of planning practice, the simple equation between mobility enhancements and urban access improvement persisted, despite half a century of contrary experience. Mobility enhancement is deeply embedded in the cost–benefit analysis (CBA) methodology employed to evaluate most urban transport projects of significant size. These projects invariably used travel time saved as a principal measure of mobility enhancement.

CBA transport methodology evolved out of a series of transport-based economic studies undertaken in the late 1950s and early 1960s when large-scale post World War II construction and reconstruction was getting underway. Its heavy reliance on time saving as the paramount benefit is so standard that, despite a constant drumbeat of criticisms of its shortcomings as a proxy for urban access, it persists in dominating the way in which official protocols for CBA are structured. However, as the economic and environmental costs of mobility are becoming difficult to sustain and there are alternative ways to create access, the critics are finding a broader audience.

Two projects in particular were seminal in the development of the CBA methodology. (Box 2.1) The CATS study undertaken in metropolitan Chicago and the 1962 study on the new Victoria Line on the London Underground which opened in 1969. Together these two projects illustrate the centrality of mobility over access in the process of transport evaluation and created the initial methodologies for estimating its value. CBA in its present form emerged out of studies such as these and formed the basis for the protocols of contemporary urban transport planning. A recent look at a cross section of transport CBAs across the United Kingdom concluded that approximately 80 per cent of the identified benefits in transport derives from the monetary value assigned to time saving.[14]

Throughout the 1960s CBA models which evolved from studies such as those described in Box 1 spawned variations on time-price models intended to correct the methodological flaws of predecessors and further refine the analysis. However, the fundamental assumption that improving travel speeds by saving time lessened the "disutility" of travel remained unchallenged. The problem with that assumption is it bears no relationship to actual travel behavior. It has long been observed that travel time saved does not get invested in other pursuits; rather it is reinvested in either longer distance journeys or further travel for other pursuits. The "Zahavi conjecture"[15] (Zahavi and Talvitie, 1980) has received renewed interest as a result of a paper by Metz (2008). Using the National Travel Surveys of the United Kingdom's Department for Transport, which covers all forms of travel, Metz found that "average travel time is 385 hours per person per year, or just over one hour per day".[16] He further found that that figure has remained constant at around that level for three decades. If travelers took the time saving benefit of all the infrastructure improvements developed over those decades as less time spent traveling, we should expect to observe a downward sloping trend in time spent in travel.

Metz's analysis bolsters the validity of the Zahavi conjecture that the benefits of transport improvements are enjoyed through more travel within the same time budget. A powerful economic implication flowing from this hypothesis is that investments in road infrastructure to support automobile travel will lead to decreasing returns to access. Cars rarely travel at their full passenger carrying capacity; single passenger occupancy is typical. Hence the added miles of lane capacity will not produce sufficient throughput for a rapidly urbanizing world in which people are traveling longer distances. Instead travel times will increase as speeds slow due to the growing

Box 2.1 The birth of cost–benefit analysis and the time value of mobility in urban transport

Although the economic theories behind cost–benefit analysis extend back into the first half of the nineteenth century (Dupuit, 1844), it was the post World War II public works construction boom that created the urgency from which an effective methodology emerged. The impetus for this was rooted in the large public works backlog that accompanied the end of hostilities and the need to find a rational way to choose priorities. Two studies in particular are noteworthy as they played a seminal role in shaping contemporary cost–benefits methods. Both were completed in 1962. These were the Chicago area transportation study (CATS) followed by London Transport's cost–benefit analysis (CBA) for its Victoria Line.

CATS is an exemplar of rational, region-wide planning and the development of pioneering methodological innovations linking metropolitan transport to land use. Until then, the notion of regional, system-wide area planning was mainly conjecture. The work reflected a concern with creating expeditious ways to move people between locational points. Reflecting the conventional wisdom of its time, it assumed that most new travel would be via automobiles; few would choose public transport. The researchers' view was

> [I]f the majority of families preferred to move to the suburbs and rely on personal autos for their travel, then these trends should be accepted. One should not criticize choices freely made in the marketplace.
>
> (Black, 1990: 35–6)

It similarly took the observed trends in land use as givens and assumed they were independent of one another. The study was criticized for its passive approach to emerging land use trends and not having a land use planning component. The studies' authors defended this by arguing that there was no land use plan for such a large metropolitan area and hence the best they could do was to project future land uses based on a knowledge of trends at the time. Five of its six goals reflected an unquestioning concern with enhanced efficient mobility: 1) greater speed, 2) increased safety, 3) lower operating costs, 4) economy in new construction and 5) minimizing disruption. Its sixth goal, promoting better land development, although laudable, had little to do with the highway plans that were its principal outcome and the author's acknowledgement that there were no such plans.

Construction on London Transport's Victoria Line began in 1962 and was largely completed by 1972. The idea for a new line first surfaced in 1948. However, it was in 1955 that a bill was introduced into Parliament to add a deep tunnel line to the London Underground. The Victoria Line originally ran from Victoria Station to Walthamstow and was soon extended south to Brixton. Economists Christopher Foster and Michael Beesley developed a detailed cost–benefit model to evaluate the project. The important innovation of their work was the development of a model for evaluating the impacts of capital improvements on one transport mode across others under conditions in which the effective social costs of each diverge as do the effective prices paid by users. This situation is of course generic to all of the world's urban areas.

They concluded that in a dense location like central London, both users and non-users benefited in terms of lessened travel times, as a result of less congested travel both below and above ground. Further, those already using the Underground also benefited qualitatively from less crowding. However, it was the non-users who most benefit from the decongestion on the streets of London. The authors made it clear that it would not be the fare revenues gained by London Transport that made this project worthwhile, but the travel time saving accruing to both public transport users and motorists. These savings were not easily, if at all captured by the travel charges that were collected from Underground users for providing improved travel time at no added cost to auto users. The Foster and Beesley study established the notion of saved travel time as a key benefit of a transport improvement project.

Both CBAs established the notion of travel time saving as a principle benefit of transport improvement and both provided methods for measuring and monetizing it. In the case of the Victoria Line, almost 90 per cent of all the ascribed benefits were travel time saving regardless of whether travelers used the tube, passenger rail or roadways in buses and private vehicles.

Sources: Black, 1990; Foster and Beesley, 1963; Beesley and Foster, 1965.

congestion on the roads. To the extent that access enhancement is sought through mobility, forms of modally segregated public transport, either rail-based or using exclusive vehicle lanes (for example bus rapid transit) will be needed. These modes, unlike individually driven motorcars, can provide increasing returns to scale via shortened journey times and faster travel speeds when there is adequate volume demand.

A powerful social implication also ensues. One result of the post-war globalization of automobile travel and expansion in highway networks has been urban sprawl in the high-income countries, and peri-urban expansion in low- and middle-income nations. This spatial fragmentation of urban life

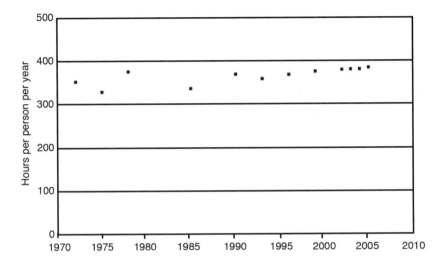

Figure 2.4 Average travel time (hours per person per year)
Source: Reproduced from Metz, 2008

in which families live significant distances from work, school and shopping results in social fragmentation that negates the integrative benefit of urban access.

At the time of the Victoria Line study in 1962, Foster and Beesley could conceive of no way to internalize the benefits and costs of this cross modal project. Organizationally, London Transport and the streets were operated by separate agencies. The best they could do was point out that London Transport was creating a benefit for the above ground travelers that needed to be taken into account. However, at about the same time that they were completing their study, Columbia University economist and future Nobel Prize winner William Vickrey was undertaking preliminary path-breaking work about what, in the twenty-first century came to be congestion pricing. Vickrey observed that "...in no other major area are pricing practices so irrational, so out of date, and so conducive to waste as in urban transportation".[17] The notion of creating forms of cross-modal subsidy as both a matter of equity and efficiency emerged from this thinking.

2.7.2 Unpacking access benefits

Although the methodological debate opened up by Metz's article is recent, the value of access has long been understood. The word "access" might not have been part of Adam Smith's 1776 lexicon but the key to his notion of how increases in productivity are created was precisely that. Smith held that the ability to expand productivity by introducing specialization into the manufacturing process was the crucial element: the larger the market, the more economically feasible it was to invest in labor specialization and mass production. For Smith the limit on such productivity gain was the size of the market. Put in terms of access, either a dense, co-located concentration or an easily reachable geographic spread of buyers would drive expansion in social wealth. This was a demand-driven productivity increase. The value via scale economies in production came from access enhancement either through co-location or mobility.

But there was a supply side driver as well. Alfred Marshall (1920), an important progenitor of modern microeconomics, observed that when firms in an industry are able to locate with easy access to other firms in their industry, productivity gains are generated thanks to the ease of specialization by firms throughout the production process. For Marshall most importantly this occurred through more efficient face-to-face transmission of ideas and innovations. Silicon Valley in Northern California is the prime contemporary example of these "Marshallian" or localization economies. Taken together, these economies of market and supplier density are now known as the "agglomeration economies of urbanization". We can simply call these the benefits of access.

To the extent that transport improves the ability of an urban area to capture these access benefits, it adds significant value to the local economy. A working definition of the benefits of agglomeration would be the increase in productivity per worker or gross value added (GVA) as a result of the milieu in which work is performed. Productivity is typically seen as a measure of output per worker relative to the capital stock and raw materials with which they work. GVA takes this measurement to the next level. It is not just a question of the skill and discipline of the individual worker relative to the context of the firm or agency, though these are important, but of the entire context in which the worker and the organization operates, extending beyond their individual equipment to the urban environment and the access it provides to a range of supports. In a comparison of the GVA for metropolitan London with the whole of the United Kingdom, it was found that metropolitan London's GVA was 69 percent higher than the nation's. If only central London is considered, the local–national differential was 186 per cent.[18] This data provides an order of magnitude with which we can value the access or agglomeration that urban density provides.

Taking accessibility to the next level, Jenkins et al. (2010) cite a recent study of London's Crossrail project that, like the Victoria Line study of a half-century ago, promises to break new ground methodologically in attempting to capture access benefits along with travel time saving benefits. Adding these agglomerative benefits to the more traditional time cost savings benefits raised the traditional time savings based benefit–cost ratio

(BCR) between 36 and 93 per cent. We can debate the methodologies used to measure these effects, but the important point is that, as with the measurement of GVA, these are order of magnitude estimates that provide an empirical basis for the sizable benefits that access conveys and they far outweigh the narrower concerns with mobility-based time saving that occupy so much of the CBA literature. Most importantly they open up the possibility of improving access and hence economic well-being through improving the co-locational characteristics of places. This includes more reliance on pedestrian and bicycle access as well as more and better public transport options; both of which are critical to an economics of sustainable urban transport.

2.8 Access and value capture

The potential specific revenue sources for financing urban access will vary with the range of specific forms of conveyance (motorcycle taxis to high speed rail), patterns of co-location (mixed uses), fiscal arrangements and effectiveness of local land use regulation. Much of this variation results from the evolution of local institutions of social, economic and political governance. Despite the richness of all this variation, it is nonetheless the case that there are only a few very consistent economic principles to which these revenue generation patterns respond. At a general level, there are only two ways to support urban transportation: direct charges to users (fares and tolls) for the private benefit rendered – which is mobility – and charges to the indirect beneficiaries of the public good – which is access.[19]

Because we are seeking to develop finance models that link costs to the broader benefits, there is a need to move beyond thinking in terms of traditional revenue sources such as allocations from general taxation or revenue sources tied to specific taxes such as those on local payroll and sales.[20] It is the attempt to address the challenge of long term financing that explains the interest in value capture approaches to raising revenue. Value capture seeks as directly as possible to capture the locational value of the access created. Value capture mechanisms can be linked to the capitalized value (the real estate values) of locations that benefit from better access. The most obvious form has been the growing awareness of the feasibility of imposing charges for the capitalized access value that segregated, typically rail-based forms, of urban transport create by enhancing the differential rental or market value of locations in the vicinity of station stops and terminals. In the desire to ensure systems are as self-supporting as possible, such value capture offers a fruitful way forward. Hong Kong, with its linkage of development and rental values around stations presents the best-known example. At the same time Hong Kong is unique given its particularly strong travel flows, densely populated areas and specific forms of strong governance. However, it is possible to conceive of other, simpler ways to capture access value to support public transport-based mobility. For example, locational value can be captured through a range of property taxes, tax increment financing,[21] parking charges and congestion pricing mechanisms.[22] Value capture targeted on property rather than on drivers ensures the indirect beneficiary contributes towards paying for the transport facility. Put another way, focusing on property-based charges supports access through a co-locational approach while charging drivers does it through a mobility-based approach.

2.9 Concluding observations

This chapter opened with a discussion of the famous 1960s battles between Jane Jacobs and Robert Moses over the nature of urbanism. The enduring importance of this debate resides in the paradigmatic way these two epic figures cast up mobility and co-location as alternatives. But they are not. Modern cities everywhere need both mobility and co-location to create the vital social access that gives urban life such enduring social value to human society. The argument made in this chapter can be summarized as follows. For a growing majority of the world's population urban life is increasingly the preferred living option. People choose to live and work in urban places for the access it affords to opportunities for a richer life. In simplest terms access is a physical quality, the reduction in the time–space friction of accomplishing the activities of daily life. Because urban life is characterized by diversities of income, wealth, education, ethnicity and gender, access takes on powerful social characteristics too. These diversities in turn lead to differentials in the quality of physical access which different groups of urban residents are able to enjoy. The physical challenge of urban planning is to ensure that access to important locations is made as widely available as possible. This can be justified in both efficiency (economic) and equity (social justice) terms. To accomplish good access for all, it is necessary to address the challenges of social equity and economic efficiency embedded in the system of incentives and disincentives that finance urban transport and land use.

For much of the last century the expansion of urban mobility became conflated with the expansion of urban access – more mobility supposedly equaled more access. Co-location was an afterthought. Over the course of the second half of the twentieth century there was a transformation of the dominant means of mobility away from space efficient public modes that characterized the late-nineteenth and early-twentieth centuries to space consuming automobile-based and largely private modes. The result has been sprawled patterns of low-density development, in many ways the antithesis of the access that urban life promises. This transformation exposed the limits of the assumption that more mobility automatically meant more access.

The central challenge for the present century is not to turn the clock back to a time when access was almost solely achieved through the dense, pedestrian-based co-location of people and activity that characterized the pre-industrial and early industrial city. Rather it is one of re-balancing the options among existing travel modes and land use and urban design possibilities. The desired outcome is to enhance the opportunities for urban access for the diverse social groups that comprise modern global urban society.

As a matter of public policy, the challenge is to create incentives for behaviors that enhance rather than diminish access. Over the course of the last century the financial incentives built into our models for urban development have disproportionately encouraged automobile-based mobility rather than co-location in the development of metropolitan regions. This has come at the expense of creating high-quality public transport and safe, non-motorized transport. If that is to change, we need to change the incentive structures. The goal must be to move towards replacing mobility as the dominant policy goal with access. It is necessary to begin to balance a system of charges and revenue streams on the finance side of the social ledger with an integrated mobility-land use system on the product side.

The term "transport system" requires an integrative re-conceptualization. At present what is called urban transport could more accurately be described as urban anarchy; a collection of independent and individual routes and modes of conveyance that as often work at cross purposes as complement one another. This is the present state-of-the-art and it must be incentivized to change. The more options that urban residents have to access work, education, shopping and social connections through combinations of integrated mobility modes and co-location, the more value is added to the city-region. The greater the degree of system integration within and across modes, the higher the degree of access the system creates. To achieve that valuable goal requires public-led investments in infrastructure, equipment and service delivery as well as urban designs that both accommodate these modes and provide alternatives in the form of pedestrian access and safe, non-motorized transport.

In pursuit of an integrated, socially equitable and environmentally sustainable approach to the creation of enhanced urban access there are a number of research challenges that must be pursued further.

Although access is easy to define as a geographic concept, it is far more difficult to pin down as a matter of either economic development or social integration. Furthermore although the importance of economic development and social integration are well understood in their own terms, what are the dynamics that connect them to one another in the urban context? More work is needed to fully explore this connection.

Moving from understanding the notion of access as a social and economic good, we are also challenged by a need to create practical ways to calculate the value of access that are comparable to the measures we use to assess the quantity and quality of mobility. How can we evaluate the comparative social and economic impacts of transport or other access enhancing efforts? What are "moveable" lessons that we can take from experiences in some places to improve finance for urban access in others? How do we employ cross-subsidy approaches to ensure that they are being employed to keep travel times reasonable, travel quality good and access to mobility open to all urban residents?

There are also many institutional and organizational questions that need further exploration. How can we connect changes in land uses and land value to changes in access-based investments? What are practical and easily adaptable organizational forms to ensure that value capture from these changes is at least in part used to sustain the access created? These are questions that are easy to answer in the abstract, but in terms of the challenge of how we transform theory and concept into on-the-ground institutional and organizational forms become questions that require a great deal of further inquiry.

Political-economics are not divorced from questions of social class, gender and ethnicity. It becomes important that the dimensions of these issues are well understood and embedded in the values that define the financial models we design. The role of the middle class is central to this. The key to re-balancing mobility and co-location in twenty-first century cities is the quality of public transport. Unless public transport is seen as a safe, speedy, reliable means of metropolitan travel by the middle classes of society, it is going to be impossible to build the political base for designing cities in which access is achieved in an environmentally sustainable manner as well as one that is socially equitable. Thus meeting the needs of middle class urbanites is the necessary condition, but ensuring that the urban poor have equal and easy access as well is the sufficient one.

Notes

1   Path dependence theory in economics originally developed to explain how technological processes and industries evolved in relation to one another (see Nelson and Winter, 1982). For a good review of the larger social science and political science implications of the concept see Pierson, 2000. In the present case we witness the way in which a late nineteenth century technical innovation, the automobile, led to the responsive evolution of urban land use patterns that accommodate its technical requirements as it provides an urban public service.
2   World Health Organization data 2011, author's calculations.
3   Quotation from Talvitie, Antti (2000) *Lessons from Urban Transport: Selected Proceeding from a World Bank Seminar* The World Bank: Washington, DC, p.50.
4   For a thorough introductory formal discussion of the nature of public and private goods see Weimer and Vining, 2010.
5   "Excludability" is the fact that the owner of a transport vehicle is able to deny passage to anyone for any reason, typically for non-payment of a fare. "Rivalrous consumption" refers to the fact that if I am sitting on a seat in the bus you cannot occupy the same seat.
6   Non-rivalrous is the opposite of rivalrous. It refers to the idea that two of us can access a good and not destroy its value for the other.

7   "Cities on the Move: A World Bank Urban Transport Strategy Review" (2002) World Bank: Washington, DC. Quoted from the Executive Summary.
8   While it is possible to create something akin to a "competitive" market for the generation of electric power, the delivery mechanism remains of necessity a natural monopoly. Although electric power can be generated in many ways, (fossil fuel, wind, nuclear) once created it is a homogeneous product. Its transmission to users occurs over a single physically fixed network or grid.
9   Property taxes paid by residents and property owners do represent an indirect charge to some beneficiaries for the value that the streets and roads bestow.
10 http://en.wikipedia.org/wiki/Farebox_recovery_ratio (accessed on 11-02-12).
11 www.mtr.com.hk/eng/investrelation/annualresult2007/MTR_annual_2007_final_web.pdf#page=21 (accessed on 11-02-12).
12 ibid.
13 See footnote 10.
14 Metz, 2008.
15 Zahavy Y. and A.Talvitie, 1980, "Regularities in Travel Time and Money", *Transportation Research Record*, 750: 13–19.
16 Metz, 2008, p. 323.
17 Vickrey, 1963, p. 452.
18 Data from Office for National Statistics, "Statistical Bulletin: Regional, Sub-regional, and Local Gross Value Added", (Dec 2009), in Jenkins, J., M. Colella and F. Salvucci (2010) "Agglomeration benefits and transportation projects: a review of theory, measurement, and application", Paper prepared for annual meeting of TRB, January 2011.
19 In developing financial models it is also useful to consider the situation with regard to the other networked infrastructure-based urban services: water, sanitation and power. In these cases there are provisions for combining charges for actual service with charges for capacity provision. Such consideration could be helpful in linking the public goods and private goods aspects of urban transport and urban access to one another.
20 It can be argued that because these latter taxes are imposed on aspects of economic activity that they are in some way connected to the access value that transport provides. While there is validity in this argument, it is still a tenuous link. The New York Metropolitan Transportation Authority (MTA) receives significant support from such regional sales taxes and taxes on property transfers. However, when the economy contracts as it did recently it led to a severe contraction in both consumer sales property sales, hence in revenues. Sources such as these are particularly sensitive to even small cyclical ups and downs. The result is sharp and sudden cutbacks in services when they are most needed. It is therefore important to anchor access finance in sources with far less short-term cyclical sensitivity.
21 Tax increment financing or TIF attempts to tax the increase in value of a given location as a result of public goods improvement such as enhanced transport access.
22 Congestion charging involves levying a charge on automobile users that enter the most congested parts of cities at the most congested times of day. A large SUV traveling in mid-town Manhattan at midday, mid-week imposes more social costs on the street system than does a small economy car traveling late at night in an outlying district where the streets are comparatively empty.

References

Alexiou, A. (2006) *Jane Jacobs: Urban Visionary*, New Brunswick NJ: Rutgers University Press.

Ballon, H. and Jackson, K. (eds) (2007) *Robert Moses and the Modern City: The Transformation of New York*, New York: W.W. Norton.

Beesley, M.E. and Foster, C.D. (1965) "The Victoria Line: Social Benefits and Finances', *Journal of the Royal Statistical Society, Series A (General)* 128(1): 67–88.

Black, A. (1990) "The Chicago Area Transportation Study: A Case Study of Rational Planning", *Journal of Planning Education and Research*, 10(1): 27–37.

Breithaupt, M. (2004) "Economic Instruments", Module 1d of *Sustainable Transport: A Sourcebook for Policy-makers in Developing Cities*, Deutsche Gesellschaft für Technische Zusammenarbeit (GTZ) GmbH, www2.gtz.de/dokumente/bib/05-0511.pdf (accessed 25 October 2011).

Couclelis, H. (2000) "From Sustainable Transportation to Sustainable Accessibility: Can we Avoid a New Tragedy of the Commons?", in D. Janelle and D. Hodge (eds) *Information, Place, and Cyberspace: Issues in Accessibility*, Berlin: Springer-Verlag, pp. 342–56.

Cervero, R. and Murakami, J. (2008) "Rail and Property Development in Hong Kong: Experiences, Impacts and Extensions', Working Paper, Lincoln Institute of Land Policy, http://www.lincolninst.edu/pubs/dl/1388_706_Cervero Murakami Final.pdf (accessed on 25 August 2011).

Crozet, Y. (2006) "Assessing the Long-term Outlook for Current Business Models in the Construction and Provision of Urban Mass Transit Infrastructure and Services", Paper prepared for the OECD Futures Project on Global Infrastructure Needs: Prospects and Implications for Public and Private Actors, Paris, 23 June 2006.

Darido, G., Mariana, T. M. and Mehndiratta, S. (2009) "Urban transport and CO_2 Emissions: Some Evidence from Chinese Cities", World Bank Working Paper, June 2009.

Dupuit, A. J. É. J. (1844) *De la Mesure de l'Utilité des Travaux Publics*, Annales des Ponts et Chaussées, Second series, 8. Translated by R.H. Barback as *On the Measurement of the Utility of Public Works*, International Economic Papers, 1952.

Flint, A. (2009) *Wrestling with Moses: How Jane Jacobs Took On New York's Master Builder and Transformed the American City*, New York: Random House.

Foster, C.D. and Beesley, M.E. (1963) "Estimating the Social Benefit of Constructing an Underground Railway in London", *Journal of the Royal Statistical Society, Series A (General)* 126(1): 46–93.

Glaeser, E. (2011) *Triumph of the City, How Our Greatest Invention Makes Us Richer, Smarter, Greener, Healthier and Happier*, London: The Penguin Press.

Hansen, W. G. (1959) "How accessibility shapes land use", *Journal of the American Institute of Planners* 25: 73–6.

Jacobs, J. (1961) *The Death and Life of Great American Cities*, New York: Vintage Books.

Jacobs, J. (1969) *The Economy of Cities*, New York: Vintage Books.

Jenkins, J., Colella, M. and Salvucci, F. (2010) "Agglomeration Benefits and Transportation Projects: A Review of Theory, Measurement and application",

Paper prepared for annual meeting of Transport Research Board, January 2011, Washington, DC.

Marshall, A. (1920) *Principles of Economics*, Eighth Edition, 1961 reprint, London: Macmillan and Co Ltd.

Metz, D. (2008) "The Myth of Travel Time Saving", *Transport Reviews* 28(3): 321–36.

Moses, R. (1970) *Public Works: A Dangerous Trade*, New York: McGraw Hill.

Nelson, R. and Winter, S. (1982) *An Evolutionary Theory of Economic Change*, Cambridge: Harvard University Press.

Office for National Statistics UK (2011) *Statistical Bulletin: Regional, Sub-regional, and Local Gross Value Added*, December.

Pierson, P. (2000) "Increasing Returns, Path Dependence and the Study of Politics", *The American Political Science Review* 94(2 June): 251–67.

Schaeffer, K.H. and Sclar, E. (1980) *Access for All: Transportation and Urban Growth*, New York: Columbia University Press.

Sennett, R. (1970) *Uses of Disorder: Personal Identity and City Life*, New York: Knopf.

Smith, A. (1776) *An Inquiry into the Nature and Causes of the Wealth of Nations*, 1937 Edition, Modern Library Edition, New York: Random House.

Talvitie, A. (ed.) (2000) *Lessons from Urban Transport: Selected Proceedings from a World Bank Seminar*, Washington, DC: The World Bank.

Vickrey, W. (1963) "Pricing in Urban and Suburban Transport", *The American Economic Review* 53(2): 452–46, www.econ.ucsb.edu/~tedb/Courses/UCSBpf/readings/vickerymay63.pdf (accessed 25 October 2011).

Warner, S. B. Jr (1962) *Streetcar Suburbs: The Process of Growth in Boston 1870-1900* Cambridge; Harvard University Press.

Weimer, D. and Vining, A. (2010) *Policy Analysis*, London: Longman.

Zahavi, Y. and Talvitie, A. (1980) "Regularities in Travel Time and Money Expenditures", *Transportation Research Record*, 750: 13–19.

Chapter 3

Social inequalities in urban access

Better ways of assessing transport improvements

Sylvie Fol and Caroline Gallez

In the field of transport studies, research on urban access generally deals with this notion in a narrow sense. Most of the time the issue of access is analysed in terms of transportation network performance, using economic models that were designed to assess infrastructure efficiency. In this chapter we argue that the social characteristics of space and of individuals, along with the provision of urban amenities in a given urban environment, are also essential elements in the complex notion of urban access. Therefore, urban access should be analysed not only in terms of transportation networks but also from the perspective of spaces and individuals. We begin with a review of studies measuring urban access through accessibility in the field of urban geography and transport studies, without restricting our analysis to transportation networks and transport policies. By rejecting a narrow definition of urban access, we seek to broaden thinking on measuring social access inequalities and their implications for public policy. We then examine policies implemented to improve accessibility, focusing on those policies that emphasize the social dimension of urban access, and offering a critical review of the models and indicators used to assess transportation investments and policies. Finally, we suggest some possible explanations for the lack of emphasis on social accessibility and offer suggestions to help overcome current difficulties.

3.1 Introduction

Since the 1990s, the existence of a link between transport and social exclusion has been recognized (Gaffron, Hine and Mitchell, 2001) and has featured prominently in several countries.[1] This connection has been the subject of growing interest in research and policy. In the United Kingdom, for example, the creation of the Social Exclusion Unit in 1997 was a starting point for the development of many studies analysing the various factors behind social exclusion. Lack of access to facilities and services has been cited among the components of social isolation (SEU, 2003). As a result, the notion of accessibility has received renewed attention in studies aiming to understand the transportation dimension or more generally speaking the spatial dimension of social exclusion. Similarly, in the US and in France the implementation of welfare-to-work policies has placed new emphasis on the necessity for job seekers to access employment. At the same time, the transportation field has also changed its focus from policies addressing a wide range of destinations to strategies targeting deprived areas (Harzo, 1998; Sanchez, 2008). However, despite this growing interest in accessibility and its relationship with social exclusion processes, there has been more recognition of this issue than progress in evaluating its components, effects and applications to public policy.

Accessibility is indeed a complex notion, "a multifaceted concept" according to Curtis and Scheurer, 2010. It is related to the spatial dimension of social exclusion and raises the issue of the role of place and location in poverty (Farrington, 2007). However, the role of space in social exclusion is unclear and still the subject of debate (Hodgson and Turner, 2003). While most studies emphasize the fact that spatial segregation reinforces social exclusion, some authors argue that other factors like race play a more important role than space in social exclusion processes (Ellwood, 1986).

Another difficulty in dealing with the notion of accessibility is its proximity to that of mobility. The two terms are often used interchangeably without clear distinction. According to Handy (2002), there is a strong relationship between the two ideas, which probably explains the confusion: mobility refers to a potential for movement while accessibility can be defined as a potential for interaction (Hansen, 1959). Moseley (1979, quoted by Farrington and Farrington, 2005) insists that accessibility must be focused on "opportunities, not behavior", which expresses the distinction between accessibility and mobility. Farrington (2007) underlines that

> there should be no simple conceptualization which sees mobility deriving from person characteristics, with accessibility being solely an attribute of place. Accessibility is at least as much about people as places.

As mobility reflects the ability to reach a destination, policies to increase mobility will generally increase accessibility (Handy, 2002). However, this is not always the case. In the US, the focus on mobility in transportation planning has contributed to a decrease in accessibility by encouraging sprawl and a scattered pattern of urban development.

"To plan for accessibility, in contrast, is to focus on the ends rather than the means and to focus on the traveler rather than the system". For Handy (2002), accessibility planning includes a much broader range of strategies, which do not necessarily imply increasing travel. For Curtis and Scheurer (2010), "while mobility is concerned with the performance of transport systems in their own right, accessibility adds the interplay of transport systems and land use patterns as a further layer of analysis". As a result, mobility planning has traditionally been concerned with the movement of motor vehicles, people and goods, while accessibility planning includes the land use and transport connection (Litman, 2003). However, as Farrington (2007) states,

> a mobilities discourse does not conflict with an accessibility concept, which recognises the significant role that mobility plays, and will continue to play, in achieving the spectrum of people's needs for reaching and participating in activities, services and opportunities.

Thus, current reflections on accessibility converge with those of authors like Urry (2003) or Cass *et al.* (2005), which are more focused on mobility issues. The two concepts should be seen as complementary (Farrington, 2007).

Another point to bear in mind when dealing with accessibility issues is the fact that "accessibility is only one aspect of social exclusion, and the existence of a high level of accessibility does not necessarily imply that people are able to benefit from it" (Church, Frost and Sullivan, 2000). In addition, to understand the various components of accessibility, it is necessary to distinguish between direct and indirect accessibility. According to Hine and Grieco (2003) individuals with low levels of direct accessibility can gain actual access through their social networks. It is therefore important to take interpersonal interactions and involvement with the local community into account, since exclusion from mainstream society does not necessarily mean exclusion from local networks (Stanley and Vella-Broderick, 2009). At the same time, certain individuals' social isolation is likely to worsen their accessibility situation (Hine and Grieco, 2003). Social interaction is thus an important dimension of access, as underlined by Cass *et al.* (2005): "appreciating the networked nature of social life makes the notion of access more complex and less locally focused".

Certain groups are more likely to experience accessibility-related disadvantages: people on low incomes, women, older people, disabled people, and (more generally) carless individuals are the most affected by the lack of access (Hine and Mitchell, 2001; Social Exclusion Unit, 2003; Hine and Grieco, 2003). Unfortunately most of the accessibility measures currently used are area- and space-based (Hine and Grieco, 2003). Additionally, current accessibility planning is not very sensitive to issues such as gender, age, disability and ethnicity (Preston and Rajé, 2007).

Finally it is important to recognize that accessibility is a component of social justice. As Farrington (2007) pointed out, constrained access is "making more difficult the achievement of social justice". Accessibility is thus "a pre-condition for social inclusion, itself a pre-condition for social justice". The accessibility discourse should take the relationship between accessibility needs and accessibility rights into account (Farrington and Farrington, 2005). It necessarily engages reflections on equity (Young,

1994) and spatial justice (Soja, 2010). An accessibility perspective is part of "the project of inserting explicitly the notion of space into the understanding of social justice" (Farrington and Farrington, 2005). This cannot happen without integrating the various dimensions of accessibility planning. While transport policies are of course critical to achieve better accessibility, they can be viewed as a "fire-fighting" rather than a permanent solution (Farrington and Farrington, 2005).

Within the current framework of accessibility planning, the integration of land use and transport has become a key policy objective (Hine and Grieco, 2003) and has led to the development of new approaches to measuring accessibility. However, accessibility-enhancing policies are difficult to introduce and there are many barriers to their implementation. Some are technical in nature but most involve political choices and the way in which priorities are defined. In this chapter, we first review the various definitions of the notion of accessibility, as well as measurement techniques that have been proposed in the literature. The second section examines policies intended to improve accessibility, focusing on those that emphasize the social dimension of urban access. A critical review of models and indicators used to assess transportation investments and policies is then provided. Finally, based on our conclusion that the social dimension of accessibility is not sufficiently accounted for in either evaluations or policies, the last section of this chapter will suggest possible explanations for this situation and propose new ways of overcoming these difficulties.

3.2 Accessibility: definitions, measures and observations

Though accessibility is a major topic in geography, urban planning, and transport engineering, it is also "a slippery notion (...) one of those common terms that everyone uses until faced with the problem of defining and measuring it" (Gould, 1969). As noted by Dalvi and Martin (1976), the "conceptual nature" of accessibility makes it difficult to propose a satisfactory measure, and complicates its use as a variable in travel demand or urban interaction models. Examining the state of the art in the fields of transportation and urban planning studies, this chapter will first review different perspectives on measuring accessibility. Then, focusing on the relationship between accessibility and social inequality, we will evaluate the usefulness and limitations of accessibility indicators as social indicators. Finally, we will discuss a number of empirical results concerning the social dimension of accessibility.

3.2.1 Definitions of accessibility

Since the end of the 1950s, accessibility has been defined in various ways for different purposes. According to Vandenbulcke, Steenberghen and

Thomas (2009) there is no consensus on the definition and formulation of accessibility. Hansen (1959) defines it as "the potential of opportunities for interaction". Most of the early definitions of accessibility refer to the "get-at-ability" of a destination (Hillman, Henderson and Whalley, 1973, quoted by Hine and Grieco, 2003). Burns and Golob (1976) thus refer to "the ease with which any land-use activity can be reached from a location using a particular transport system". According to Burns (1979), accessibility represents "the freedom of individuals to decide whether to participate or not in different activities". For Ben-Akiva and Lerman (1979), it could be defined as "the benefits provided by a transportation/land-use system".

These different definitions concur on one point: in its simplest sense, accessibility is related to the interaction between land use and transport systems. Accessibility therefore is not only a question of transport. Indeed, accessibility is determined "by the spatial distribution of potential destinations, the ease of reaching each destination, as well as the magnitude, quality and character of the activities found there" (Vandenbulcke *et al.*, 2009). Accessibility is

> a function of the mobility of the individual, of the spatial location of activity opportunities relative to the starting point of the individual and of the times at which the activities are available (...). Accessibility therefore depends on the transportation available to individuals, the temporal and spatial distribution of activities and the social and economic roles of individuals that determine when, where and how long they must pursue various activities.
>
> (Okodi, Kerali and Santorini, 2001)

Bhat *et al.* (2000) define accessibility as "a measure of the ease of an individual to pursue an activity of a desired type, at a desired location, by a desired mode, and at a desired time". According to a recent definition, "accessibility refers to the ability of individuals to easily reach desired goods, services, activities and destinations at appropriate times using an integrated transport system without being restricted by physical, financial or safety concerns" (Wixey, Jones, Lucas and Aldridge, 2005). This definition points to the various components of accessibility. Finally, most definitions agree on four main determinants of accessibility: land use, transport, time and individual components (Vandenbulcke *et al.*, 2009).

According to Geurs and Van Wee (2004), the "land use component" of accessibility not only reflects the amount, quality, and spatial distribution of opportunities, but also the demand for these opportunities and the tension between supply and demand. The "transportation component" refers to the transport system, expressed as the disutility for an individual to cover the distance between an origin and a destination using a specific transport mode (which depends on the tension between infrastructure and transport service supply and demand). Since accessibility is related to the role of land use and transport systems in society, which "gives individuals the opportunity to participate in activities in different locations" (Geurs and Van Wee, 2004), we must consider the influence of two other components: the "temporal" and "individual" components. The former refers to the availability of opportunities at different times of the day and the time available to participate in activities in different locations. The latter relates to the needs, abilities and opportunities of individuals, which depend on several characteristics such as age, income, household situation, physical condition and availability of travel modes.

To summarize, an accessibility measure should ideally take into account these four components. It should be sensitive to changes in the transport and land use systems, to temporal constraints or opportunities such as changes in the schedules of public services and account for individual characteristics such as income, sex, age, or qualifications that could influence access to travel modes, jobs, or housing. These four components are not independent. For instance, the distribution of activities influences travel demand and may also introduce time constraints, influencing people's opportunities. The individual component interacts with the three other components: a person's sex or age determines his or her time constraints, needs, access to travel modes, and relevant activity types. As stated by Farrington (2007), accessibility is at least as much about people as places: "A place is not just 'more' or 'less' accessible, but accessible relative to people in all their different circumstances: people experience more, or less, access to places". Accessibility is also related to social groups, which vary in their needs and ability to access different goods and services (Wixey *et al.*, 2005). In practice, accessibility measures generally focus on one or more of the four components, depending on the perspective employed (Geurs and Van Wee, 2004).

3.2.2 Practical measures of accessibility

As underlined by Weber (2006), the history of accessibility is "the history of particular measures, such as topological, cumulative opportunity, population potential or space-time". From a literature review in the field of transport and urban planning (see for instance Handy and Niemeier, 1997; Geurs and Ritsema van Eck, 2001; Kwan and Weber, 2003; Vandenbulcke *et al.*, 2009), we have identified three basic perspectives[2] on measuring accessibility:

1   *Location-based measures* analyse accessibility at locations. The measures describe the level of accessibility from one place to spatially distributed opportunities around that place and are typically used in

urban planning and geographical studies. This category includes several types of indicators, which have been improved over time, such as Geurs and Ritsema van Eck, 2001:

- *Distance measures*, which are the simplest ones. For instance Ingram (1971) defines "relative accessibility" as the degree to which two places on the same surface are connected, and "integral accessibility" as the degree of interconnection for a given point with all other points on the same surface. This type of measure assumes that space is undifferentiated with respect to the distribution of opportunities, and mainly estimates the connectivity of locations derived from the transport network.

- *Contour measures*, also known as isochrone measures or cumulative opportunities, evaluate the number of opportunities from a particular point within a certain time distance or travel cost range (Wachs and Kumagai, 1973; Dalvi and Martin, 1976). Elements of land use and transport components are taken into account, but their combined effects are not evaluated.

- *Potential accessibility measures or gravity measures* have been designed to differentiate the attractiveness of opportunities by considering their distance from the origin point. In these measures accessibility decreases gradually as the travel time to destinations increases. Hansen (1959) was the first author to use the "potential concept", derived from the social physics school, to describe accessibility. Several adjustments to Hansen's formulation have been proposed, using alternative decay functions of distance or cost and weighting the potential accessibility measure according to the total number of opportunities in the zone of origin (see for instance Dalvi and Martin, 1976).

- *Competition factors and inverse balancing factors*, derived from gravity models, have been developed to take into account competition effects that result from the interaction between the demand and supply of opportunities when measuring access to opportunities. Competition factors only account for the competition for available opportunities, for instance the competition between job seekers (Shen, 1998). Inverse balancing factors also take into account the impact of other opportunities in other places, which may influence the level of accessibility to opportunities in a given place. Based on the doubly constrained spatial interaction model of Wilson (1971), inverse balancing factors are calculated by using an iterative process ensuring the number of trips to and from each zone is equal to the number of opportunities (Geurs and Ritsema van Eck, 2003).

2   *Individual-based measures* analysing accessibility at the individual level were first developed in the time–space geography of Hägerstrand (1970). They evaluate the activities that an individual can participate in

at any given time, considering constraints such as the location and duration of activities, the time budget for activities, and the travel speed allowed by the transport system (see for instance Dijst and Vidakovic, 1997).

3   *Utility-based measures* analyse the utility (benefits) that people derive from access to spatially distributed activities. The primary assumptions of this approach are found in Koenig (1974, 1980). Accessibility is measured at the individual level and takes into account user characteristics (income, demographic variables), in addition to modal or link characteristics (speed and travel costs) (see for instance Banister and Berechman, 2000).

3.2.3 Methodological problems of accessibility as a social indicator

While our literature review reveals the existence of a wide range of accessibility definitions and measures, most studies pay little attention to the social dimension of accessibility. Moreover, since accessibility has been defined primarily in terms of public transport access to key destinations, its measurement is mostly based on aggregate and unimodal approaches "when a more disaggregated, multimodal approach is required" (Preston, 2009). We will now review practical measures of accessibility, questioning (from a methodological point of view) their ability to be used as social indicators.

Location-based measures

Location-based measures represent accessibility from one location to all other destinations, and do not account for individual characteristics that influence access. This drawback can probably be overcome by disaggregating measures among different population groups (see for instance Handy and Niemeier, 1997). Nevertheless, these measures exhibit several shortcomings in accounting for individual disparities. First, neither distance, contour nor potential measures include competition effects. They do not account for the tension between opportunity, supply and demand. Inverse balancing factors, which have been designed to overcome this problem, are rarely used because they are complex to interpret and to estimate, as they result from an iterative process (Geurs and Van Wee, 2004). Furthermore, location-based measures do not account for temporal constraints.

Individual-based measures

Individual-based measures seem to be more appropriate when evaluating social access disparities, as they analyse accessibility from the viewpoint of individuals. The main purpose of the space–time geography founded by

Hägerstrand (1970) was to re-introduce the individual and time components into spatial models, examining how individuals' or households' activity programs could be carried out given time restrictions. Prisms were used to describe patterns in space and time, identifying the potential areas within which opportunities could be reached given predetermined time constraints. Individual-based measures have great theoretical advantages: in particular, they allow more sensitive assessment of variations in accessibility, such as gender or ethnic differences, and account for the "lived experience of individuals" (Kwan and Weber, 2003). Highlighting the need for new concepts and methods in accessibility research, Kwan and Weber state that "the effect of distance on the spatial structure of contemporary cities and human spatial behavior has become much more complicated than what has been conceived in conventional urban models and concepts of accessibility". However, these measures have several shortcomings for the evaluation of land use and transport investment. First, they do not account for competition effects. Second, current activity-based measures focus on short-term behavioral responses, and do not include the effect of long-term land use changes on daily household activities and travel patterns. Third, these measures are difficult to operationalize. Recent developments in space–time measures have been made using network-based GIS (Geographic Information Systems) (see for instance Kwan, 1998). Despite advances in GIS and spatial modeling, many difficulties remain, including the detailed individual activity-travel data required and the lack of operational algorithms (Kwan, 1998). Furthermore, as data on individuals' time budgets are not available in standard travel surveys, applications are often restricted to relatively small areas and subsets of the population, resulting in difficulties in extrapolating the analysis to larger population groups.

Utility-based measures

Under the utility-based approach accessibility should be measured at the individual level and computed by including individual characteristics (Banister and Berechman, 2000). Utility-based measures interpret accessibility as the outcome of a set of transport choices. The computation of individual utility takes user characteristics (income, residential location and demographic variables) into account in addition to the number of opportunities at the destination (measuring each person's freedom of choice) and transport characteristics (speed, travel costs) (Koenig, 1974, 1980; Banister and Berechman, 2000). Two main types of measures are cited in the literature (Geurs and Ritsema van Eck, 2001). The first is based on random utility theory (the logsum model) and its main advantage is that it can be integrated with microeconomic theory, allowing consumer surplus calculations. The second is based on a doubly constrained entropy model including competition effects, but this measure cannot be interpreted in terms of consumer surplus or welfare without strong restrictions. To summarize, utility-based measures satisfy most of the theoretical requirements for accessibility measurement except for temporal and schedule constraints. Furthermore, because they capture the non-linear relationships between accessibility improvements and changes in utility, they can show the existence of diminishing returns. As a result, a utility-based measure may indicate that it is more desirable to improve accessibility for individuals at locations with low accessibility than at locations already benefiting from higher levels (Koenig, 1980; Geurs and Ritsema van Eck, 2001). This is clearly relevant when undertaking social or economic evaluations of transport and land use projects. The major disadvantage of these measures is the difficulty of interpreting and disseminating them, due to their roots in complex economic theory (Koenig, 1980).

3.2.4 Incorporating the social dimension in accessibility measures: empirical results

According to many authors (Church and Frost, 1999; Gaffron *et al.*, 2001), few studies have produced useful indicators for analysing the link between social exclusion and transport. In the field of social exclusion analysis, "there are relatively few studies which directly attempt to assess levels of transport or accessibility as part of their indicators" (Church and Frost, 1999). By the same token, in the transportation field there is a paucity of empirical data to analyse the link between transport and social exclusion.

However, the social dimension of accessibility has been extensively studied and documented since the end of the 1990s due to increasing concern over social exclusion and its determinants. Since then, lack of mobility and insufficient access to urban services and resources have been included among factors that can prevent particular social or ethnic groups from fully participating in society. These studies can be roughly divided into three categories:

Individual indicators of social disparities

A significant number of studies have been dedicated to illustrating social disparities in mobility, based on individual indicators. Most of these studies analyse the relationship between individual characteristics (household income, race, gender, age, etc.) and various indicators, such as travel patterns (number of trips, distance travelled and travel modes), car ownership, or the possession of a driver's licence. These studies show that in the US (Murakami and Young, 1997; Pucher and Renne, 2003), in Great Britain (SEU, 2003) as well as in France (Mignot and Rosales-Montano, 2006; Orfeuil, 2004; Paulo, 2006), low-income households travel less and make shorter trips than their richer counterparts. Similarly, in these three countries, the rate of car ownership is much lower among low-income households, which are therefore more dependent on public transit and walking. As Pucher and Renne (2003) pointed out, this might be interpreted as a fundamental inequity in the transportation system. Many low-income households experience restrictions on individual accessibility because they cannot reach parts of metropolitan areas that are only accessible by car. This brings us to a second category of studies that goes beyond mobility to address the notion of accessibility.

Unequal access to job opportunities

Many studies have focused on the unequal access to job opportunities among different social or ethnic groups.[3] The extensive research on this topic generally combines various accessibility components and indicators: land use (location of residence and job opportunities), transportation (availability of transportation modes) and individual (income, social or ethnic group, and gender). A growing number of studies have shown that the uneven residential distribution of social and ethnic groups combined with the spatial distribution of employment opportunities creates large scale accessibility inequalities between groups. First developed in the US after the seminal work of John Kain (1968), the "spatial mismatch" literature has grown in importance since the 1996 Welfare Reform. Four types of approaches can be distinguished (Ihlanfeldt and Sjoquist, 1998) in the literature: comparisons of commuting time or distances between different ethnic or social groups; attempts to measure the impact of job accessibility on obtaining and maintaining a job and on wages; comparisons of the integration of inner-city and suburban residents in the job market; and examinations of the differences between inner city and suburban job markets. While most authors conclude that the suburbanization process has reinforced residential segregation and job access inequality, there is no consensus on the weight of the spatial mismatch factor in explaining certain social or ethnic groups' employment difficulties. Taylor and Ong (1995) show that barriers to employment opportunities for ethnic minorities are related less to spatial mismatch than to the use of slow forms of transportation: individual members of ethnic minorities have longer commute times because they use public transport more frequently and not because their jobs are further away. They conclude that the problem is one of "automobile mismatch" rather than "spatial mismatch". A body of related research has shown that car use tends to be positively correlated with a wider range of destinations, higher employment rates and salaries, and reduced disparities in inter-ethnic levels of unemployment (Ong, 1996; Blumenberg, 2002). According to Raphael and Stoll (2002), low-income people with access to a car have a better chance of finding and retaining a job than their carless counterparts.

The spatial mismatch debate has raised questions related to the role of space and access in the exclusion of certain individuals and groups from the job market. However, the conclusions are still controversial and several studies have shown that other factors like racial discrimination (Ellwood, 1986), lack of qualifications (O'Regan and Quigley, 1999), or time constraints can also play a major role in the employment difficulties of certain groups. As a consequence "decades of empirical tests have resulted in widely divergent results, with contradictory evidence that both supports and refutes the existence of spatial mismatch" (Grengs, 2010). These conflicting results can be explained not only by the use of oversimplified measures of job access but also by the fact that the concept of spatial mismatch is "ill-defined" (Grengs, 2010). Therefore, the enormous amount of research on the topic contrasts with a lack of consensus on the relevant variables to take into account and the limited policy response to the issue of job access. Actually,

> because scholars have been vague in defining the relevant independent variables in spatial mismatch studies, policy makers have interpreted the primary problem as geographic distance. But a person's prospects depend on the land-use arrangements of housing and jobs, the location of competing workers in filling a job, the availability of a car, and the effectiveness of transportation infrastructures and services. In other words, the problem is one of accessibility rather than distance itself.
>
> (Grengs, 2010)

Another problem with the spatial mismatch debate is the fact that it tends to reduce the problem of accessibility to the sole issue of job access, and the solution to social inclusion as integration in the job market.[4] However, there has been a recent movement toward a "wider 'access to services' understanding" of social exclusion (Hodgson and Turner, 2003), leading to a broader understanding of accessibility.

Unequal access to services

Several recent studies have attempted to measure lack of access to a wide range of services as a component of social exclusion (Caubel, 2006). Studies in this category use a larger set of indicators than those in the previous one, especially regarding the land use component (location of various urban resources and opportunities). As low-income households are often concentrated in locations with sparse facilities and poor public transport services, the question of accessibility for residents living in deprived neighborhoods has been given emphasis.

In Great Britain, the appearance of the Social Exclusion Unit in 1997 created opportunities to analyse the various dimensions of social exclusion, as well as the relationship between mobility and social exclusion (Church *et al.*, 1999, 2000; Hine and Mitchell, 2001; SEU 2003; Grieco, 2003; Lyons, 2003; Lucas, 2004). Church *et al.* (2000) list seven types of transport-related exclusion: physical, geographic, economic, time-based, fear-based, space and exclusion from facilities. Wixey *et al.* (2005) list six main types of transport exclusion: spatial, temporal, personal, financial, environmental, infrastructural and institutional. Although these typologies help us better understand transportation-related social exclusion processes, they must develop empirical measures in order to be operationally useful.

Among the indices of local deprivation used by the Social Exclusion Unit is a measure of accessibility. However, as Grieco (2003) points out, the Index of Multiple Deprivation introduced by the SEU has a very limited accessibility component as it considers only four items: access to a food store, primary health care, a primary school, and a post office. Moreover, this kind of measure is restricted to "identifying outcomes without identifying the processes which produce them" (Grieco, 2003). Another weak point is the paucity of data on the cost of transportation and its effects on accessibility (Preston and Rajé, 2007).

Several studies have suggested that indicators using GIS databases should be developed. For example, Church *et al.* (1999, 2000) proposed a method of local access mapping based on the location of facilities (post offices and shops) and transport infrastructure. Their approach involves identifying areas with high levels of deprivation based on the Index of Local Deprivation devised by the Social Exclusion Unit. By calculating the average time needed to travel to specific destinations from a given area (using a mapping tool called CAPITAL), a cumulative indicator identifies the time needed to access a range of facilities and services. While this type of area-based accessibility indicator is interesting, it does not take into account the individual dimension of accessibility. As Hine and Grieco (2003) point out, the fact that people have access to opportunities does not necessarily mean that they will be able to take advantage of them. In addition, while the mapping technique is very useful for identifying and measuring a lack of accessibility within clusters of individuals affected by social exclusion, it does not help detect more scattered individuals or groups (Hine and Grieco, 2003; Preston and Rajé, 2007). Consequently the focus on area-based measures rather than individual measures may be considered problematic.

As a result of the complexity of these measures, "examples of the actual use of accessibility measures in planning are relatively scarce" according to Handy and Clifton (2001). Traditional measures do not take some characteristics of the local environment into account, though they might have a major impact on transportation mode choice. In fact, accessibility assessment would require data that is very difficult to collect. There is a gap between the data required to obtain a satisfactory measure of accessibility and the data available to planning departments. In addition, "the more complex the measure the more data and analysis skill required, limiting the ability of most planning departments to develop such measures" (Handy and Clifton, 2001). It is thus a major methodological challenge "to make the bridge from theory to practice" (Preston, 2009) and to find "the right balance between a measure that is theoretically and empirically sound and one that is sufficiently plain to be usefully employed in interactive, creative plan-making processes where participants typically have different degrees of expertise" (Bertolini *et al.*, 2005). According to Bertolini *et al.* (2005, cited by Curtis and Scheurer, 2010), "in order to be useful for practical planning purposes, an accessibility measure must meet two basic requirements: it must be consistent with the uses and perceptions of the residents, workers and visitors of an area, and it must be understandable to those taking part in the plan-making process". This emphasizes the need to build a common language between the different participants in the planning process, be it policy-makers, technicians or citizens.

3.3 Transport policy and social inequalities

Studies show that the way in which social inequalities have been addressed as a subject for public policy in general (Castel, 1995; Paugam, 1996) and for transport policy in particular has changed over time. In the 1960s, transport policies in most European countries focused on the development of road infrastructure, in order to meet expected growth in demand and individual mobility. In France at the beginning of the 1970s, the priority given to the development of urban public transport networks was a response to different concerns: preventing a loss of attractiveness in urban centers, ensuring access to the city center (in the context of rapidly increasing car traffic) and providing access to urban amenities for the many (especially those without a car). During this period, prior to the growth in suburbanization, transport studies paid little attention to the problem of socio–spatial inequalities. Many authors have pointed out that, similarly, much literature on social exclusion (or inclusion) had long neglected its spatial or mobility-related aspects (Kenyon, Rafferty and Lyons, 2003, cited by Farrington, 2007; Church *et al.*, 2000).

Over the past four decades, the policy discourse on social issues gradually evolved from the fight against social inequalities to the problem of social exclusion (Jones and Smyth, 1999; Levitas, 2000). At the same time, the dimension of transportation and accessibility has slowly found its place among factors cited as contributing to social exclusion. As a result, instead of aiming to provide extensive access, transportation policies have been increasingly focused on specific territories, targeting the needs of the most deprived neighborhoods which are seen as being particularly vulnerable to social exclusion. Since the 1990s, improving urban access for disadvantaged groups has become a component of strategies put in place to tackle social exclusion, partly through Workfare-type policies.[5]

Similarly, the question of social inequalities in access has been reformulated since the 1960s, influencing the design and application of models and indicators used in the assessment of transport and land use investments. Despite growing concern over social exclusion and recognition that a lack of accessibility can prevent people from taking part in social activities, equity considerations are still poorly integrated in the *ex-ante* assessment of transport investment projects. On the other hand, an analysis of recent transport-specific policies in different countries shows their limited success in the fight against social exclusion, emphasizing the need for cross-sector policies.

In this section, we review policies intended to improve urban access, focusing on policies that have been implemented since the 1990s to tackle social exclusion through improved accessibility. Then we examine the various tools used to assess transport policies and their limitations. Finally we discuss social access as a policy priority.

3.3.1 Tackling social exclusion through accessibility policies

Over the past twenty years, the perceived link between low accessibility to urban resources and the risk of social exclusion resulted in specific policies in most countries. Since the 1990s, in France policies have been implemented to promote improved access to public transit in disadvantaged areas (Harzo, 1998). In the UK, after the creation of the Social Exclusion Unit, lack of access to various services was identified as a factor behind social exclusion. Many studies have set out the various dimensions of social exclusion that limit "access to basic necessities of life" (Strategy Action Team, 1999, quoted by Gaffron *et al.*, 2001). The 2003 Report of the Social Exclusion Unit states that "recent years have seen a growing recognition that transport problems can be a significant barrier to social inclusion" (SEU, 2003). As a result, the UK has introduced policies to improve access to public transport in socially deprived areas. However, the main innovation is the introduction of "accessibility planning" (SEU, 2003). In 2004, the Department for Transport published a guidance note which required accessibility strategies to be included in local transport plans. A five-step approach was recommended: strategic accessibility assessment, local accessibility assessment, option appraisal, accessibility plan preparation, performance monitoring plus evaluation (Preston and Rajé, 2007). As a result, while developing their 2006–2010 local transport plans, local transport planners had to work with land use planners, service providers and agencies, the private sector and major employers:

> the key aims for accessibility planning are to ensure that local decision-makers have improved information on the areas where accessibility is poorest and the barriers to accessibility from the perspective of the

people who are living there. It is also designed to create a more transparent, integrated and equitable process for transport and land-use decisions. Transport planners are encouraged to 'think out of the box' and work more collaboratively with their partner agencies, so that a wider range of solutions to accessibility problems can be identified and greater value for money achieved through their combined and synchronized efforts.

(Lucas, 2006)

In the US, transportation policy started addressing social justice goals in the 1990s, in a break with what has been called the "Interstate era" of high-way-building (Jakowitsch and Ernst, 2004). A landmark measure, the Intermodal Surface Transportation Efficiency Act (ISTEA) was passed in 1991, and helped balance investment between roads and public transport infrastructure (Goldman, Deakin, 2000). Improved access for disadvantaged groups and individuals was to be achieved "through intermodal connections between people and jobs, goods and markets, and neighborhoods" (Bullard, 1996, cited by Sanchez, 2008). It also made cooperation with citizens and transportation bodies compulsory. The Transportation Equity Act for the 21st Century (TEA-21), which followed ISTEA in 1998, continued in the same vein making the travel needs of the poor and ethnic minorities a priority. The role of citizens and users in decision-making was strengthened. Meanwhile, the welfare system reform passed in 1996 emphasized the mobility needs of welfare recipients. Some of the "welfare-to-work" funds provided by the Federal Government were dedicated to improving transportation services. They were used to adapt public transit routes and schedules to the needs of welfare recipients, but also to create specific programs intended to improve access to employment.

Recently, due to the rising importance of "Workfare" policies in several industrialized countries, the ability to get around is presented as an important factor in maximizing the employability of poorer people. Therefore, accessibility and transportation are now seen as key in getting people back to work (Gobillon, Selod and Zenou, 2007; Patacchini and Zénou, 2003). At the same time, mobility is increasingly considered to be a personal asset and resource. In this context, public policies increasingly target individuals through dedicated tools like car ownership programs (Wachs and Taylor, 1998; Blumenberg and Waller, 2003) or targeted fare policies (Mignot and Rosales-Montano, 2006).

3.3.2 Social disparities, equity and the appraisal of transport investments

Since the 1990s, the spread of sustainable development ideas has raised the issue of environmental and social assessment of transport projects as well as their economic impact. While substantial efforts have been made to include environmental impacts in the appraisal of transport projects, the social dimension has received far less attention. Recent studies examine the evaluation of transport's social impacts (Geurs, Boon and Van Wee, 2009) or equity considerations in transport infrastructure appraisal[6] (see for instance Van Wee, 2012; Litman, 2011; Thomopoulos, Grant-Muller and Tight, 2009). Based on this review of current practices, we will first identify the limitations and advantages of the two main approaches to transport project evaluation, particularly their ability to take distributional impacts into account. Then, we will show that valuing mobility rather than accessibility in transport project appraisal may prevent better inclusion of the social dimension in transport and urban planning.

Cost–benefit analysis

Cost-Benefit Analysis (CBA) is a method where the benefits of a given project are weighed against its costs. If the benefit to cost ratio (BCR) is greater than one, the project is considered a worthy investment. One major advantage of the method (which probably explains its popularity) is that it allows multiple options to be compared on the basis of a single value: the BCR. Today CBA is the standard method of transport project evaluation in most Western countries. Despite its popularity, the methodology of cost–benefit Analysis has been criticized for several reasons (Thomopoulos *et al.*, 2009; Grant-Muller, Mackie, Nellthorp and Pearman, 2001), some ethical and others technical. Here, we will focus on criticism of measuring social impacts and disparities, and the ethical basis of these methods.

First of all, CBA is criticized for ignoring distribution effects. The underlying theory of CBA, utilitarianism, does not distinguish between the different beneficiaries of a project – the aim is to maximize the total amount of welfare in society as a whole. Focusing on total welfare does not account for lost welfare among certain regions or population groups. CBA is based on the underlying assumption of an optimal distribution of income, neglecting the fact that, in practice, the marginal utility of one monetary unit decreases with wealth.

Furthermore, to be included in CBA, the effects of transport must be expressed in monetary terms, which is difficult for environmental effects and almost impossible for social effects. In practice, only a very limited number of social impacts are included in CBA as monetary values. This is generally done through the estimation of compensation, after a willingness to pay (WTP) or a willingness to accept compensations (WTA) survey has been conducted. However, this type of *a posteriori* compensation does not take into account other potentially damaging effects, such as the relative loss of access for certain regions or population groups resulting from the choice of one option over another. In other cases, social impacts are either omitted or assessed using a qualitative appraisal (see for instance Geurs *et al.*, 2009). Moreover, the overall benefit of a particular project is highly sensitive to the chosen discount rate and the time horizon of benefits. Furthermore, these choices may have intergenerational equity implications.

Another limitation is that in most transport project evaluation methods, direct effects are estimated in terms of travel time savings[7] (Metz, 2008; Geurs *et al.*, 2009; CGPC, 2005; Grant-Muller *et al.*, 2001). Several authors have criticized this methodological approach to benefits (see for instance Neuberger, 1971; Poulit, 1974; Koenig, 1974; Metz, 2008), emphasizing the fact that short-term improvements in transport conditions may not result in a long-term reduction in travel time, but rather an increase in mean or total travel time. The additional travel time resulting from new transport infrastructure has long been recognized as a result of "induced traffic", which arises from increasing the capacity of the system (Goodwin, 1996). Since the seminal comparative study of Zahavi and Talvitie (1980) on travel time budgets, several studies based on travel surveys have shown that over the long term, the average time an individual spends on daily travel has remained almost constant, while daily travel distance has increased. This hypothesis of a near-constant time budget for daily mobility is known as the "Zahavi conjecture". It suggests that individuals and firms use the increase in travel speed resulting from improved transport conditions to increase their access (by choosing new locations, or reaching new opportunities) and not to gain time.[8] Based on these observations, some authors have high-lighted the link between the improvement of transport conditions (which can be summarized as an increase in average speed) and urban sprawl (see for instance Bieber, Massot and Orfeuil, 1993; Wiel, 1999). From a social justice perspective, the main criticism of this approach is that it assumes a positive correlation between the total number of trips and the benefits generated: "the more trips are forecasted for a specific link for a certain year in the future, the more travel time savings can be earned by improving that link and the higher the total benefits related to that improvement" (Martens, 2006). As underlined by several authors (Martens, 2006; Litman, 2007), such a principle works to the advantage of well-off social groups with high levels of car ownership.

Multi-criteria analysis

Multi-criteria analysis (MCA) is a multi-objective decision making process that was developed following criticism of the single-criterion CBA approach. Here, multiple criteria are taken into account simultaneously, and the goal is to optimize with respect to a set of socially-based objectives defined by the decision makers, for example maximize accessibility for certain population groups. Unlike with CBA, the achievement of given objectives can be assessed using both quantitative and qualitative measures

(Grant-Muller *et al.*, 2001). A project's various impacts are ranked on an intensity scale, and the comparative desirability of each project can be evaluated via an overall project score, the weighted sum of all impacts.

MCA techniques have several advantages in estimating the indirect impacts of transport, especially social and environmental impacts which cannot easily be translated into monetary calculations. The participation of decision makers in the appraisal process (rather than only technicians) is central to this approach, and can be viewed as a significant advantage when assessing equity considerations (Thomopoulos *et al.*, 2009). MCA has seen new developments recently in Great Britain, where monetized effects are used as inputs to a partial CBA estimating cost–benefit ratios, which in turn are inputs to a MCA (Geurs *et al.*, 2009). More generally, MCA has been used to assess projects' environmental impacts. According to Thomopoulos *et al.* (2009), MCA "has the potential to be an appropriate evaluation methodology to accommodate the equity considerations of large transport infrastructure projects".

A large number of MCA methodologies have been developed, according to the different needs of each context and discipline (Thomopoulos *et al.*, 2009; Grant-Muller *et al.*, 2001). Among the most commonly used is the analytical hierarchy process (AHP), which was developed by Saaty (1980). The key input to this method is decision makers' choices in relation to a series of pairs of various alternatives. These responses, which may be either verbal or numeric, are coded on a nine-point intensity scale and used to derive weights for criteria and performance scores for various options. This method has faced criticism over the use of a nine-point scale, which may not be compatible with all relevant pairs of comparisons, and the fact that the relative weight of criteria may be established by decision-makers before the measurement scale is set. Several improvements have been made to overcome these drawbacks, including breaking down the process into individual steps. The basic steps can be summarized as: (1) Establishing a hierarchy of objectives, where sub-objectives are linked to main objectives, (2) Eliciting responses to sets of pairs of comparisons from the decision-makers, (3) Deriving weights for each element using mathematical analysis of the pairs in the decision matrix (Thomopoulos *et al.*, 2009).

Criticism of MCA methods concentrates on their subjectivity and lack of robustness (Crozet, 2004; Olson, 1995). According to Grant-Muller *et al.* (2001), as "the choice and use of weights in a MCA may be somewhat arbitrary (...) there may be a sense that the MCA is *making the decision* rather than *supporting the decision-maker*". One way to overcome or lessen these potential problems is to contrast the results of the pairs of comparison with the project's objectives. Additionally, a decrease in total welfare is not necessarily reflected in MCA outputs. For Thomopoulos *et al.* (2009) this may be considered an acceptable risk "as regards equity concerns as they are principally based on value judgments of decision and policy makers".

Shortcomings of the confusion between mobility and accessibility in transport plans

Current planning practices tend to use the terms 'accessibility' and 'mobility' together without clear distinction (Handy, 2002) and to assess the benefits of transport projects in terms of mobility rather than accessibility. A review of recent urban studies literature shows that mobility variables are used more frequently than accessibility indicators to measure social disparities and risk of social exclusion. The focus probably falls on mobility because it is easier to measure than accessibility. However, it has major shortcomings.

It is rather difficult and ambiguous to interpret differences in mobility patterns in terms of social inequalities. In fact, a high level of mobility may correspond with a large number of constraints, especially for certain job categories such as cleaning personnel (who are most often women) or precarious workers (Jouffe, 2007). On the other hand, low levels of daily mobility are often observed for high-income people who can afford central residential locations or who reduce their travel time to work to preserve their quality of life. More generally, travel time budgets are not a direct function of social status. Disadvantaged social groups sometimes have longer travel times but on the other hand many studies have shown that low-income individuals tend to travel less and make shorter trips than well-off individuals (Pucher and Renne, 2003; SEU, 2003; Orfeuil, 2004). Therefore, it is not a relevant objective to reduce daily travel time, especially where poor people are concerned, because this could mean reduced access to jobs or other urban opportunities. There is a contradiction between the short-term view (how to travel more easily or rapidly from one location to another) and the medium- or long-term view (how to access better jobs and opportunities within a daily time constraint). Consequently, accessibility is a better indicator of social disparities in the sense that it accounts for land use patterns as well as social and individual characteristics including time availability.

In transport modeling, forecasts of future travel demand are based on current travel patterns. By doing so, transport models reproduce current imbalances in transport provision between population groups:

> The models use the high trip rates among car owners in the present to predict high trip rates among car owners in the future. These predictions favor policies that cater to this growth through improved services for car owners (for example road building or investment in costly rapid rail).
>
> (Martens, 2006)

This inherent feedback loop was highlighted early by Dupuy (1978), who showed that by incorporating increasing motorization rates in the generation step, four-step models inevitably predicted an increase in transport infrastructure needs. As far as distributional impacts are concerned, such an analysis suggests that classic transport models tend to generate transport improvement plans that benefit highly mobile population groups at the expense of the mobility-poor (Litman, 2003).

Furthermore, the improvement of transport conditions does not systematically result in an improvement of accessibility. This relation depends on the considered spatial and temporal scales. For instance high-speed transport infrastructures give priority to long rather than medium or short distance access. Accessibility depends on the connectivity properties of the transport network (highly performant versus highly connected). High-speed transport infrastructures generally produce cut-off effects for people living in close proximity. Moreover, the improvement of access changes over time and differs between the short term and the long term. Experience shows that in the medium or long term, improvements to transport systems lead to changes in residential or activity locations, resulting either in induced traffic (and possibly in infrastructure congestion) and urban sprawl (resulting in residential areas with poor access).

As suggested by Wachs and Kumagai (1973), one reason that accessibility analyses have frequently not been included in social reports is "the common notion that the demand for movement is a 'derived' demand: movement is rarely considered an end in itself, but rather a cost which is normally born in order to achieve these objectives". Because transport and physical accessibility systems were considered means to reach spatially distributed opportunities, accessibility has not been singled out in city or regional social reports. This probably explains why accessibility is still seen in terms of reducing distances, and addressed by transport policy rather than other fields of public policy.

3.3.3 Are current accessibility policies effective in tackling social exclusion?

Although social issues have appeared on transport policy agendas in most countries, the results are still disappointing or difficult to assess (Sanchez and Schweizer, 2008; Féré, 2011). Studies have attempted to measure the impact of public transit on the social integration of low-income individuals and have produced mixed or even contradictory results (Sanchez, 1999; Cervero, Sandoval and Landis, 2002; Holzer, Quigley and Raphael, 2003; Sanchez, Shen and Peng, 2004; Kawabata and Shen, 2007). Research findings on how car ownership affects employment opportunities are more conclusive but their implications for public policy are controversial (Ong, 1996; Raphael and Stoll, 2002; Ong, 2002; Blumenberg, 2002; Blumenberg and Waller, 2003). The first studies on alternative policies like car ownership programs show that while their cost is very high their results are uncertain and they often "miss their target" (Fol, Coutard and Dupuy, 2007; Féré, 2011). For example, demand responsive services are very expensive but do not offer the flexibility of alternative means of transportation like taxis (Gaffron *et al.*, 2001). Overall, the cost–benefit ratio of such programs is often questionable (Sanchez and Schweizer, 2008). According to Sanchez (2008), there is very little evidence of these programs "creating opportunity or improving the well-being of families in the grip of poverty". One explanation is the lack of resources to evaluate the effectiveness of programs with social implications. The scale and fragmentation of these programs, which are scattered among many private and public agencies, do not make comprehensive evaluations of their effects easy. In addition, most of them rely on fragile, non-guaranteed funding, which prevents a long-term view of their effectiveness (Fol, 2010; Féré, 2011).

The effects of the accessibility planning implemented in the United Kingdom are difficult to assess. According to Lucas (2006), "accessibility planning for social inclusion is still in its infancy in the UK and it will be some time before it will be possible to assess whether the aspirations for the method can be realized". This lack of evidence raises the question of whether real political will exists to improve social access. It is also reflects the lack of a common language shared by the different participants in the planning process.

3.3.4 Is social access really a priority?

Although the literature on the social dimensions of urban access has become quite abundant in the past few years, policy makers seem hesitant to make this issue a priority. Unlike other aspects of urban provision, which have been the subject of innovative solutions to better serve poor households and deprived areas, the field of transport is still struggling with basic difficulties in dealing with this issue. This can be partly explained by the complexity of the accessibility concept itself and the problems posed by its measurement, especially where the social dimension is concerned. In addition there are some specific characteristics of both transportation networks and accessibility planning that make it difficult to implement better and more efficient policies. Another possible explanation may be found in the distinct "technical cultures" of the transportation and urban planning fields. Transportation planning has long been structured around two main disciplines: economics and traffic engineering. Both emphasize the functioning of transportation networks in relation to the short-term problem of organizing urban traffic flows. However, urban planners, who often come from a social science background, are more inclined to adopt a long-term perspective and address "soft" issues like urban form and social disparities.

Transportation networks hold a distinct place among urban provision, and accessibility issues have never been addressed in the same manner as in other sectors. The idea of "universal coverage" is common to most networks including transport, and based on continuous improvement of supply through technical and economic progress and political will (Coutard, 1999). However, access to transportation does not carry the same weight nor is seen in the same light as access to water, for example, which has been defined as a basic human need internationally (Jaglin and Zérah, 2010).[9] While some innovative experiments in water or sewage services have been designed to reach poor populations in the developing world, the transportation field seems reluctant to renounce the network concept. For example, in the water services sector, "pro-poor" solutions have been implemented, relying on the participation and work of the users themselves and not necessarily on a network connection (Jaglin and Zérah, 2010). Although these innovations are subject to strong criticism (Spronk, 2009), the emphasis placed on community participation and non-network solutions is interesting.

Another distinguishing characteristic of transportation networks is their high cost compared with other networks, in terms of infrastructure investment as well as operation costs. When investment choices are to be made, social concerns must compete with transportation's other goals. As observed and demonstrated by several authors, as long as the principles of welfare economics are applied, there is a major contradiction between the objective of efficiency (optimum allocation of resources) and the objective of equity (see for instance Martens, 2006; Bonnafous and Masson, 2003). The case of a light rail line extension in Lyon (France) studied by Cécile Féré (2011) is very informative: instead of implementing a long-term extension project designed to serve one of the most deprived areas of Lyon's urban region (Vénissieux), local authorities decided to give priority to a new line serving a brand-new regeneration project (Lyon Confluence), despite the fact that the initial scheme was expected to be well-patronised. Similarly, in the current discussion on Greater Paris the recent choice between the two public transportation options was the scheme that had less effect on job accessibility for carless residents. Improving urban access for low-income individuals might not be a priority for some local actors if it means allowing young people from deprived neighborhoods to travel anywhere anytime.

Moreover, in recent years the rising importance of environmental issues has tended to reduce interest in social questions, though the social dimension of sustainable development and environmental justice should keep these issues alive. In some respects, there are even tensions and contradictions between social and environmental goals in the field of transportation (Féré, 2011). The 'rail versus bus' debate in Los Angeles is a good example of the potential contradictions between limiting car use by expanding public transit for middle-class suburban commuters (the rail option) and better serving low-income and minority inner city residents (the bus option). In many cases, policy makers tend to favor pro-environment choices that can be detrimental to disadvantaged groups (Taylor, Wachs, Luhrsen, Lem, Kim and Mauch, 1995; Garrett and Taylor, 1999; Bullard and Johnson, 1997; Bénit-Gbaffou *et al.*, 2007; Fol and Pflieger, 2010).

Certain global trends have also hindered the introduction of good practice on accessibility planning. Insufficient planning regulations have allowed residential, employment, retail and service sprawl to continue. In parallel, the "rationalization" of many public services such as hospitals, health services, and post offices has resulted in longer travel distances for most users. In rural areas the ongoing streamlining of public and private services as a result of globalization has had a dramatic impact on accessibility (Nutley, 2003). This is also the case in urban locations. As Lucas (2006) points out,

> many planning decisions are taken out of the hands of land-use planners by the private sector or other more powerful public sector agencies (. . .), which do not include transport and accessibility in their location assessments. Moreover, the deregulation of transport systems, particularly in the UK, has led to a reduction in bus services.
>
> (Gaffron *et al.*, 2001)

The current context of an "underfunded and fragmented public transport network" (Lucas, 2006) does not favor better integration of land use and transportation. Grieco (2003) underlines a policy paradox where the role that transport and land use organization can play in reducing social exclusion has been recognized just when the means of intervention (municipal transport, social housing, public sector employment) "have been subject to radical erosion".

However, we shall argue that these obstacles to a better understanding of accessibility and more efficient implementation of accessibility planning can be overcome.

3.4 How can the role of social indicators in accessibility assessment be improved? How can accessibility policies be improved?

Many recent studies have proposed new accessibility assessment methods that better account for the social component. These new approaches are taking place in pre-decision accessibility measurement, as well as in the evaluation of accessibility policies themselves. Some improvements have already been tried in the planning process, too. We will first suggest some practical ways to better account for social issues in the appraisal of transportation projects and policies. Then we will make some recommendations for improving the planning process.

3.4.1 How can social criteria be given greater weight in the appraisal of transport projects and policies?

As mentioned above, social issues have until recently rarely been included in transportation planning, despite the fact that transport decisions often have significant social and equity impacts. In this section, we suggest three ways to increase the weight of social criteria, all of which assume the improvement of social access as an explicit objective of the decision-making process. The first aims to clarify which type of equity is pursued, in order to choose adequate measurements of social or spatial inequality. The second emphasizes the importance of shifting from a demand-based transport planning approach to one based on needs. The third seeks to identify the losers and the winners in the implementation of transportation projects.

Defining equity objectives in a comprehensive and effective way

Our first proposal is **to define clearly which equity objectives are being pursued in order to clarify the types of indicators that may be used**. As underlined by Litman (2011), "transportation equity analysis can be difficult because there are several types of equity, various ways to categorize people for equity analysis, numerous impacts to consider, and various ways of measuring these impacts". Different measures of social disparity correspond to different conceptions of social equity. According to Young (1994), three fundamental approaches reflect the main theories of equity (cited in Thomopoulos *et al.*, 2009):

- Egalitarian: everyone has equal rights or benefits for a particular service or scheme.
- Utilitarian: the aim is to maximize the total welfare of the society as a whole.
- Rawlsian: the aim is to retain the existing status quo between those better- and worse-off, improving the situation for the worse-off as much as possible after everyone's fundamental rights are secured.

The utilitarian approach has prevailed in transport infrastructure appraisal through references to welfare economics and the use of CBA. As mentioned above, this approach takes little or no direct account of equity and social exclusion. Litman (2002) notes that the egalitarian approach has also been applied in various situations, but the Rawlsian approach has not yet been widely used. Talen (1998, cited by Apparicio and Séguin, 2006) defines four conceptions of equity that correspond to four types of accessibility: equity in terms of equality (everyone receives the same public benefit); equity in terms of needs (the distribution of public benefit is based on needs, which refers to a 'compensatory equity'); equity in terms of demand (which would probably favor wealthy neighborhoods, where the expressed demand is greater); and market-based equity (where cost is the key factor determining the willingness and ability of users to pay).

Following Litman (2011), we suggest that these various views of equity be grouped into three main types:

- Horizontal equity: requires that public resources be allocated equally to each individual or group unless a targeted subsidy is specifically justified. Furthermore, it requires that consumers pay costs incurred by their activities as much as possible. Horizontal equity relates to the egalitarian theory of equity.
- Vertical equity with respect to income and social class: requires that disadvantaged people (according to the level of income or social class) be identified and given special consideration (or protection) in planning. People should be burdened according to their ability to contribute. Vertical equity relates to the Rawlsian theory of equity.
- Vertical equity with respect to need and ability: same as previous, except that people's disadvantages are not estimated in terms of income or social class, but in terms of needs and ability.

As Litman (2011) points out, equity evaluation is significantly affected by the chosen definition of equity (Table 3.1), along with the categories used to measure social differences (demographics, income class, geographic locations and ability), the social impacts of transport project or policy (prices,

Table 3.1 Equity evaluation variables

Types of equity	Categories	Impacts	Measurement units
Horizontal	Demographics (age,	Price or fare	Per capita
Vertical with	gender, race, ethnic	structure	Per vehicle-mile or
respect to income	group, family status,)	Tax burdens	kilometre
and social class	Income class	Transportation	Per passenger-mile or
Vertical with	Geographic location	service quality	kilometre
respect to need	Ability (physical	External costs (crash	Per trip
and ability	disabilities, driving	risk, congestion,	Per peak-period trip
	licence)	pollution)	Per dollar paid in fare
	Travel mode	Access	or tax subsidy
	Vehicle type	Economic opportunity	
	Industry (truckers,	and development	
	transit, taxis, vehicle	Transport industry	
	manufactures)	employment and	
	Trip type and value	business opportunities	

Note: in this table we added "access" to the list of impacts in order to distinguish the accessibility improvements from "economic opportunity and development" and "business opportunities".
Source: Litman, 2011

tax burdens, transport service quality and external costs) and the units used for these measurements (per capita, per vehicle-kilometre and per trip).

Acknowledging the fact that "there is no single correct way to evaluate transportation equity" (Litman, 2011), we recommend, as suggested by Litman, considering various perspectives, impacts and methods.

Basing transport planning on the principle of needs

Following Martens (2006), we state that given the importance of mobility and accessibility, transport-modeling approaches – which are implicitly based on the distributive principle of demand – should be based on the principle of need.

Many authors have underlined the importance of a needs-based approach to transport planning, derived from the Rawlsian idea of equity. Rawls (1971, 1982) discussed optimizing primary social goods as an alternative to optimizing welfare.[10] Sen (2009) disagrees with Rawls, arguing that it is important to take people's actual capabilities into account. More generally, there is an ongoing debate concerning the measurement of vertical equity. As underlined by Litman (2011),

> there is general agreement that everybody deserves 'equity of opportunity', meaning that disadvantaged people have adequate access to education and employment opportunities. There is less agreement concerning 'equity of outcome', meaning that society ensures that disadvantaged people actually succeed in these activities.

Considering that transport affects equity of opportunity, it therefore meets the most "conservative" test of equity, according to Litman. Following this principle, transport projects can be evaluated and prioritized according to the degree to which they provide basic access (Litman, 2011).

There are some practical barriers to evaluating present and future collective needs. For instance, it is necessary to define which types of goods, services and activities are considered essential. Moreover, it may be difficult to define the level of access that is sufficient to avoid a reduction in life opportunities without making normative judgments (Martens, Golub and Robinson, 2012).

While we appreciate the difficulty of taking present and future collective needs into account, we suggest that several methodological and empirical changes be made in transport planning.

First of all, we suggest to replace travel time-savings with accessibility gains in CBA analysis. Following Martens (2006) and other authors who emphasize the shortcomings of time saving as a criterion in transport benefit assessment (see for instance Litman, 2003; Metz, 2008), we propose that travel time savings be replaced with accessibility gains as the key benefits of a transport project in CBA analysis. By doing so, "the monetary value of accessibility gains is not related to income group dependent wage levels, but in large part to the existing level of accessibility of a person". Using a utility-based measure of accessibility that incorporates the principle of diminishing marginal utility (see Koenig, 1980 for empirical applications), "an individual with a large choice set of destinations may be expected to attach a lower value to the addition of an extra destination, than a person with a relatively small choice of destinations, all else being equal." The use of "accessibility gains" as the primary benefit of transport improvements would have two major advantages in relation to equity principles: the first is to break the direct link between quantity of trips and benefits; the second is to direct attention in transport planning and cost–benefit analysis towards equity in terms of accessibility (Martens, 2006; Geurs and Ritsema van Eck, 2001).[11] Martens (2006) observes that the challenge here is to develop a practically feasible method to assess accessibility gains in terms of monetary values.

Despite the fact that utility-based measures are probably the most satisfactory to measure social inequalities, their foundations are in complex theory (random utility theory or the doubly constrained entropy modal) making them difficult to implement by non specialists. Therefore, there is a need for measures that are usable by planners at the local level – relatively simple indicators that could be used alongside classical CBA assessment in a multi-criteria analysis. Place-based indicators are more readily accessible to local planners. Compared to individual-based measures, which require comprehensive local surveys (whose results are difficult to generalize on a larger scale), this type of measurement is easy to conduct. However, it results in a rather rough measure of urban access based on assessing which places or resources are reachable from a given location in a given amount of time To overcome its obvious limitations, we suggest that this measure be disaggregated according to the needs of specific groups. This method requires locally available place-based data (location of urban resources, transportation provision) to be combined with individual census data (income, social position, possession of a car). This combined method has been used in several studies (Handy and Niemeier, 1997; Wenglenski, 2004; Preston and Rajé, 2007[12]) and appears promising.

Our last point concerns trade-offs between different objectives including equity, cost-efficiency, and environmental protection in transportation planning. As there is no single way to determine how much weight should be given to a particular objective, it should reflect community needs and values (Litman, 2011). To achieve this, we suggest that quantitative and qualitative methods of assessment be combined. While the use of quantitative data seems essential when measuring accessibility, qualitative approaches are necessary to understand the real experience of deprived groups or individuals, the way they perceive their personal accessibility and that of their neighborhood, and the barriers which matter most to them. To implement this kind of approach, we suggest that focus groups be put in place, with participants describing the types of activities they take part in, their location, the routes and transportation modes used, frequencies and costs. (McCray, 2009). This could result in the establishment of a detailed accessibility database by disadvantaged residents (Handy and Clifton, 2001). As Lyons (2003) pointed out, while levels of access are rather easy to measure through quantitative parameters, quality of access relates to the individual's experience. Some barriers to access are not necessarily objective but can be subjective or cognitive (Beaucire, 2011) and it is important to find out about these barriers, which could undermine the efficiency of policies aiming to improve accessibility. As Bertolini *et al.* (2005, cited by Curtis and Scheurer, 2010) state, taking various kinds of expertise into account is critical "not just because of a generic democratic concern, but also because of the importance of mobilizing the (tacit) knowledge of different participants in the identification of problems and the search for solutions".

Identifying losers and winners

Most transportation projects are based on the naïve assumption that they will benefit all users whatever their social position, income or location of residence. The reality is of course different.

To change the current situation where the social dimension of accessibility is a low priority, Farrington (2007) suggests that "accessibility rights" be defined and placed on the urban and transportation actors' policy agendas. This is particularly relevant in relation to sustainability. According to Farrington (2007), the accessibility concept "is capable of both making a significant contribution to the conceptual development of sustainability discourses, and also helping to articulate the social and economic dimension of sustainability and implementation".

To take this into account, we suggest that the principle that there are losers as well as winners when transportation projects are implemented should be accepted. This recognition requires a significant amount of political vision and courage, and a willingness to submit the issue of cost/benefit distribution to public debate. The "rail versus bus" conflict in Los Angeles is an interesting example of what happens when this principle is not taken into account. The Bus Riders Union sued the Metropolitan Transportation Authority over its extension of the rail system, arguing that this extension would mostly benefit the "white suburban commuters". The allocation of resources to the project would therefore be detrimental to users of the inner city bus system, most of whom are low-income people and minorities. Garrett and Taylor (1999) argued that for carless, transit-dependent people, bus services were vital for access to jobs, schools, medical care and other necessities. They suggested that by "accommodating the political interests and desires of a more mobile, dispersed, and largely white, suburban-based electorate", investment in the rail system would not increase accessibility but rather draw resources away from bus services that were vital for low-income residents. By failing to take transit ridership patterns into account, subsidy policies reinforced existing segregation.[13]

3.4.2 Improving the planning process by escaping the limits of transport-based approaches

As stated by Church *et al.* (2000), overcoming the access difficulties of some groups and individuals requires not only changes to the transport system, but also policies that tackle the factors behind this lack of access. In this last section we suggest that the planning process itself can be adapted, encouraging better integration of the various dimensions of accessibility planning, and promoting public and community participation.

Coordinating transport and land use policies

We suggest promoting integrated transportation and land-use policies. While this requires a multi-agency approach,[14] we are convinced that this goal cannot be attained by institutional procedures alone, as it requires better coordination of public transport services and various community transport operations (Hine and Mitchell, 2003). Overcoming the traditional divide between transportation providers and land use planning agencies is indeed a challenge (Handy, 2002). As Lucas (2006) points out, "a great deal of political will is needed, both within central and local governments and across all the relevant sectors" to achieve accessibility planning. In addition to improving linkages between land use, service location, and transportation decisions, an integrated approach would "optimize scarce resource use" (Farrington, 2007).

Beyond the limitations of transport policies themselves, the necessity to coordinate different policy sectors better derives from the need to reduce undesired impacts resulting from the improvement of transport systems, especially urban sprawl. The current separation of housing and transport policies, for instance, increases the risk of conflicting policy goals. In France, the creation of a zero-rate loan intended to facilitate homeownership for low-income households has had major urban sprawl repercussions, as low-income households were encouraged to buy homes in suburban areas where housing is more affordable than in the city centre.

The notion that coordinated transport and land use planning is a necessary condition for sustainable urban development has spread throughout academic and professional circles. During the last decade, considerable research has evaluated the links between land use patterns and public transportation use, favoring compact cities, "transit cities" or "transit oriented development" (Cervero, 1998). Despite their focus on sustainability, these studies rarely take social inequalities into account (Jemelin *et al.*, 2007). In addition, key issues for coordination such as land policy, local taxation, or economic development are often neglected in the analysis (Gallez *et al.*, 2013). However, promising new planning tools have emerged that seem to allow for better coordination of transport and urban development. In France, these tools take the form of contracts between the State or regional authorities in charge of public transportation, and the local authorities responsible for land use planning. In accordance with the 2010 law on Greater Paris development, "territorial development contracts" (*contrats de développement territorial*) are being signed between the State and municipalities that will accommodate future metro stations, in order to define quantitative residential and economic development objectives. The aim is to encourage increases in density around stations. We suggest that these arrangements should include public housing objectives, in order to allow as many people as possible to benefit from improved access to public transportation and urban opportunities.

Introducing accessibility indicators in the design of regeneration policies

We suggest a stronger emphasis on the accessibility criterion in the design of regeneration policies. In France, current policies in disadvantaged neighborhoods mainly target transportation improvements based on the simple diagnosis of spatial isolation. While it is necessary to improve the mobility of disadvantaged residents through transportation, we recommend that accessibility should also be understood in terms of proximity. This means that regeneration policies should take into account the local provision of services, shops, and jobs. Similarly, social housing policies would benefit from coordination of residential location with urban resources.

Encouraging community participation in the planning process

We recommend local or neighborhood-level transportation planning, which would allow greater participation of the community and of the groups affected by accessibility issues (Hodgson and Turner, 2003). However, planning at the local level can "represent a challenge for a profession traditionally concerned at maintaining integrity of a transport network at as large a geographic scale as possible" (Hodgson and Turner, 2003). Some successful examples of this kind of planning practice already exist. In the US, the appearance of environmental justice in political debate and policy-making processes constituted a turning point (Fol and Pflieger, 2010). Not only does the issue of accessibility need to be explicitly addressed in transportation planning, it also must be discussed with the concerned groups. Beyond equal access to transportation networks and a fair distribution of transportation-related burdens, this means the participation of communities in the planning process (Cairns *et al.*, 2003). The planning process can greatly benefit from hearing the citizens' point of view, which must be recognized as a real form of expertise.

3.5 Conclusion

The multidimensional and complex nature of the concept of accessibility explains both its capacity to enrich reflection on the social aspects of spatial exclusion, and the difficulties encountered when using it operationally. The notion of accessibility should be distinguished from that of mobility. Accessibility involves mobility as well as proximity, transportation as well as land use planning. Accessibility is a component of social justice, and as a precondition for social inclusion it is part of the "right to the city".

Approaching accessibility in relation to social disparities or social exclusion is a work in progress. While some effort has been invested in building indicators, the measurement of accessibility is still a challenge for both academics and planners. In terms of public policies, although a link between low accessibility and the risk of social exclusion has been widely recognized, policy results still seem disappointing and their effectiveness is difficult to assess.

In the appraisal of transportation projects, the social dimension of accessibility is not taken into account and poses difficult challenges. Expressing the benefits of transport projects in terms of "potential access" seems the best way to assess transport projects and their distributive effects.

Notes

1   The role of transportation in social exclusion processes was recognized quite recently, compared to other services like health or education.
2   Unlike Geurs and Van Wee (2004), we do not consider simple infrastructure-based measures (evaluating the performance of the transport system, such as congestion level or the average speed on the road network) as reflecting accessibility. In our opinion, accessibility is a transversal notion, resulting from interaction between at least the land use and the transport systems.
3   In the context of the Workfare policies implemented in many industrialized countries, recent analyses have stressed the importance of access to employment opportunities for poor households. The ability to get around is presented as an important factor in maximizing the employability of poorer people.
4   It is indeed problematic to reduce social integration to the sole issue of access to the job market, and to reduce employability to a question of mobility and transportation. While the lack of adequate transportation is a significant barrier to employment, there are other obstacles that probably have a stronger impact on the employment outcomes of disadvantaged individuals: racial discrimination (Ellwood, 1986; Massey and Denton, 1993) or individual characteristics like education and qualification (O'Regan and Quigley, 1999) are among the

key barriers to employment. Policies aiming at improving physical access to job opportunities would probably be more efficient if they were complemented by strategies tending to improve access to health, childcare, education and training facilities.

5   In Workfare policies, the emphasis is put on the objective to get people back to work. As a result, unemployed people are given incentives to seek and maintain a job. Recipients have to meet certain requirements to continue to receive their Welfare benefits.

6   The evaluation of social impacts and the question of equity are closely linked, although some authors recommend making a distinction between the measure (objective) and the interpretation (subjective) of social disparities. Questioning the social impacts of transport is related to estimating changes in a transport system that may (positively or negatively) affect the preferences, well-being, behavior, or perceptions of individuals or groups (Geurs et al., 2009). On the other hand, equity refers to the distribution of a project's impacts (benefits or costs) and whether that distribution is considered appropriate (Litman, 2002).

7   In Great Britain, for instance, travel-time savings have accounted for around 80 per cent of the monetized benefits of major road scheme CBAs (Metz, 2008).

8   Of course this conjecture does not hold at a disaggregate level, but results from a combination of different individual situations.

9   An obvious explanation lies in the fact that lack of access to water and sewage has direct implications on health.

10 According to Rawls, primary social goods include: basic liberties (freedom of association, liberty, etc.), freedom of movement and choice of occupation, powers and positions of responsibilities, income and wealth, the social bases of self-respect (quoted by Van Wee, 2012).

11 In classical CBA analysis, the more trips are predicted for a given link, the more travel savings can be accrued to this specific link and the higher the total benefits related to that improvement. This principle works to the advantage of populations with high levels of car ownership, since they have higher trip rates than people with lower car ownership (Martens, 2006; Litman, 2011). On the other hand, as Martens (2006) points out "the identification of accessibility gains as the prime benefit of transport investments has profound consequences for cost–benefit analysis. The monetary value of accessibility gains is not related to income group dependent wage levels, but in large part to the existing level of accessibility of a person. More specifically, the value of an additional destination that comes within reach due to a transport improvement will depend on the choice set of destinations already within the reach of an individual. Following the principle of diminishing marginal utility, an individual with a large choice set of destinations may be expected to attach a lower value to the addition of an extra destination, than a person with a relatively small choice set of destinations, all else being equal".

12 In their case studies of Bristol, Nottingham and Oxfordshire, Preston and Rajé (2007) have identified three criteria to assess accessibility-related exclusion: the level of travel in the area as a whole (area mobility); the level of travel made by particular individuals or groups (individual mobility) and the overall accessibility of the area.

13 The Bus Riders Union won the case and in the following years, the

Metropolitan Transportation Authority had to dedicate more funds to bus services and less to suburban rail.

14 According to Farrington (2007), this multi-agency approach "involves horizontal integration between the different sectors in which policy is made and delivered, as well as vertical integration between stakeholders and partners in community, governance and policy-making".

References

Apparicio, P. and Séguin, A.-M. (2006) "Measuring the accessibility of services and facilities of residents of public housing in Montréal", *Urban Studies,* 43(1): 187–211.

Banister, D. and Berechman, J. (2000) *Transport Investment and Economic Development,* London: University College London Press.

Beaucire, F. (2011) "Sur l'accessibilité aux ressources offertes par la ville", *Les Cahiers de l'IAU IdF,* 157: 20–2.

Ben-Akiva, M. and Lerman, S.R. (1979) "Disaggregate travel and mobility choice models and measures of accessibility", in Hensher, D. A. and Sopher P.R. (eds) *Behavioural Travel Modelling,* Andover: Croom Helm, pp. 654–79.

Bénit-Gbaffou C., Fol, S. and Pflieger, G. (2007) "Des pauvres aux écologistes: le front anti-métro en Californie. Crises et controverses autour des politiques de transports en commun à Los Angelès et San Francisco", *L'Espace Géographique,* 2: 115–130.

Bertolini, L., Le Clercq, F. and Kapoen, L. (2005) "Sustainable accessibility: a conceptual framework to integrate transport and land use plan-making. Two test-applications in the Netherlands and a reflection on the way forward", *Transport Policy,* 12: 207–20.

Bhat, C., Handy, S., Kockelman, K., Mahmassani, H., Chen, Q. and Weston, L. (2000) *Development of an Urban Accessibility Index: Literature Review,* Report for the Texas Department of transportation, University of Texas, Austin, TX Center for Transportation Research. www.utexas.edu/research/ctr/pdf_reports/ 4938_1.pdf

Bieber, A., Massot, M.-H. and Orfeuil, J.-P. (1993) Questions vives pour une prospective de la mobilité quotidienne, *INRETS,* Synthèse 19: 76.

Blumenberg, E. (2002) "On the way to work: welfare participants and barriers to employment", *Economic Development Quarterly* 16(4): 314–25.

Blumenberg E. and Waller M. (2003) "The long journey to work: a federal transportation policy for working families", *Transportation Reform Series,* Washington, DC: The Brookings Institution.

Bonnafous, A. and Masson, S. (2003) "Evaluation des politiques de transport et équité spatiale", *Revue d'Economie Régionale et Urbaine,* 4: 547–72.

Bullard, R. (1996) "Introduction: environmental justice and transportation", *Environmental Justice and Transportation: Building Model Partnerships*: Proceedings Document, Clark Atlanta University.

Bullard, R. and Johnson, G. (eds) (1997) *Just Transportation: Dismantling Race and Class Barriers to Mobility,* New York: New Society Publishers.

Burns, L. D. (1979) *Transportation, Temporal and Spatial Components of Accessibility,* Lexington/Toronto: Lexington Books.

Burns, L. D. and Golob, T.F. (1976) "The role of accessibility in basic transportation choice behavior", *Transportation*, 5: 175–98.

Cairns S., Greig J. and Wachs M. (2003) *Environmental Justice and Transportation: A Citizen's Handbook,* Institute of Transportation Studies at the University of California, Berkeley.

Cass, N., Shove, E. and Urry, J. (2005) "Social exclusion, mobility and access", *Sociological Review,* 53(3): 539–55.

Castel, R. (1995) *Les Métamorphoses de la Question Sociale: Une Chronique du Salariat,* Paris: Fayard.

Caubel, D. (2006) *Politiques de Transports et Accès à la Ville Pour Tous ? Une Méthode d'Evaluation Appliquée à l'Agglomération Lyonnaise,* Doctoral thesis, Université de Lyon II.

Cervero, R., Sandoval, O. and Landis, J. (2002) "Transportation as a stimulus to welfare-to-work: private versus public mobility", *Journal of Planning Education and Research,* 22: 50–63.

Cervero, R. (1998) *The Transit Metropolis: A Global Inquiry,* Washington, DC: Island Press.

Church, A. and Frost, M. (1999) *Transport and Social Exclusion,* Report for London Transport Planning.

Church, A., Frost, M. and Sullivan, K. (2000) "Transport and social exclusion in London", *Transport Policy,* 7: 195–205.

CGPC (2005) *Analyse Comparative des Méthodes d'Evaluation des Grandes Infrastructures de Transport,* Rapport no. 2005-0353-01 du groupe de travail présidé par Claude Gressier, July 2005.

Crozet, Y. (2004) "Calcul économique et démocratie: des certitudes technocratiques au tâtonnement politique", *Cahiers d'économie politique,* 47(2): 155–72.

Currie, G., Richardson, T., Smyth, P., Vella-Brodrick, D., Hine, J. and Lucas, K. (2007) "Investigating links between transport disadvantage, social exclusion and well-being in Melbourne: preliminary results", *Transport Policy,* 16(1): 97–105.

Curtis, C. and Scheurer, J. (2010) "Planning for sustainable accessibility: developing tools to aid discussion and decision making", *Progress in Planning,* 74: 53–106.

Coutard, O. (1999) "L'accès des ménages à faible revenu aux services d'eau et d'énergie en France et en Grande-Bretagne", *Flux,* 36–37: 7–15.

Coutard, O. and Rutherford, J. (2009) "Les réseaux transformés par leurs marges: développement et ambivalence des techniques décentralisées", Flux, 76–7: 6–13.

Dalvi, M. Q. and Martin, K. M. (1976) "The measurement of accessibility: some preliminary results", *Transportation,* 5: 17–42.

Dijst, M. and Vidakovic, V. (1997) "Individual action space in the city", in Ettema, D. F., Timmermans, H. J. P. (eds) *Activity-based Approaches to Travel Analysis,* Pergamon, Kidlington/New York/Tokyo, 117–34.

Dupuy, G. (1978) *Urbanisme et Technique : Chronique d'un Mariage de Raison,* Centre de recherche sur l'urbanisme, Paris.

Ellwood, D. T. (1986) "The spatial mismatch hypothesis: are there teenage jobs missing in the ghetto?" in Freeman, R. B. and Holzer, H. J. (eds) *The Black Youth Unemployment Crisis,* Chicago: University of Chicago Press.

Farrington, J. (2007) "The new narrative of accessibility: its potential contribution to discourses in (transport) geography", *Journal of Transport Geography,* 15: 319–30.

Farrington, J. and Farrington, C. (2005) "Rural accessibility, social inclusion and social justice: towards conceptualisation", *Journal of Transport Geography*, 13: 1–12.

Féré, C. (2011) Concilier accès à la mobilité pour tous et mobilité durable. La prise en compte des inégalités d'accès à la mobilité dans les politiques urbaines de l'agglomération lyonnaise, Doctoral thesis, Université Lyon II Louis Lumière.

Fol, S. (2010) *La Mobilité des Pauvres*, Paris: Belin.

Fol, S., Coutard, O. and Dupuy, G. (2007) "Transport policy and the car divide in the UK, the US and France: beyond the environmental debate", *International Journal of Urban and Regional Research*, 31–4: 802–18.

Fol, S. and Pflieger, G. (2010) "Environmental justice in the US: construction and uses of a flexible category. An application to transportations policies in the San Francisco Bay Area", *Justice Spatiale / Spatial Justice* I 2 October, www.jssj.org

Gaffron, P., Hine, J.-P. and Mitchell, F. (2001) *The Role of Transport on Social Exclusion in Urban Scotland. Literature Review*, Transport Research Unit, Napier University.

Gallez, C., Kaufmann, V., Maksim, H., Thébert, M. and Guerrinha, C. (2013) "Coordinating transport and urban planning: from ideologies to local realities", *European Planning Studies* 21(8): 1235–55.

Garrett, M. and Taylor, B. (1999) "Reconsidering equity in public transit", *Berkeley Planning Journal*, 13: 6–27.

Geurs, K. T. and Van Wee, B. (2004) "Accessibility evaluation of land-use and transport strategies: review and research directions", *Journal of Transport Geography*, 12: 127–40.

Geurs K. T., Boon, W. and Van Wee, B. (2009) "Social impacts of transport: literature review and the state of the practice of transport appraisal in the Netherlands and the United Kingdom", *Transport Reviews*, 29(1): 69–90.

Geurs, K. T. and Ritsema van Eck, J.R. (2001) *Accessibility measures: review and applications*, RIVM report 408505006, National Institute of Public Health and the Environment, Bilthoven. www.rivm.nl/bibliotheek/rapporten/408505006.html

Geurs, K. T. and Ritsema van Eck, J.R. (2003) "Accessibility evaluation of land use scenarios: the impact of job competition land use and infrastructure developments for the Netherlands", *Environment and Planning B*, 10: 69–87.

Gobillon, L., Selod, H. and Zenou, Y. (2007) "The mechanisms of spatial mismatch", *Urban Studies*, 44(12): 2401–27.

Goldman, T. and Deakin, E. (2000) "Regionalism through partnership? Metropolitan planning since ISTEA", *Berkeley Planning Journal*, 14: 46–75.

Goodwin, P. (1996) Empirical evidence on induced traffic: a review and synthesis, *Transportation*, 23(1): 35–54.

Gould, P. (1969) *Spatial diffusion*, Resource paper 17, Association of American Geographers, Washington, DC.

Grant-Muller, S. M., Mackie, P., Nellthorp, J. and Pearman, A. (2001) "Economic appraisal of European transport projects: the state of the art revisited", *Transport Reviews*, 21(2): 237–261.

Grengs, J. (2010) "Job accessibility and the modal mismatch in Detroit", *Journal of Transport Geography*, 18: 42–54.

Grieco, M. S. (2003) "Transport and social exclusion: new policy grounds, new policy options", Keynote paper, *10th IATBR Moving through nets: the physical and social dimensions of travel*, Lucerne, 10–15 August 2003.

Hägerstrand, T. (1970) "What about people in regional science?" *Papers of the Regional Science Association*, 24: 7–21.

Handy, S. (2002) "Accessibility- vs. mobility-enhancing strategies for addressing automobile dependence in the US", Paper presented at the *European Conference of Ministers of Transport* (ECMT), Paris, May 2002.

Handy, S. and Clifton, K. (2001) "Evaluating neighborhood accessibility: possibilities and practicalities", *Journal of Transportation and Statistics*, 69–78.

Handy, S. L. and Niemeier, D. A. (1997) "Measuring accessibility: an exploration of issues and alternatives", *Environment and Planning A*, 29: 1175–94.

Hansen, W. G. (1959) "How accessibility shapes land use", *Journal of American Institute of Planners*, 25(1): 73–6.

Harzo, C. (1998) *Mobilité des populations en difficultés: connaissance des besoins et réponses nouvelles,* Document de synthèse, Paris, DIV et Ministère de l'Emploi et de la Solidarité.

Hillman, M., Henderson, I. and Whalley, A. (1973) *Transport Realities and Planning Policy*, London: PEP.

Hine, J. and Grieco, M. (2003) "Scatters and clusters in time and space: implications for delivering integrated and inclusive transport", *Transport Policy*, 10: 299–306.

Hine, J. and Mitchell, F. (2001) "Better for everyone? Travel experiences and transport exclusion", *Urban Studies*, 38(2): 319–22.

Hine, J. and Mitchell, F. (2003) *Transport Disadvantage and Social Exclusion: Exclusionary Mechanisms in Transport in Urban Scotland*, Aldershot: Ashgate.

Hodgson, F. and Turner, J. (2003) "Participation not consumption: the need for new participatory practices to address transport and social exclusion", *Transport Policy*, 10: 265–72.

Holzer, H., Quigley, J. and Raphael, S. (2003) "Public transit and the spatial distribution of minority employment: evidence from a natural experiment", *Journal of Policy Analysis and Management,* 22(3): 415–42.

Ihlanfeldt, K. and Sjoquist, D. (1998) "The spatial mismatch hypothesis: a review of recent studies and their implications for welfare reform", *Housing Policy Debate*, 9(4): 849–92.

Ingram, D. R. (1971) The concept of accessibility: a search for an operational form, *Regional Studies*, 5: 101–7.

Jakowitsch, N. and Ernst, M., (2004) "Just Transportation", in Bullard, R., Johnson G. and Torres, A. (eds) *Highway Robbery, Transportation Racism and New Routes to Equity,* Cambridge, MA: South End Press.

Jaglin, S. and Zérah, M. H. (2010) "Eau des villes: repenser des services en mutation", *Revue Tiers-Monde*, 203: 7–22.

Jemelin, C., Kaufmann, V., Barbey, J., Klein, T. and Pini, G. (2007) "Politiques de transport et inégalités sociales d'accès. Analyse comparative de huit agglomerations européennes", EPFL-Prédit 3, *Cahier du LaSUR* 10.

Jones, A. and Smyth, P. (1999) "Social exclusion: a new framework for social policy analysis", *Just Policy*, 17: 11–20.

Jouffe, Y. (2007) *Précaires Mais Mobiles. Tactiques de Mobilité des Travailleurs Précaires Flexibles et Nouveaux Services de Mobilité,* Doctoral thesis, Ecole Nationale des Ponts et Chaussées.

Kain, J. (1968) "Housing segregation, negro employment and metropolitan decentralization", *Quarterly Journal of Economics,* 82: 175–97.

Kawabata, M. and Shen, Q. (2007) Commuting inequality between cars and public transit: the case of the San Francisco Bay area, 1990–2000", *Urban Studies,* 44(9): 1759–80.

Kenyon, S., Rafferty, J. and Lyons, G. (2003) "Social exclusion and transport: a role for virtual accessibility in the alleviation of mobility-related social exclusion?", *Journal of Social Policy,* 32(3): 317–38.

Koenig, J. G. (1974) "Théorie économique de l'accessibilité urbaine", *Revue Economique,* 25(2): 275–97.

Koenig, J. G. (1980) "Indicators of urban accessibility: theory and applications", *Transportation,* 9: 145–72.

Kwan, M. P. (1998) "Space-time and integral measures of individual accessibility: a comparative analysis using a point-based framework", *Geographical Analysis,* 30(3): 191–216.

Kwan, M. P. and Weber, J. (2003) "Individual accessibility revisited: implications for geographical analysis in the twenty-first century", *Geographical Analysis,* 35(4): 341–53.

Levitas, R. (2000) "What is social exclusion?" in Gordon, D. and Townsend, P. (eds) *Breadline Europe: The Measurement of Poverty,* Bristol, Policy Press, pp. 357–83.

Lewis, D. (2011) "Economic perspectives on transport and equality", Paper presented at International Transport Forum, OECD, Paris, April 2011 (Discussion paper no. 2011-09, www.internationaltransportforum.org/jtrc/DiscussionPapers/jtrcpapers.html)

Litman, T. (2002) "Evaluating transportation equity", *World Transport Policy and Practice,* 8(2): 50–65.

Litman, T. (2003) "Measuring transportation: traffic, mobility and accessibility", *ITE Journal,* 73(10): 28–32, www.vtpi.org/measure.pdf

Litman, T. (2011) "Evaluating transport equity. Guidance for incorporating distributional impacts in transportation planning", Victoria Transport Policy Institute, 24 November 2011, www.vtpi.org/equity.pdf

Lucas, K. (2004) (ed.) *Running on Empty: Transport, Social Exclusion and Environmental Justice,* Policy Press, Bristol.

Lucas, K. (2006) "Providing transport for social inclusion within a framework for environmental justice in the UK", *Transportation Research Part A,* 40: 801–9.

Lyons, G. (2003) "The introduction of social exclusion into the field of travel behaviour ", *Transport Policy,* 10: 339–42.

Martens, K. (2006) "Basing transport planning on principles of social justice", *Berkeley Planning Journal,* 19(1): 1–17.

Martens, K., Golub, A. and Robinson, G. (2012) "A justice-theoretic approach to the distribution of transportation benefits: implications for transportation planning practice in the United Staes", *Transportation Research A,* 46: 684–95.

Massey, D. and Denton, N. (1993) *American Apartheid: Segregation and the Making of the Underclass,* Harvard University Press.

McCray, T. (2009) "Engaging disadvantaged populations in transport studies: linking modal use and perceptions of safety to activity patterns", *Research in Transportation Economics,* 25: 3–7.

Metz, D. (2008) "The myth of travel time saving", *Transport Reviews*, 28(3): 321–36.

Mignot, D. and Rosales-Montano, S. (2006) *Vers un Droit à la Mobilité Pour Tous. Inégalités, territoires et vie quotidienne*, La Documentation Française, Paris: PUCA.

Moseley, M. J. (1979) *Accessibility: The Rural Challenge*, London: Methuen.

Motte, B. (2006) *La Dépendance Automobile Pour l'Accès aux Aervices aux Ménages en Grande Couronne Francilienne*, Doctoral thesis, Université Paris Sorbonne.

Murakami, E. and Young, J. (1997) "Daily travel by persons with low income", Paper for NPTS Symposium, Betheda, MD, 29–31 October, 1997.

Neuberger, H. (1971) "User benefits in the evaluation of transport and land-use plans", *Journal of Transport Economics and Policy*, 5(1): 52–75.

Nutley, S. (2003) "Indicators of transport and accessibility problems in rural Australia", *Journal of Transport Geography*, 11: 55–71.

Okodi, J., Kerali, H. and Santorini, F. (2001) "An integrated modal for quantifying accessibility-benefits in developing countries", *Transportation Research Part A*, 35: 601–23.

Olson, D. (1995) *Decision Aids for Selection Problems*, Springer, Berlin.

Ong P. (2002) "Car ownership and welfare-to-work", *Journal of Policy Analysis and Management*, 21(2): 239–52.

Ong, P. (1996) "Work and car ownership among welfare récipients". *Social Work Research* 20(4): 255–62.

O'Reagan, K. and Quigley, J. (1999) "Accessibility and economic opportunity", in *Transportation Economics and Policy*, Washington, DC: The Brookings Institution.

Orfeuil, J. P. (ed.) (2004) *Transports, Pauvretés, Exclusions. Pouvoir Bouger Pour s'en Sortir*, La Tour d'Aigues, Editions de l'Aube.

Paez, A., Gertes Mercado, R., Farber, S., Morency, C. and Roorda, M. (2010) "Relative accessibility deprivation indicators for urban settings: definitions and application to food desert in Montreal", *Urban Studies*, 47(7): 1415–38.

Patacchini, E. and Zénou, Y. (2007) "Spatial dependence in local employment rates", *Journal of Economic Geography*, 7(2): 169–91.

Paugam, S. (ed.) (1996) *L'Exclusion. L'état des Savoirs*, Paris: La Découverte.

Paulo, C. (2006) *Mobilité et Inégalité: Une Mesure à Différentes Échelles Spatio-Temporelles*, Doctoral thesis, Université de Lyon II.

Poulit, J. (1974) *Urbanisme et Transport : Les Critères D'accessibilité et de Développement Urbain*, Ministère des Transports-SETRA (Division urbaine), Paris.

Preston, J. (2009) "Epilogue: transport policy and social inclusion. Some reflections", *Transport Policy*, 16: 140–2.

Preston, J. and Rajé, F. (2007) "Accessibility, mobility and transport-related social exclusion", *Journal of Transport Geography*, 15: 151–60.

Pucher, J. and Renne, J., (2003) "Socio-economics of urban travel: evidence from the 2001 NHTS", *Transportation Quaterly*, 57(3): 49–77.

Raphael, S. and Stoll, M. (2002) Can boosting minority car ownership rates narrow inter-racial employment gap?, *Working Paper, no. W00-002*, IBEN, UCB.

Rawls, J. (1971) *A Theory of Justice*, Boston, MA: Harvard University Press.

Rawls, J. (1982) "Social unity and primary goods", in Sen, A. and Williams, B. (eds)

Utilitarianism and Beyond, Cambridge, MA: Cambridge University Press.

Saaty, T. L. (1980) *The AHP: Planning, Priority Setting Resource Allocations*, New York: McGraw-Hill.

Sanchez, T. (1999) "The connection between public transit and employment", *Journal of the American Planning Association*, 65(3): 284–96.

Sanchez, T. (2008) "Poverty, policy, and public transportation", *Transportation Research Part A*, 42: 833–41.

Sanchez, T., Shen, Q. and Peng, Z. (2004) Transit mobility, jobs access and low-income labour participation in US Metropolitan Areas, *Urban Studies*, 41(7) 1313–31.

Sanchez, T. and Schweizer, L. (2008) *Assessing Federal Employment Accessibility Policy: An Analysis of the JARC Program*, Transportation Reform Series, Brookings Institution, Washington, DC.

Sen, A. (2009) *The Idea of Justice*, Allen Lane, London.

Social Exclusion Unit (2003) *Making the Connections: Final Report on Transport and Social Exclusion*, London: SEU.

Shen, Q. (1998) "Location characteristics of inner-city neighborhoods and employment accessibility of low-wage workers", *Environment and Planning B: Planning and Design*, 25(3): 345–65.

Soja, E. (2010) *Seeking Spatial Justice*, Minneapolis, MA: University of Minnesota Press.

Spronk, S. (2009) "Making the poor work for their services: neo-liberalism and 'pro-poor' privatization in El Alto, Bolivia", *Canadian Journal of Development Studies*, 28(3–4): 397–413.

Stanley, J. and Vella-Brodrick, D. (2009) "The usefulness of social exclusion as a theoretical concept to inform social policy in transport", *Transport Policy*, 16(1): 90–6.

Talen, E. (1998) "Visualizing fairness: equity maps for planners", *Journal of the American Planning Association*, 64: 22–38.

Taylor, B. and Ong, P. (1995) Spatial mismatch or automobile mismatch? An examination of race, residence and commuting in US metropolitan areas, *Urban Studies*, 32(9): 1463–94.

Taylor, B., Wachs, M., Luhrsen, K., Lem, L.L., Kim, E. and Mauch, M. (1995) Variations in fare payment and public subsidy by race and ethnicity: an examination of the Los Angeles Metropolitan Transportation Authority", UCLA Institute of Transportation Studies (UCTC), *Working Paper*, no. 704.

Thomopoulos, N., Grant-Muller, S. and Tight, M. R. (2009) "Incorporating equity considerations in transport infrastructure evaluation: current practice and a proposed methodology", *Evaluation and Program Planning*, 32(4): 351–9.

Urry, J. (2003) "Social network, travel and talk", *British Journal of Sociology*, 54: 155–75.

Vandenbulcke, G., Steenberghen, T. and Thomas, I. (2009) "Mapping accessibility in Belgium: a tool for land-use and transport planning?" *Journal of Transport Geography*, 17: 39–53.

Van Wee, B. (2012) "How suitable is CBA for the ex-ante evaluation of transport projects and policies? A discussion from the perspective of ethics", *Transport Policy*, 19: 1–7.

Wachs, M. and Kumagai, T.G. (1973) "Physical accessibility as a social indicator",

Socio-Economic Planning Sciences, 7: 437–56.

Wachs, M. and Taylor, B. (1998) "Can transportation strategies help meet the welfare challenge?" UCTC Working Paper no. 364, Berkeley, CA: University of California.

Weber, J. (2006) "Viewpoint: reflections on the future of accessibility", *Journal of Transport Geography*, 14: 399–400.

Wenglenski, S. (2004) "Une mesure des disparités sociales d'accessibilité au marché de l'emploi en Île-de-France", *Revue d'Economie Régionale et Urbaine*, 4: 539–550.

Wiel, M. (1999) *La Transition Urbaine. Le Passage de la Ville Pédestre à la Ville Motorisée*, Editions Mardaga.

Wilson, A.G. (1971) "A family of spatial interaction models, and associated developments", *Environment and Planning*, 3(1): 1–32.

Wixey, S., Jones, P., Lucas, K. and Aldridge, M. (2005) "Measuring accessibility as experienced by different socially disadvantaged groups. User needs literature review", EPSRC FIT Programme, Working paper no. 1.

Young, H. P. (1994) *Equity: In Theory and Practice*, Princeton, NJ: Princeton University Press.

Zahavi, Y. and Talvitie, A. (1980) "Regularities in travel time and money expenditures", *Transportation Research Record*, 750, 13–19.

Chapter 4

Access as a social good and as an economic good

Is there a need for a paradigm shift?

Rosário Macário

4.1 Introduction

Accessibility is usually referred to as the ease of reaching goods, services, activities and destinations, which together are often recognized as opportunities for individual and societal development. While mobility is concerned with the performance of transport systems in their own right, accessibility adds the interaction of transport systems and land use patterns for a further layer of analysis. Therefore, accessibility measures are capable of assessing feedback effects between transport infrastructure and services, urban form and the spatial distribution of activities. It is thus inevitable that accessibility is used as an indicator of quality of living and competitiveness in urban areas due to its impact in business and social activities.

The concept of "accessibility" has been dealt with by planners and politicians all over the world for many years. However, gaps in material perception, valuation and consequently, representation of accessibility remain. Economically, accessibility has been mostly measured on the basis of generalized costs from the users' perspective, and total costs (including indirect and non-market costs) from society's perspective. On the benefit side the key concept has been travel time savings which are quantified and valued for the purpose of social appraisal. To illustrate this approach, Metz (2008) reports that in Britain travel time savings have accounted for around 80 per cent of monetized benefits registered in cost–benefit analysis of major road schemes. This has contributed to the shift of transport policy away from the concept of access, which is in fact the main purpose of transport, to provide access solely to desired destinations.

However, none of these concepts is able to encompass the views of the different stakeholders on transport and reconcile tensions between these interests, the necessary tradeoffs between them, and the complexity of associated information. We still lack a market evaluation of accessibility, a hypothetical compromise area where the interests of users, authorities and society could converge or at least see some similarity in their levels of tolerance. It is also within this conceptual and theoretical market area that we are able to understand the added value provided by every increase of accessibility to economic and social services and real estate, and also the reduced value that any degradation of accessibility imposes on those urban services and assets (for example congestion is a factor of subtracted value) as well as the loss of social opportunities (for example access to employ-ment and consequent increase of poverty). The first is very commonly referred to but only rarely considered as a financing mechanism, the latter is neither considered nor accounted for in the assessment of investment nor in the evaluation of political decisions.

This chapter suggests that the economic valuation of accessibility, in the light of public and private provision of goods and services, should be considered as an implicit funding and financing mechanism of urban mobil-ity systems to reposition transport as an urban utility, just like electricity, water and sewage. Furthermore we propose ways to hone down this strate-gic formulation to the tactical and operational levels, shifting the accessibility concept to the political analysis of the benefits of investment in access. The economic valuation of accessibility acts simultaneously as a market factor and as a social factor. The analysis builds on previous research work and accommodates this new formulation proposing alterna-tives to tackle the elements required to introduce this change of paradigm in financing and funding urban access. This chapter is structured in five main sections. After this introduction, accessibility concepts are discussed in Section 4.2, highlighting the evolution of the planning perspective over accessibility. Section 4.3 focuses on social aspects and impacts accruing from accessibility, and assesses the relationship between social exclusion and economic development while Section 4.4 compares mobility-based and accessibility-based policies and finally, Section 4.5 presents the main elements of change required to introduce the proposed paradigm.

4.2 Accessibility: is there a leading stakeholder?

4.2.1 The different meanings of accessibility

Accessibility definitions and their related indicators have been widely stud-ied for the past five decades. One of the most influential works on accessibility definitions and corresponding mathematical formulations was produced by Hansen (1959), who defines accessibility as a measure of potential opportunities for interaction. In 1974, Vickerman defined accessi-bility as a combination of two elements: location on a surface relative to suitable destinations, and the characteristics of the transport network or networks linking points on that surface. In another interpretation (Niemeier, 1997) accessibility is seen as the "ease" with which desired desti-nations may be reached and is frequently measured as a function of the available opportunities moderated by some measure of impedance. Opportunities may be expressed as employment levels and retail or non-retail square footage. In line with this Cervero et al. (1997) defined entropy as a measure of diversity, where low values indicate single-use environments and larger ones denote a variety of land uses. Diversity, in turn, is related to the number of different land uses in an area and the degree to which they are balanced, represented in land area, floor area, or employment.

More recently Bhat *et al.* (2000) defined accessibility as a measure of the ease of an individual to pursue an activity of a desired type, at a desired location, by a desired mode and at a desired time. In the following year, Geurs and van Eck (2001) referred to land use and transport, on the basis that accessibility is closely connected with transport infrastructure and urbanization patterns. For them accessibility is the extent to which the land use-transport system enables groups of individuals or goods to reach activities or destinations by means of a combination of transport modes, reinforcing the idea of Wachs and Koenig (1979) that a transport network offers a vector of opportunities which is rather similar to Cervero's concept of entropy. In this respect Crozet (2009), in a study relating economic development and travel time, observes that the advantage of extending the range of travel lies in the potential to segregate urban functions but he also highlights the fact that this dissociation of functions contributed to increase social distance between groups, questioning the rationale of the Athens Charter.[1]

An example to illustrate this argument is the difference between North American and European cities. North American cities offer higher average speeds but accessibility is lower than in European cities, despite having much higher GDP per capita and longer commuting times. This study also shows that the growth trend in both GDP and distance made US cities much more extensive than those in Europe, where a more intensive pattern is found. According to Crozet (2009) job density in Europe almost always exceeds the threshold of 15 jobs per hectare allowing accessibility without increased travel time, whereas in North America and Oceania, the lower density leads to longer travel times, which means a much lower net utility for the user. It seems evident that there is a positive correlation between increase of income, car ownership and travel time budget, both in the USA and Europe. Worth noting is the seminal work of Yacov Zahavi (referred to by Metz, 2008) who found constancy of travel time across several studies and interpreted this as the existence of a stable travel time and money budget – in other words people tend to spend both the same amount of time and of money on travel.[2] Metz (2008) develops the work of Zahavi to examine the relationship between income and money spent on travel. He found that in Britain average expenditure on travel and transport as a proportion of total household expenditure, remained steady at 16 per cent during the past 20 years.

Recognizing that there are limitations related to comparability of surveys covering 20 years Metz extended his observation to other countries and world regions in different stages of development and concludes that:

households without a car devote on average, 3–5 percent of their income to travel. As income grows, and cars become more affordable, travel expenditure rises with increased car ownership, stabilizing in the range of 10–15 per cent of household income once ownership reaches about one per household. As households continue to get richer the number of cars per household continues to rise but the proportion of expenditure devoted to travel does not.

(Metz, 2008)

Other studies in the USA and Europe find evidence that urban sprawl results in a trade-off between low income households searching for cheaper houses at the cost of higher transport spending.

The conclusions of these studies suggest that GDP growth, as correlated to rises in average income, contributes to increased daily commuting travel distance but not spending on travel time budget, which is a very significant outcome in terms of impact on productivity and urban performance. In addition, the conclusions of these research studies also question the idea that the traveler's strategy is travel cost minimization (Schaffer and Victor, 2000). This in turn weakens, or at least questions, the adequacy of traditional modeling approach of minimization of generalized cost, and suggests that in the long term travel behavior may not be one of utility-maximization (Avineri and Prashker, 2005). In addition, there is also widespread evidence that car ownership is often used as a second alternative to house acquisition. Together these reflections raise doubts over whether consumer behavior should be assessed in relation to the available household budget for transport and housing which represent a substantial part of the household fixed costs in the short and medium term. This means looking at utility maximization through citizens' eyes.

The current evidence from across the world (Schafer and Victor, 2000) allows us to suggest that there are doubts about the validity of the paradigm that has underpinned current economic analysis, in particular cost–benefit analysis supported by generalized cost approaches for infrastructure investment decisions. In fact, traditional transport models have assumed that travelers minimize their generalized costs (the combination of money and time costs calculated using monetary values of travel time) (Wardrop's equilibrium, de Dios Ortúzar and Willumsen, 2001) which is consistent with the idea that travelers use improved infrastructures to save travel time that consequently results in increased productivity. But this is not consistent with the idea that in the long run travel time is maintained as a trade-off for lower housing prices.

However, we have no evidence to state for sure that short term transient behaviors of utility maximization do not occur – so in the short term the theory of Wardrop's equilibrium may remain valid. Despite this uncertainty, it seems that a more realistic modeling approach could, as proposed by

Metz (2008), assume that travelers aim to maximize access, subject to money and time constraints in relation to housing and transport costs. Nonetheless to date no register exists of any behavioral framework developed to link long term land use changes (changes of house and job location) with daily household activities and travel patterns (Waddell, 2001), implying that there is a serious lack of multidisciplinary research in this domain.

Accessibility measures are therefore spatial and economically relevant for assessing the relationship between transport infrastructure and modal participation on the one hand, and urban form and the spatial distribution of activities on the other. This has long been used by planners. However, to a certain extent this rationale led to the disregard of the segments of population without economic activity dependent on social care schemes, as well as those with limited or no access to dominant modes of travel, such as cars. Koenig proposed the strengthening of the use of accessibility indicators in urban and transport planning studies (Koenig, 1980). He argues that accessibility indicators provide a sound tool for evaluating transport policies, particularly at a disaggregated level, and could be a key variable in traffic or urban development models.

The accessibility concept is recognized to be complex and difficult to express, with a considerable amount of research having been dedicated to this field. Several review articles on accessibility measures can be found in the literature, with various focus, such as: location accessibility (for example Song, 1996; Handy and Niemeier, 1997), individual accessibility (for example Pirie 1979; Kwan, 1998); economic benefits of accessibility (for example Koenig, 1980; Niemeier, 1997); and the use of accessibility in evaluations of transport and land use change and respective impacts (for example Geurs and Wee 2004). Moreover, Alan *et al.* (2005) synthesized the literature regarding relations between public infrastructure and economic development as follows (Martinez and Viegas, 2010):

- spatial advantages provided by transportation infrastructure (Hartgen, Stuart *et al.* 1990; Arsen 1997; Forkenbrock, Benshoff *et al.* 2001);
- productivity and output effects (Aschauer 1989; Coffey and Shearmur 1997);
- reduction of production costs (Nadiri and Mamuneas, 1998); and
- impacts on externalities and enhancement of regional economic equity and social welfare (Isserman and Rephann, 1995).

From these reviews we can say that there are two main strands for understanding the accessibility concept. Accessibility as a social indicator in social exclusion or inclusion (see Barton, Horswell *et al.* (2007); Farrington, J. and Farrington, C. (2005); Mackett, R. (2008); and accessibility as an economic indicator, demonstrating land value capture of immobilized assets and thus inducing that these additional captured values can be directed to transport funding and financing schemes (see Levinson, Istrate *et al.* (2011); Martinez and Viegas (2010)) or economic potential of activities (see Suárez (2008); Geurs and van Wee (2003).

According to the literature survey, the focus of accessibility as an economic indicator is property value or the economic potential for development of areas or regions. Market evaluation of accessibility is never referred to. On the accessibility benefits generated by the transportation system these are reported by several authors and can be divided into:

- internal benefits of improved accessibility (enhancements in travel time and connectivity) of the users (Martinez and Viegas, 2010);
- external benefits of the system, which include (Martinez and Viegas, 2010):
  - increase of the city competitiveness;
  - benefits captured by the private sector:
    - property values increase;
    - expansion of the catchment's area of skilled workers;
    - enlargement of the catchment's area of customers for shops and consumer-oriented services;
- benefits captured by the public sector:
  - increased fiscal income resulting from the rise in property value (although this is partially lost by fiscal evasion);
  - reduction of social exclusion and related negative effects;
  - increased aggregated productivity.

According to Geurs and van Eck (2001) accessibility consists of four components: transport; land use; temporal; and individual (see Table 4.1). These authors argue that the transport component is concerned with measures such as travel time, cost and effort of movement. The land use component measures the spatial distribution of activities or opportunities, and contains an assessment of the competitive nature of demand for activities at destinations, and of supply of potential users. The temporal component examines the time constraints users experience in their activity patterns, and the availability of activities or opportunities according to the time of the day, week or year. And finally, the individual component investigates the needs, abilities and opportunities of transport users and thus takes into account socio-economic and demographic factors.

Ideally an accessibility measure should include all these components and the relationship between them. This interpretation raises the question of variability of access value along time and motivation. When authors such as Koenig (1980) argue that accessibility can be used as a key variable for policy and urban development models, they still miss the point that the economic value of accessibility is widely undervalued when the respective differentials are not considered in cost–benefit analysis, or multi-criteria

Table 4.1 Type of accessibility measures and components

Measure \ Component		Transport component	Land-use component	Temporal component	Individual component
Infrastructure-based measures		Average travel time; Travelling speed; Vehicle hours lost in congestion		Peak hour period 24-hr period trips)	Trip-based stratification (e.g. home-work, business
Activity-based measures	Geographical measures	Travel time and/or travel costs between locations of activities, typically using a distance decay function	Distribution of opportunities in space (e.g. number of jobs per zone or grid)	Travel time and costs may differ between hours of the day, between days of the week, or seasons	Stratification of the population (e.g. by income, educational level)
	Time-space measures	Travel time	Distribution of opportunities in space	Temporal constraints for activities and time available for activity participation are accounted for	Accessibility is analysed at individual or household level
Utility-based measures		Travel costs between locations of activities, using a distance decay function	Distribution of opportunities in space	Travel time and costs may differ between hours of the day, between days of the week, or seasons	Utility is estimated for population groups or at individual level

Source: Geurs and van Eck (2001)

analysis for public decision on investment. This means that – *in ceteris paribus* conditions – an investment generating greater business potential through accessibility should be given priority, and return a part of that additional economic value to the transport system. Following the same rationale, investment providing access to more social opportunities of interaction (Hansen, 1959) should also be given priority and the respective benefits accounted for, even if no travel time savings exists.

In fact a market component should examine accessibility from several stakeholders' perspectives considering the respective economic values resulting from accessibility differentials An example is the fact that property values provide the evidence that increases in property and land values derived from accessibility enhancement are an added value, and not simple double counting of the transport-induced benefits, as several supporters of current cost–benefit analysis suggest (Banister and Berechman, 2003). Ultimately, if doubts persist on double counting, time saving metrics could be skipped given the current uncertainty surrounding this potential effect, while variations in property value remain effective. Tables 4.2 to 4.4

Table 4.2 Property value impacts of rail proximity (Part I) in Europe

Case/Location	Impact on	Impact	Source
Belfast	House prices	+2%	(Adair, McGreal et al., 2000)
Bremen	Office rents	+50% in most cases	(Hass-Klau, Crampton et al., 2004)
Croydon Tramlink	Residential property	Some localized positive impacts	(Atisreal, Geofutures et al., 2004)
Freiburg	Office rent	+15–20%	(Hass-Klau, Crampton et al., 2004)
Freiburg	Residential rent	+3%	(Hass-Klau, Crampton et al., 2004)
Greater Manchester	Not stated	+10%	Hass-Klau, Crampton et al., 2004)
Hannover	Residential rent	+5%	(Hass-Klau, Crampton et al., 2004)
Helsinki Metro	Property values	+7.5–11%	(Hack, 2002)
London Crossrail	Residential and commercial property	Positive	(Hillier Parker, 2002)
London Docklands LRT	Residential and commercial property	Positive	(Hack, 2002)
London JLE	Residential and commercial property	Positive	(Chesterton, 2000) (Pharoah, 2002)

Source: Martinez and Viegas, 2010

Table 4.3 Property value impacts of rail proximity (Part II) in Europe

Case/Location	Impact on	Impact	Source
Manchester Metrolink	House prices	Unable to identify +10%	(Forrest, Glen et al., 1996; Dabinett, 1998) (Hass-Klau, 2006b)
Montpellier	Property values	Positive	(Hass-Klau, Crampton et al., 2004)
Nantes LRT	Commercial property	Higher values	(Hass-Klau, Crampton et al., 2004)
Nantes LRT	Not stated	Small increase	(Hass-Klau, Crampton et al., 2004)
Nantes LRT	Number of commercial premises	+13%	(Hack, 2002)
Nantes LRT	Number of offices	+25%	(Hack, 2002)
Nantes LRT	Number of residential dwellings	+25%	(Hack, 2002)
Newcastle upon Tyne	House Prices	+20%	(Hass-Klau, Crampton et al., 2004)
Orléans	Apartment rents	None-initially Negative due to noise	(Hass-Klau, Crampton et al., 2004)
Paris	House prices	+3.3%–5.2%	(Hass-Klau, 2006b)
Paris	Offices prices	+57%	(Hass-Klau, 2006b)
Rouen	Rent and houses	+10% most cases	(Hass-Klau, Crampton et al., 2004)
Saarbrucken	Not stated	None	(Hass-Klau, Crampton et al., 2004)
Sheffield Supertram	Property values	Unable to identify	(Henneberry, 1998) (Dabinett, 1998)
Strasbourg	Office rent	+10–15%	(Hass-Klau, Crampton et al., 2004)
Strasbourg	Residential rent	+7%	(Hass-Klau, Crampton et al., 2004)
Tel Aviv	House Prices	Positive	(Gat, 1996)
Turin	House Prices	Positive	(Corto, Bravi et al., 1993)
Tyne and Wear Metro	Property values	+2%	(Pickett and Perrett, 1984)
Vienna S-Bahn	Housing units	+18.7%	(Hack, 2002)

Source: Martinez, 2010

Table 4.4 Property value impacts of rail proximity in North American cities

Case/Location	Impact on	Impact	Source
Atlanta	Office rents	Positive	(Bollinger, Ihlanfeldt et al., 1998) (APTA, 2002)
Baltimore LRT	Not stated	Unable to identify	(Hack, 2002)
Boston	Residential property	+6.7%	(APTA, 2002) (Armstrong Jr, 1994)
Buffalo, New York	House prices	+4–11%	(Hess and Almeida, 2006)
Chicago MTA	House prices	+20%	(Gruen, 1997)
Dallas DART	Commercial rents	+64.8%	(Weinstein and Clower, 1999)
Dallas DART	Property values	+25%	(Kay and Haikalis, 2000) (Weinstein and Clower, 1999)
Linden, New Jersey	Residential property	Positive	(Diaz, 1999)
Los Angeles	Property values	Higher values	(Fejarang, 1994)
Miami	House prices	+5%	(Gatzlaff and Smith, 1993)
New Jersey SEPTA rail	House prices	+7.5–8%	(Voith, 1991)
New Jersey PATCO rail	House prices	+10%	(Voith, 1991)
New York	Not stated	Positive	(Anas and Armstrong, 1993)
Pennsylvania SEPTA rail	House prices	+3.8%	(Voith, 1991)

Source: Martinez and Viegas, 2010

(Martinez and Viegas, 2010) provide evidence on studies which have found positive effects produced by public transport accessibility on land and property value.[3] Besides the diversity of valuation methods applied and the possibility of having a standard approach to this metric – market pricing is likely to be a good candidate – the key question is how is that added value applied, and whether that is consistent with development strategies and policies put forward by those cities and regions.

Moreover, whenever the valued asset is an intangible (for example services) the differential value of accessibility is not identified and there is no possibility to return it as a transport source of financing, although this could be calculated through time saving benefits and their impact in both productivity and improvements in the labor market. In practical terms this means answering the question, "what is the differential in business potential, or social interaction potential that results from increased accessibility in the case of services?" The recognition of this additional economic value also in services, enables internalizing the value of accessibility in market dynamics to the benefit of the user, the society and consequently the authorities that should seek the benefits of the previous two. Even if the existence of imperfect information leads to deficiencies in market internalization, having only an approximate valuation is better than having no valuation since that suggests there is no impact which is obviously a serious distortion. These concepts must be included not only in the management of sources of funding for transport but also in public decisions on investments.

The main drawback of this approach is the weakness of empirical evidence for the link between infrastructure provision and economic activity. This is an area where substantial research work is still needed, especially due to the findings of studies in several countries which reveal that infrastructure impacts are mostly short term (for Sturm *et al.*, 1998, Mamatzakis, 2007) and their economic performance depends on the public or private nature of investment and the state of public accounts. The added complexity of the issue of agglomeration effects must also be considered. In most countries the issue of the additional property value that accrues to real estate from transport developments is ignored and left as a positive externality that benefits only real estate investment and, to some extent, assuming efficient fiscal settings, the State budgets through general taxation mechanisms on property transactions. One key exception is Japan where funds for railways are obtained through value capture from real estate rents. As we can see from Tables 4.2 to 4.4 the estimates of positive impacts reported in the review done by Martinez and Viegas (2010) are significant and can even reach outstanding impact values as reported by Weinstein and Clower (1999) who examined the Dallas DART. There is thus the potential to ensure authorities and investor satisfaction but other stakeholders, like users and society at large, have no benefit, to the extent they are not attached to property or business value.

Failing to apply cross subsidisation means that social exclusion is not addressed. Cross subsidy is practised in many areas of the economy (for example education and health) and since prevention of social exclusion or, rather, guarantee of social inclusion, should be a public service obligation of the State, there is no distortion of competition if this is ensured through added value created by public investment carried out on the basis of public service obligations. There is evidence across the world that social exclusion rises when there are market failures (as formulated by Rothstein, 2011), defined as a misalignment of supply and demand.

The objective should be the prevention of negative or degradation effects. In addition, several authors report that social exclusion hinders competitiveness of cities, quality of life and well-being (for example Stanley and Stanley, 2007),[4] although this is a field where sound quantitative approaches have still not been developed.

4.2.2 Different measures of accessibility

The different meanings of accessibility and the diversity of associated stakeholders require an extensive understanding of differences between accessibility indicators, with the help of a structuring classification. Definitions, measures and applications found in literature can be categorized in several ways. Three basic perspectives on accessibility measures are identified:

- *Infrastructure-based measures* These measures focus on the characteristics of infrastructure and sometimes on its use. They are used to analyse the observed or simulated performance of transport infrastructure. Examples include: "average speed on the road network", "level of congestion" or "average delays". Some of these measures and applications are only related to the supply of infrastructure, while others include demand factors. For example, travel times and risk of congestion depend on both supply and demand but can also be used in social terms for the ease of access to areas of employment.

- *Activity-based measures* These measures are related to activities such as living, working, recreation and shopping. They are used to analyse the number of available opportunities with respect to their distribution in space and the restrictions on travel between origins and destinations. These measures can be further subdivided into geographic and time–space measures, as well as into macro-level or micro-level indicators. An example of a geographical accessibility indicator offering simultaneously economic and social information for decision makers is the number of jobs within 30 minutes travel time. This type of measure is often used in urban planning and time–space measures.

- *Utility-based measures* This is a mixed group, related to both activities and infrastructure. These measures are used to analyse the benefits which individuals obtain from the land use-transport system. Most of these measures integrate aspects related to: travel costs, not only monetary costs, but also travel time, risks, comfort and other quality characteristics; volume aspects, such as number of people, jobs and shops and location aspects. These measures are typically used in economic studies and urban planning. Examples include "distance from housing locations to public transport infrastructure" or "distance or travel time from working locations to a roadway junction".

The main methodological approaches to accessibility are outlined in Table 4.5, based on the work of Bhat *et al.* (2000), Geurs and van Eck (2001) and Baradaran and Ramjerdi (2001), focusing on their characteristics, their main utilization and their constraints. Infrastructure-based accessibility measures, such as journey times, congestion and operating speed on the road network, play a crucial role in the implementation of transport policies. In fact they are at the interface between land use and transport and the power struggle between these two policy domains is perhaps a result of inadequate institutional design resulting in the unwillingness to address policy on access. In European national transport policies, improving accessibility is generally considered to be important for economic development or to reduce economic deprivation in particular for regions or parts of the population (Geurs and van Eck 2001). Nevertheless there are several advocates of a "paradigm shift" from traditional infrastructure-based measures to activity-based measures (Cervero *et al.* 1997).

Spatial separation measures were identified by Bhat *et al.* (2000) and

Table 4.5 Approaches to measurement of accessibility

	Methodological category	Approach	Metrics
Spatial Separation Measures	Spatial Separation Model (Bhat *et al.*, 2000) Infrastructure Measures (Geurs K.T., van Eck J.R. 2001) Travel Cost Approach (Baradaran S, Ramjerdi F., 2001)	Travel impediment or resistance between origin and destination on between nodes. 'relative accessibility"	physical distance travel time average speed
Contour Measures	Contour Measures (Geurs, K.T., van Eck, J.R., 2001) Cumulative Opportunity Model (Bhat *et al.*, 2000)	Definition of catchment areas (by drawing one or more travel time contours around a node and measures the number of opportunities without each contour (jobs, employees, customers, etc.)	distance travel time costs location of facilities
Gravity Measures	Gravity Model (Bhat *et al.*, 2000) Potential Accessibility Measure (Geurs, K.T., van Eck, J.R., 2001)	Definition of catchment area by measuring travel impediment on a continuous scale	distance travel time costs location of facilities
Time-space Measures	Time-space Measures (Bhat *et al.*, 2000 and Geurs, K.T., van Eck, J.R., 2001) Person-based Measures (Geurs, K.T., van Eck, J.R., 2001)	Travel opportunities within pre-defined time constraints	distance travel time costs time budgets space-time
Utility Measures	Utility Measures (Bhat *et al.*, 2000 and Geurs, K.T., van Eck, J.R., 2001) Utility Surplus Approach (Baradan S., Ramjerdi F., 2001)	Individual or societal benefits of accessibility	distance travel time costs income demographic variables

Source: Galelo and Macário, 2011

categorised as an infrastructure-based measure by Geurs and van Eck (2001). They are considered to be the simplest type of accessibility measure as they use only the physical distance between infrastructure elements and thus are suitable for the analysis of nodes and network structures. This type of measure relies solely on information related to the transportation system. Baradaran and Ramjerdi (2001) refer the TCA (travel cost approach) measures which can be included in spatial separation measures as they do not consider land use patterns and spatial distribution of opportunities. A common aspect for this class of accessibility indicators is determined by their configuration, where the indicator is a proxy of transport cost (for example network or Euclidean, distance, travel time, or travel cost). A major criticism is that spatial separation measures do not take into account either behavioral aspects of travel choices, or the different attraction levels of activities and the value of time to different groups of people making the trip (Scheurer and Curtis, 2007).

Contour measures, also called "cumulative opportunities" in Bhat *et al.*

(2000) indicate the number of opportunities reachable within a given travel time or distance, defining thresholds of maximum desirable travel times for different types of activities: catchment areas of jobs, employees, customers, visitors and other members of the traveling public are mapped out as contours for each node under consideration. With this type of measure, accessibility increases if more opportunities can be reached within a given travel time or distance. This increase can be the result of a change in the ease of reaching destinations (for example a shortening of travel times due to infrastructural improvements) or land use changes (for example densification of destinations within reach) (Geurs and van Eck, 2001). These measures are often used in urban planning and geographical studies. Contour measures aim to describe the transport and land use system from the user's point of view. They incorporate the transport component (travel time, costs and distance) and the land use component (location of facilities) but do not attempt to evaluate their combined effect or consider the value people attach to each of these components separately (Geurs and van Eck 2001). Moreover, this methodology cannot capture variation in accessibility between activities within the same contour.

Indicators based on spatial opportunities available to travelers were among the first attempts to address the behavioral aspects of travel. The "potential to opportunities" or the "gravity" approach is the most used technique among accessibility indicators (Baradaran and Ramjerdi, 2001). These measures have their root in Hansen's (1959) work, the first author to use the concept to describe accessibility to employment opportunities and who defined accessibility as *"the potential of opportunities for interaction"*. This concept is closely associated with the gravity models based on the interaction of masses and has been extensively discussed by Rich (1978).

Gravity measures according to Bhat *et al.* (2000), are loosely related to "potential accessibility measures" discussed by Geurs and van Eck (2001). They set out to overcome the deficit of rigid or arbitrary contour lines by treating opportunities differently along a continuum of time and distance. In most cases, this is done by identifying the actual travel time for each opportunity and using a relatively generic distance decay function as a proxy for the disutility experienced by transport users with increasing travel time, cost or effort (Geurs and van Wee 2004).

Despite their widespread use, accessibility indicators still have weaknesses. The major limitation of the gravity measure is that it neglects variations between individuals such as differing time constraints. The temporal component of accessibility involves the availability of activities at different times of the day and the times in which individuals seek to participate in specific activities. Time–space measures, discussed by Bhat *et al.* (2000) and Geurs and van Eck (2001), and further refined into person-based measures by Geurs and van Wee (2004), focus specifically on time budgets, or space–time paths, of transport users. An advantage of this approach is that it is a disaggregated model which allows personal characteristics to be taken into account. On the other hand, this disaggregated model is also the main disadvantage of space–time accessibility measures since it requires large amounts of data that usually are not available from standardized travel surveys and often need to be collected specifically. This limits the opportunities for data aggregation over larger areas, and the compatibility of data sets collected in different surveys, raising barriers to long term comparability of travel behavior patterns. These limitations reveal the need to design standardized travel surveys, although the costs tend to discourage most practitioners. Another disadvantage of these measures is that the recognition of time constraints alone does not do justice to the full spectrum of motivations for individual travel choices, as noted by Metz (2008).

Another perspective on accessibility is given by utility-based accessibility measures based on economic theory. Random utility theory assumes that people choose the alternative with the highest utility. However, utility is not known with certainty to the analyst, and therefore is treated as a random variable (Dong, Ben-Akiva et al. (2006)). Utility measures (Bhat et al. (2000) and Geurs and van Eck (2001)) are designed to capture the benefit to users from accessibility to opportunities. This can occur in a monetized form as a measure of economic utility, or as an indicator for social equity. It can also be applied as a behavioral indicator, measuring the value individuals ascribe to the accessibility of particular activities (Scheurer and Curtis, 2008). Geurs and van Eck (2001) also point to the weakness of empirical evidence for the link between infrastructure provision and economic activity, and the relative inability of this approach to capture feedback effects between transport patterns and land use changes, which largely accrue from the different patterns of user behavior over short and long terms. Bhat et al. (2000) highlight the bias in defining a set of choices for activities and opportunities to be included in this approach, and its "inherent conservatism", as they call it, for the model cannot predict the emergence of new choices and their effect on travel behavior. Baradaran and Ramjerdi (2001) also mention the problematic integration of income effects in this approach. While disregarding such effects restricts the efficacy of the model, their inclusion and consequently the allocation of a higher utility value on activities performed by higher-income earners, raises equity concerns (Geurs and van Eck, 2001), that can only be compensated through cross funding mechanisms. Finally, it is worth noting the variation of relative value utility impacts with the income of users which is never considered in the assessment of infrastructure projects.

From this review, briefly summarised in Table 4.5, we can conclude that the attempts to measure accessibility have become more sophisticated over time, but there are still numerous possible classifications. Nonetheless, there is sufficient evidence of a misrepresentation of accessibility as a factor of social exclusion (or inclusion). Sources of funding and financing through the generation of value capture are equally misrepresented and that justifies the need to call for a paradigm shift which takes into account the diversity of land uses (such as the entropy concept of Cervero, 1997) and the economic and social potential they represent. This leads to seek a sustainable source of funding (generated from the added value produced by accessibility) and to establish equitable cross subsidy mechanisms, to ensure that low income areas and users are not left out of the equation. This suggests the need for a shift from mobility policies to access policies.[5]

4.2.3 Accessibility as a factor of spatial-economic competition

Another necessary perspective in this discussion is to examine accessibility in terms of its effect on business: to consider accessibility as a factor of competitiveness for cities and regions. Many authors argue that transport infrastructure improvements result in signficant impacts on the competitiveness of firms (for example Rietveld and Bruinsma, 1998). Other authors (Forkenbrock and Foster, 1996; Cairncross, 1997; Banister and Berechman, 2003) argue that transport infrastructures do not represent as important a factor in choice of location as in the past, due to the lowering of transport costs and the increasing participation of information rather than physical flows. Still others (Leitham et al., 2000; Preston, 2001; Holl, 2001), suggest that the current industrial reorganization, where time factor is of major importance, has made the distribution and production systems more dependent on transport and, therefore, on high quality access too. For example, Smith and Florida show that in 1994, Japanese companies setting up in the automobile sector in the USA cited ease of access to the highway system as the main factor determining location.[6]

To understand the rationale at the core of this discussion it is necessary to take into account the effects through which transport infrastructures determine the organization of the companies, the respective space distribution and, therefore, the levels of development of the regions where they are located (Silva, 2005). The potential impact that transport can have in the process of creation of value encompassed in the business models of companies relating to the provision of transport infrastructure is summarized below:

- *Location decision* The choice of location is a strategic decision for companies. Weber (1929), considering the issue of minimization of costs, argued that companies choose a location according to the relative cost of transporting raw materials and manufactured items to the main supply market. There are other influencing factors such as the acquisition and the storage of stocks, or taxes and lower costs of installation, and cheap power but these are already influenced by agglomeration effects.

- *Market area dimension and level of competitiveness* Holl (2004a) advocates that "(...) a reduction in transport costs can enable firms to increase their competitiveness and to expand their markets, by lowering prices or profitably serving markets at greater distance where they were formerly excluded on cost ground". This can induce companies to widen the area in which they traditionally operate. The type of company and maturity of market conditions the emergent reactions. Very dynamic and specialized firms and those with the potential to exploit economies of scale are most likely to benefit from transport improvements by increasing their ability to sell over a larger market area or increasing their labor recruitment area.
- *Organization of the production and the structure of the supply chain* Transport is considered as an input factor in the production processes. During the past decade transport decisions have tended to be made higher up in the supply chain. A reduction of the transport costs can reflect in the production planning process and lead to outsourcing to other firms in a better competitive position.

The labor market is often referred to as a factor of competitiveness affected by accessibility. Holl (2004b) underlines that there are important effects accruing from transport that affect the size of the local and regional labor market in relation to specialized labor skills. Following a similar line of thought, Vickerman structures these impacts at two levels: first physical access must exist for any activity to take place and, second, "transport affects labor both as an input to production (commuting), and as an input to other activities (social, leisure, etc.) which constitute the final demand for activities" (Vickerman, 2000).

Thus they create a chain reaction. In the first reaction, the area of the labor market increases: with the reduction of cost of travel which means workers can now travel longer distances for the same (total) cost. This mechanism induces, in general, a higher competitiveness in the local labor market, often causing (if no constraining social agreement exists) reduction of wages or an increase in unemployment. But it enables local workers to reach other markets, in other regions, and consequently is a two-way effect. In the second wave reaction, a reduction in costs can transform the region by making it more attractive to work there. This can be a catalyst for urban sprawl. This may lead to wage reduction possibly counterbalanced by emigration.[7] Prud'Homme warns of a common pitfall (1996): if jobs and homes are poorly located, or if the transport system breaks down, then the city will break up into several independent small markets without sufficient scale to induce increased productivity. So, the positive interaction between land use and transport is in itself a factor that influences the potential of a city to become a major source of productivity and, consequently, its long term sustainability will result from good city management (Macário, 2011).

The impact of a reduction in transport cost, particularly for commuters, makes clear the direct advantages that labor and housing markets obtain from transport which, in most cities make no return to one of the community's essential systems: accessibility. According to Vickerman (2000), in the long run restrictions on the housing market, more than migratory movements, become the main driver for the commuting movements in many cities of the developed world. Following the same line of thought the UK study by Cameron and Muellbauer (1998), underlines the influence that the housing market has on the migratory movements between regions and provides evidence that "(...) differential labour market effects in contiguous regions lead to commuting being substituted for migration, and for nearby regions there is a stronger labour market effect on commuting decisions and a stronger housing market effect on migration decisions", (Vickerman, 2000). This is a clear element of competition between cities.

In fact several authors (see Scheurer and Curtis, 2007; Van Wee et al., 2001) refer to competitive measures as an independent cluster of measures. These measures incorporate capacity constraints of activities and users into accessibility measures and typically provide a regional perspective on accessibility. We consider that these competitive measures result from the combined use of any of the three first groups of measures (those being spatial separation measures, contour measures and gravity measures) and do not represent an independent cluster, but only intelligent combinations of the groups. The question is whether competition measures should take the lead at strategic policy decision-making level and be incorporated into the three other groups at the planning level. This approach allows for an easier understanding that transport is an instrument of competitiveness of cities.

Another group that has been recently explored is network measures. According to Porta et al. (2006) these measures look at the whole network movements to analyse accessibility. The approach is based on the identification of nodes and boundaries as the twin components of any network. These measures capture the network topology and can be used to assess its spatial readability, and also the coverage of the whole mobility system (considering the multimodal dimension) as proposed by Garcia and Macário (2012).

In conclusion, in the study of accessibility measures each new measure has tried to overcome the limitations of the previous ones. Nevertheless, there are still fields to explore, mostly related to the systemic character of accessibility, and the need to provide decision-makers with information on feedback effects of possible measures. In this we include the measurement of accessibility through its market value capturing the economic and societal benefits generated. The utility of the integrated network of the mobility system serving a city or an urban area seems to be a good starting point but for it to be a socially inclusive concept, accessibility must be a public service obligation, and it should be given due importance within the legal institutional framework.

4.3 Social exclusion: the downside of accessibility

Mobility plays an essential role in urban life. Without mobility it is impossible to lead a normal urban life and to perform daily activities that current societies demand in the developed world. This creates the idea that mobility should be a "good" accessible to everyone. In some countries it is considered a "public good". Nonetheless, even when that is the case, some people cannot afford to use the transport system, which hinders their economic and social capacities, while others, able to pay for the services, have a physical impairment that prevents them from using the system. Finally, there are others who, while experiencing neither of the previous constraints, simply lack the knowledge required to use the system. All these issues contribute to push these people into social exclusion which might range from a slight increase of difficulty in mobility to a total lack of access to relevant daily activities. These ranges differ from country to country and the operational focus of social exclusion varies considerably with the level of development revealed in a given society.

Like other authors we argue that the concept of social exclusion has universal validity, whilst its operational execution may have specific social and local contexts. The implications of transport-related social exclusion vary according to the availability of resources to tackle the problem. The great predominance of some disadvantaged groups cannot be neglected and must be dealt with by adequate public responses. Furthermore, it is ineffective to tackle deprivation and the problems of the various social groups separately. The European Union[8] adopted the following wide scope definition for social exclusion:

> Social exclusion is a process whereby certain individuals are pushed to the edge of society and prevented from participating fully by virtue of their poverty, lack of basic competencies and lifelong learning opportunities, or as a result of discrimination. This distances them from job, income and education opportunities as well as social and community networks and activities. They have little access to power and decision-making bodies and thus often feel powerless and unable to take control over the decisions that affect their day-today lives.

Developing countries have generally not considered the concept of social exclusion (Bhalla and Lapeyre, 1997) as this has only recently been recognized as a problem that concerns the transport system. The absence of a welfare state in these societies can be explained by the different perceptions on the relative weight that should be attached to economic, social and political dimensions of poverty and deprivation. In this respect, Kowarick (2003) describes the non-accountability of the state in Latin American countries, in which social exclusion is characterized by phenomena such as unemployment, informal work, loss of identity, urban violence and lack of access to goods and services.

Once the link between social exclusion and transport is understood, the issues hindering access to transportation and consequently contributing to social exclusion must be examined. Exclusion from transport may not just be related to poverty but may also be associated with numerous factors: physical exclusion, geographical exclusion, exclusion from facilities, time-based exclusion, fear-based exclusion, and space exclusion (Hine and Mitchell, 2001). These factors mostly affect particular disadvantaged social groups, according to gender, age and marital status: physically impaired, elderly, single-parent families and illiterate people. Despite the strong interest in social exclusion, there is no agreement about its meaning and impacts apart from the fact that income distribution is associated with social stratification. Some of the ideas commonly related to social exclusion are poverty, unemployment and deprivation. There is indeed some overlap between these concepts, but social exclusion itself encompasses deprivation in a much broader sense reflecting several different forms of inequity, not necessarily caused by simple lack of money.

There is a lack of information on measuring and monitoring social exclusion which has been recognized by several authors (Bhalla and Lapeyre, 1997, Anand and Sen, 1997) who suggest that countries can be divided into groups corresponding with different levels of development. Following this line of thought a set of indicators focused on the distributional aspects are applied to developing countries, recognizing income and economic exclusion as the departure point, whereas a more complex set of indicators, based on relational aspects of social exclusion, would be applied to developed countries. Many other approaches to this concept are reported in the literature. According to Bhalla (1997), social exclusion embraces the distributional and relational aspects of poverty. These aspects include income, employment and participation in family, community and society. Social exclusion reflects the existence of barriers which make it difficult or impossible for people to access and participate fully in society. In other words, according to the seminal work of Sen (1973), it is not a matter of lack of opportunities, but a lack of access to the opportunities. From the literature we can identify a number of access-related barriers that generate social exclusion, which are according to Stanley and Vella-Brodrick, 2009:

- the availability and physical accessibility of transport;
- the cost of transport;
- services located in inaccessible places;
- safety and security – fear of crime;
- travel horizons – people on low incomes were found to be less willing to travel to access work than those on higher incomes.

We need, however, to balance the discussion and stress that for full participation in society, other conditions need to be met rather than merely access
to transport which provides the physical accessibility to economic and
social activities. Nonetheless, transport may be by itself a factor of exclusion, because it has environmental and physical impacts (for example noise
and air pollution, barriers to circulation caused by infrastructure) and
because the negative impacts tend to be concentrated in more deprived
areas (Pennycook *et al.* 2001). This is a consequence of the fact that
transport infrastructure often degrades its surrounding areas, decreasing the
local land value, which then attracts low income populations (for example
historically surroundings of railway stations, even though they are obviously well-connected, provide evidence for this argument). The evidence of
this degradation process brings an additional complexity to the discussion.
While we have seen that accessibility adds value to land use and business,
now, through the social dimension, the lack of transport is identified as a
factor causing degradation and consequently subtracting value to both land
use and business development. More visible in developed countries, congestion also impacts negatively on land use and business. In fact the quality of
the mobility system is one of the factors considered by international corporations when selecting locations for their offices. Congestion therefore is
damaging to the competitiveness of urban areas.

Social exclusion may encompass social, spatial, environmental, economic
and political dimensions. The work of Sinclair (2001) focused on the spatial
and locational dimensions which are mainly perceived through transport
availability. In fact, the ability to access society's offerings is a key component of social inclusion. There is indeed a close relation between social
exclusion and transport as they are linked in a cause–effect relation. This
relationship is demonstrated through two factors: access and impact
(Pennycook *et al.*, 2001). Those without access to transport (mobility
restrained) for either economic, personal or social reasons, are excluded
from actively participating in society.

The key seems to be developing cities and urban mobility systems towards
social inclusion, eliminating the combination of circumstances which prevent
people from fully participating in society. In the past some authors have
supported the transit-oriented development (TOD) of the city and location
of activities near access corridors to enhance accessibility. This concept has
become popular in the USA by providing residents with easy access to public
transport rather than having to rely on their cars. TOD however, addresses
only one type of accessibility and does not address the issue of deprived
groups of the population. Similar limitation also applies to financial schemes
to subsidize mobility, for example *"versement de transport"* (France), or
"vale transporte" (Brazil), which catered only for working people. The difficulties of increasing numbers of deprived groups have only recently begun to
be addressed. This illustrates how little transport is effectively considered as

a public utility compared with policies on education or health which are designed to serve all income groups in the population.

4.4 Mobility-based and accessibility-based policies

The terms "mobility" and "accessibility" are sometimes used to justify the operational objectives of transportation policies. However, a clear distinction must be made between these two concepts. According to Levine (2002) mobility is defined as ease of movement, and accessibility as ease of reaching destinations. Jones (2005) states that the term "accessibility" is used in two different contexts in the UK: the ease of reaching (a set of opportunities); and the set of features in the transport systems that inhibit or promote their use by people with physical and mental impairments. In other countries, such as Brazil, for instance, the term "accessibility" is commonly used in the latter meaning. In Europe, conversely, it is the former meaning that is mostly used.

Levine (2002) states that mobility improvements induce the relocation of activities to more distant places, since car ownership and the greater provision of road infrastructure (based on "predict and provide" policies) stimulate urban sprawl and impact on land values. Hence, the mobility gains for the affluent can result in accessibility losses for lower income groups without access to cars. This is exacerbated because the low density makes it more difficult to provide accessibility to everyone, since public transport requires a minimum scale of operation to be financially viable. Mobility-based policies generally prioritise the use of private vehicles, and tend to concentrate benefits for more affluent people. Conversely, in congested areas, investment in public transport increases access both for the users of public transport and for car users by reducing congestion.

It is commonly agreed that every individual deserves a basic level of accessibility (Preston, 2006; Murray and Wu, 2003), but to achieve this, policies must focus on ensuring minimum levels of accessibility rather than mobility. This implies that the level of mobility depends on the needs of each individual or group of individuals. Such needs may vary in time. In some cases, people can have low mobility and good accessibility, if all their desired activities are near their households. In this case, there is no need for a material dimension of transport (Preston, 2006). This must be distinguished, however, from the example of people who are restricted to activities within walking distances from their home, due to low mobility levels or, when people are obliged to undertake long daily trips via non-motorized modes because of the unaffordability of transport, which is common in South America and Asia.

Social inclusion is therefore better achieved through equity of access, which in turn depends on the combination of land use, transport, environmental aspects and income distribution. From the review on policy documents it is clear there are three reasons why there needs to be a focus on social exclusion: the need to increase equity in society, to raise the productive potential of society and to reduce risk of friction between groups in society.

To some extent current appraisal methods for transport investment projects are in contradiction to this philosophical stance. First the widely-used cost–benefit analysis approach relies on travel time savings as the main part of the quantifiable economics benefit. In other words, a decision on long life cycle infrastructure is based on short term travel savings. Besides, there is evidence that long term user strategy does not match travel cost minimization strategies (Metz, 2008). Second, agglomeration and business benefits must be included in the cost–benefit computation, as well as monetised and non-monetised effects. Third, travel time is considered a cost in the CBA approach, and the main strategy used to reduce this cost has been to increase average speed. However, economic development is related to access rather than to travel speed (Crozet, 2009). For these reasons CBA is becoming less useful in the decision-making process. Policy should focus on cost-effective solutions to achieve social inclusion objectives, through policy impact assessment procedures.

4.5 Sticking necks out: towards market evaluation of accessibility

4.5.1 Understanding minimum structural conditions and make it operational

The previous sections take us to the conclusion that current policies are not favorable to social inclusion and some even lead to exclusion. To achieve change, politically defined objectives must be broken down into planning and design at the tactical level and later into implementation at the operational level. In a market each agent (individuals and institutions) tends to pursue its own objectives. In a system with several agents concerned with, for example, urban mobility, it is the interaction of numerous elements that leads to an outcome, largely driven by the market dynamics since there is no hierarchy to establish a formal coordination. This is the typical situation leading to decisions being made on the design and implementation of an access or mobility policy.

So, understanding change is a matter of understanding the interaction between the entities that form a specific organizational field and their environment. In mobility systems the symbiotic relationship between actors forces the system to have structural consistency to evolve in a sustainable way. Decisions lie on the border of domains that usually represent autonomous political powers: environment, land use, social and transport policy. The structural consistency entails a horizontal and a vertical dimension (Macário, 2011). Horizontally consistency is provided through the equifinality[9] of action between the different agents since cities have several mobility providers with varying roles in the supply chain. Horizontal consistency can be provided by elements such as regulatory frameworks, contractual relations, quality monitoring procedures and enforcement. Vertical consistency is achieved through three system attributes : coherence, efficiency and accountability, and determines the interdependency between organizations playing roles at different decision levels (strategic, tactic and operational) and the common awareness that decisions taken at one level by one organization not only affect other organizations at that same level, but also the ones acting at other decision levels. Feedback ensures consistency of action. Lack of consistency is a very common problem between decisions taken within the land use sector and their effects on the transport sector, or between environment and any of the others. A good example of lack of vertical consistency is reported by Crozet (2009) regarding decisions that aimed to increase accessibility but instead resulted in the increase of average speed which in turn led to congestion and eventually segregation and conflict between groups of society.

The relationship between horizontal and vertical specialization in a mobility system leads to a complex network of institutions and organizations with different degrees and forms of interaction, but all should be linked by a set of quality performance objectives. Given this tight net of interactions, fitness of purpose and action is an indispensable attribute that can only be assured by a continuous adjustment of institutional design to policy and regulatory changes, that can be adapted through changes in goals, instruments or settings. A clear distinction between policy making and executive decisions is required and both should be accountable. The first aims to provide direction, coherence and continuity to the course of actions, while executive decisions are aimed at giving effect to policies. The complexity accruing from policy making lies in the fact that the basic problem of how to assimilate change with the greatest net gain of value, while preserving the balance of the system, must be identified before a course of intervention is defined.

The analysis made by Buchanan (Buchanan, 1963, in Vickers, 1965) on the impact of increased demand for traffic movements in United Kingdom towns, provides a good example. The terms of reference for the Buchanan committee were to study the long term development of roads and traffic in urban areas and their influence on the urban environment. The report started by showing that the relation between traffic and other human related activities is not self-regulated on any acceptable level thus opening the way for more interventionist regulation.

Four propositions were advanced to embody the "optimizing-balancing" problem involved in policy-making: traffic density is a function of density of use of land; traffic pattern is a function of the spatial relation between buildings and their uses; quality of buildings requires some environmental characteristics; and traffic is damaging for buildings. This formulation was considered at the time a masterpiece for making informed judgments, stressing the relationship between the level of investment and its effects. It makes it possible to assess the contradiction between the value of good environment and exclusive value for accessibility. By setting the problem before the public, revealing its complexity and showing efficient, verifiable and accountable solutions, it points to possible courses of action in a transparent way.

The four propositions used to build the construct reduce the conflict to the interaction of two variables put forward by Buchanan, 1963, (in Vickers, 1965), being accessibility and good environment, where a minimum standard for environment implies a high standard for accessibility. Capacity to bear associated costs of accessibility will determine how high good environment standards can be set. The Buchanan example suggests[10] that there are two perspectives on change: the narrow focus on service or production, that is the operational decision or planning level; and the wider whole system spectrum covering the three planning levels, strategic, tactical and operational. The first perspective is largely dominated by the effects caused by different forms of market access, while the later focuses on the overall system performance in terms of how the mobility system contributes to the economic, social and environmental objectives and how the needs of urban performance are reflected and implemented at the three decision levels. In both cases change is a permanent transition process that adjusts institutions to the dynamic environment in which they are embedded, that can be materialized in changes in goals, instruments or settings.

The definition of objectives starts thus with the decision-makers' interpretation of several elements, namely:

- the importance of the needs (or aspirations) of the citizens; and
- the importance of the problems to be solved, measured through their impacts on social and economic live of the city; and
- the assessment of the probability of success of each of the actions and policies.

A condition for vertical consistency referred to above is that strategic objectives should be defined upstream of the prioritization of actions and policies and should be part of the accountability process. Access must be dealt at the aggregate program level, and not at the operational level with fragmented measures, and across all related domains and institutions to emphasise that inclusion (or prevention of exclusion) is a top strategic priority. Indeed, whatever the context, the formulation of a strategy requires the establishment of a hierarchy of objectives and the setting of the level for their realisation. It is at this decision level that accessibility should be considered as a factor of social inclusion and competitiveness of the city. It should be seen as a public service obligation and the market value approach to accessibility (value capture) should be the main source of funding.

Cities differ substantially in their development strategies. Even if they are dealing with similar problems, in any given moment each city is conditioned by the choices made in the past that configure a different departure point and consequently decision makers will have different perceptions on which are the main problems that need to be addressed and which are the best solutions to mitigate them.

However the intertwined relationships between accessibility, land use, environment and social aspects suggest that institutional design should develop in such a way that decision-making within these sectors lies on articulated processes that over time can build the necessary institutional trust that guarantees long term thinking and vertical and horizontal consistency.[11]

4.5.2 Initiate vectors of change to build institutional trust

After ensuring access and social inclusion as strategic priorities it is then important to define these options within other decision levels. At the tactical and operational levels a number of vectors must be initiated in a consistent way. These are:

- *Access as a public service obligation* To ensure social inclusion accessibility must be defined at the top level of governance and dealt with at a tactical and operational level like other utilities that support urban living such as electricity, sanitation, water and waste. In this way accountability is pushed upstream in the provision supply chain. This means that investment decisions on access cannot be made on the basis of private decision-making criteria and that access in a zone with high willingness to pay will have to be used to cross subsidise access in other areas, in particular socially deprived areas. However, this cannot be used as an argument for lack of decision-making transparency or accountability, nor to prevent the market from operating in an efficient way. The state obligation to guarantee social inclusion should not be not a synonym for direct interference in the market of provision of services. In fact, such interference can be seen as the outcome of regulatory failure.

- *Cities as competitive economic agents* The city must recognise how it is perceived by individuals and corporations, and be managed under that perception of competitive pressure. However, a holistic view of land use and mobility is needed. As Crozet (2009) states, addressing mobility as an exclusive transport issue resulted in policies from the 1960s to the 1980s which overlooked the side effects of drivers being encouraged to travel more. The transport network represents a vector of opportunities. Consequently access and mobility must be seen as development issues and instruments of city competitiveness.

- *Fiscal decentralisation or fiscal federalism* The city must have tax raising powers to ensure it can pursue strategic objectives in a responsible and accountable way, and improve its competitiveness to the benefit of its citizens. A minimum level of service should be provided through money from development funds (cross funding) based on principles and mechanisms defined at the national level to ensure equity beyond city borders.

- *Value capture of urban assets* Property value and use should make a contribution to an investment fund to ensure cross funding of accessibility in deprived areas and help maintain equitable conditions of accessibility in urban areas. Special concern should be given to metropolitan areas where these capture mechanisms may introduce significant imbalances in the region and lead to relocations of households and firms seeking more affordable, yet still accessible, locations. These movements may lead to less sustainable configurations, increasing travel times and added costs through urban sprawl. Value capture must be seen as an evolution of the beneficiary-pay principle that should include not only users of services and infrastructures but also to the beneficiaries.

- *Comprehensive appraisal of investments and policy decisions* Changing the cost–benefit analysis approach will have a significant impact on appraisal of investments to consider the market value of accessibility (through value capture and social inclusion) using net utility ratios applied to different weighted segments of society, reflecting income differences across society, and providing a way of ranking investments based on their impact on people's welfare.

- *Establish continuous feedback mechanisms* A continuous monitoring process is required to ensure adjustment to the natural evolution of the city and its respective needs but also to address the reaction of stakeholders to the change process. It is through these monitoring mechanisms that vertical and horizontal consistency over time can be maintained.

Despite much evidence, most countries ignore the variation on property value that accrues to real estate from transport investment which is a positive externality that benefits real estate investors and owners and, assuming efficient fiscal settings, indirectly the State budgets through general taxation mechanisms on property transactions. Therefore, for the most part of society people are unaware of the social impacts of transport investment. Moreover, it is impossible to assess the impact of variations in access until both positive (increase of access) and negative (decrease of access through level of service) effects can be taken into account. Value of time, property values, business potential and local welfare generation are certainly important variables to research and will offer new challenges to the old paradigms. On top of this – and history is there to show how much we are repeating it – once again financial bottlenecks will be the trigger for paradigm shift.

Acknowledgements

The author wishes to express her appreciation for the valuable comments and inputs received from Måns Lönnroth and Elliott Sclar in their review of previous versions of this paper.

Notes

1   The Athens Charter (Charte D'Athènes), is a document about urban planning published by the Swiss architect, Le Corbusier, in 1943. The document contains the results of the work undertaken by the Congrès International d'Architecture Moderne (CIAM) in the early 1930s, largely based on the concept of the functional city. Due to the war constraints the congress, originally planned to be held in Moscow in 1933, took place on board the SS Patris, on a return journey from Marseilles to Athens, giving the name to the Charter. The Athens Charter has had a major influence in post war urbanism (Mumford, 2000) and the deployment of the functional city.

2   This stability has to be considered in short time periods when households have difficulties in reorganizing mobility budgets and logistics.

3   Martinez (2010), identified also three factors that influence the effects of public transport investment in property values, these are: the transport network context and the spatial distribution of effects; the timing of impacts; the contextual and local economic factors.

4   Stanley and Stanley (2007) reports on-going research in Australia seeking to understand the association between transport, social exclusion and well-being.

5   It is worth mentioning that the last decade revealed already some evidence of this shift of paradigm in South America (for example Brasil, Ministry of Cities), where the framework law from urban mobility (adopted by the Council of Cities in 2003 and approved by the Senate in 2012) sets as objectives equitable access requirements to the cities and their infrastructures.

6   "Related research shows how locating at the primary road network can also act as a publicity factor" (Holl, 2001).

7   A third wave reaction to the reduction of the costs of the commuting movements can be congestion in some points of the network, allowing the reduction of the impact initially estimated by certain investment in infrastructures of transport.

8   Joint Report on Social Inclusion, European Comission, 2004.

9   Equifinality is understood in this text as a consistency property. Following Drischel (1968) formulations in his "Formal Theory of Organisation", equifinal systems are the ones which have the property of reaching the same final goals (or state) regardless of the initial state, input sequence or evolving pathway. That is, consistency through equifinality can be achieved even if initial state and selected processes are different (Macário, 2011a).

10   The Committee clearly stated that existing institutions could not do the job on the required scale and recommended the creation of executive agencies.

11   There are different ways of translating these concepts to the field. One example of this approach can be found in Brazil with implementing the Ministry of Cities, in January 2003, to ensure a coherent approach to the different sectors within urban life. At the time of writing this paper, that institutional design is still operating.

References

Anand, S. and Sen, A. (1997) *Concepts of Human Development and Poverty: A Multidimensional Perspective*, New York: UNDP.

Arsen, D. (1997) *Is There Really an Infrastructure/Economic Development Link? Dilemmas of Urban Economic Development: Issues in Theory and Practice* Bingham, R. and Mier, R. (eds), Newbury Park, CA: Sage Publications.

Aschauer, D. A. (1989) "Is public-expenditure productive?" *Journal of Monetary Economics* 23(2): 177–200.

Baradaran, S. and Ramjerdi, F. (2001) "Performance of accessibility measures in Europe", *Journal of Transportation and Statistics*, 4(2/3): 31–48.

Banister, D. and Berechman, J. (2003) *Transport Investment and Economic Development*, UCL Press.

Barton, H., Horswell, M. *et al.* (2007) "Social inclusion and outer urban neighbourhoods: access to local facilities", Solutions Annual Conference, University College London.

Bhalla, A, and Lapeyre, F. (1997) "Social exclusion: towards an analytical and operational framework", *Development and Change* 28(3): 413–33.

Bhat, C., Handy, S. *et al.* (2000) "Development of an urban accessibility index: literature review", Research project conducted for the Texas Department of Transportation, Center for Transportation Research, University of Texas, Austin, TX.

Buchanan, C. J. (1963) "Report on traffic in towns", London: HMSO.

Cairncross, F. (1997) "The death of distance", 19(9): 7, Harvard University Press.

Cameron, G. and Muellbauer, J. (1998) "The housing market and regional commuting and migration choices", *Scottish Journal of Political Economy* 45(4): 420–46.

Cervero, R., Rood, T. and Appleyard, B. (1997) "Job accessibility as a performance indicator: an analysis of trends and their social policy implications in the San Francisco Bay Area. Working paper 692, University of California, Berkeley.

Coffey, W. J. and Shearmur, R. G. (1997) "The growth and location of high order services in the Canadian urban system, 1971–1991", *Professional Geographer* 49(4): 404–18.

Crozet, Y. (2009) *The Prospects for Inter-urban travel Demand,* No. 2009/14. OECD Publishing.

de Dios Ortúzar, Juan and Willumsen. L. G. (2001) *Modelling Transport 7.* Chichester: Wiley.

Dong, X., Ben-Akiva, M. E. *et al.* (2006) "Moving from trip-based to activity-based measures of accessibility",*Transportation Research Part A*, 40(2): 18.

Farrington, J. and Farrington, C. (2005) "Rural accessibility, social inclusion and social justice: towards conceptualisation", *Journal of Transport Geography* 13: 12.

Forkenbrock, D. J., Benshoff, S. and Weisbrod, G. E. (2001) *Assessing the Social and Economic Effects of Transportation Projects*, NCHRP Web Document 31. National Cooperative Highway Research Program, Transportation Research Board, National Research Council.

Forkenbrock, D. J. and Foster, N. S. J. (1996) "Highways and business location decisions", *Economic Development Quarterly* 10(3): 239–48.

Garcia and Macário, R. (2012) "The sustainable accessibility concept applied to strategic planning of urban mobility networks", submitted to the CASPT conference, July 2012, Santiago de Chile.

Geurs, K. T. and van Eck, J. R. (2001) *Accessibility Measures: Review and Applications*, Rijksinstituut voor Volksgezondheid en Milieu (National Institute of Public Health and the Environment, RIVM) and Urban Research Centre, Utrecht University.

Geurs, K. T. and van Wee, B. (2004) "Accessibility evaluation of land-use and transport strategies: review and research directions", Journal of Transport Geography 12(2): 127–40.

Groote, P., Jacobs, J. and Sturm, J. E. (1995) *Output Responses to Infrastructure Investment in the Netherlands, 1850-1913*, University of Groningen, Faculty of Economics, Groningen Growth and Development Centre.

Isserman, A. and Rephann, T. (1995) "The economic-effects of the Appalachian-regional-commission: an empirical assessment of 26 years of regional-development planning", *Journal of the American Planning Association* 61(3): 345–64.

Koenig, J. G. (1980) "Indicators of urban accessibility: theory and application", *Transportation* 9: 145–72.

Kwan, M.-P. (1998) "Space–time and integral measures of individual accessibility: a comparative analysis using a point-based framework", *Geographical Analysis* 30(3): 191–216.

Handy, S. L. and Niemeier, D. A. (1997) "Measuring accessibility: an exploration of issues and alternatives", *Environment and Planning A* 29: 1175–94.

Hansen, W. G. (1959) "How accessibility shapes land use", *Journal of the American Institute of Planners* 25: 73–6.

Hartgen, D. T., Stuart, A. W., Walcott, W. A. and Clay, J. W. (1990) "Role of transportation in manufacturers' satisfaction with locations", *Transportation Research Record* 1274: 12–23.

Hine, J. and Mitchell, F. (2001) *The Role of Transport in Social Exclusion in Urban Scotland*, Scottish Executive.

Holl, A. (2001) "Transport Infrastructure in Lagging European Regions", PhD Dissertation, University of Sheffield.

Holl, A. (2004) "The role in firm's spatial organization: evidence from the Spanish food processing industry", *European Planning Studies*, 12(4): 537–50.

Kowarick, L. (2003) "On the vulnerability and socioeconomic status: United States, France and Brazil", *Brazilian Journal of Social Sciences* 18: 51.

Leitham, S., McQuaid, R. and Nelson, J. (2000) "The influence of transport on industrial location choice: a stated preference experiment", *Transportation Research A*, 34: 515–35.

Levine, J. and Garb, Y. (2002) "Congestion pricing's conditional promise: promotion of accessibility or mobility?." *Transport Policy* 9(3): 179–88.

Macário, R. (2011) "Managing Urban Mobility Systems", Emerald Group Publishing Limited (a previous version was published in 2005, as a PhD at Instituto Superior Técnico, Lisbon Technical University).

Macário, R. and Silva, J.M. (2009) "Regional airports and local development: the challenging balance between sustainability and economic growth", in Uleguin F. (ed.) *Prospects for Research in Transport and Logistics on a Regional: Global Perspective*, pp 189–95.

Macário, R. and Galelo, A. (2011) "Accessibility: user satisfaction, authority satis-faction, or society satisfaction?" 12th Thredbo Conference, 11–15 September 2011, Durban and VREF CoE Workshop 26–29 October 2011, Beijing.

Mackett, R. (2008) Using transport to increase social inclusion. M.U.-S.R.i.T.S.C. Institute of Transport Studies. London, London TravelWatch Accessibility Committee.

Mamatzakis, E. C. (2007) "An analysis of the impact of public infrastructure on productivity performance of Mexican industry", CESifo working paper, No. 2099, http://hdl.handle.net/10419/26144

Martinez, L. M. and Viegas, J. M. (2010) "Land value capture potential of the Lisbon subway: estimation and integration with the current fiscal system", 12th WCTR, July 11–15. Lisbon.

Metz, D. (2008) "The myth of travel time savings", *Transport Reviews*, 28(3): 321–36.

Mumford, E. (2000) *The CIAM Discourse on Urbanism, 1928–1960*, The MIT Press.

Murray, A. T. and Wu, X. (2003) "Accessibility tradeoffs in public transit plan-ning", *Journal of Geographical Systems* 5(1): 93–107.

Nadiri, M. I. and Mamuneas, T. P. (1998) *Contribution of Highway Capital to Output and Productivity Growth in the U.S. Economy and Industries*, FHWA, US Department of Transportation.

Niemeier, D. A. (1997) "Accessibility: an evaluation using consumer welfare", *Transportation* 24(4): 377–96.

Pennycook, F., Barrington-Craggs, R., Smith, D. and Bullock, S. (2001) *Environmental Justice: Mapping Transport and Social Exclusion in Bradford*, Friends of the Earth, online at: www.foe.co.uk/resource/reports/env_justice_bradford.pdf

Pirie, G. H. (1979) "Measuring accessibility: a review and proposal", *Environment and Planning A* 11: 299–312.

Porta, S., Crucitti P. and Latora, V. (2006) "The network analysis of urban streets: a primal approach", *Environment and Planning B: Planning and Design* 33.

Preston, J. (2001) "Integrating transport with socio-economic activity: a research agenda for the new millennium", *Journal of Transport Geography* 9(1): 13–24.

Prud'Homme, R. (1996) "Managing megacities", *Le Courier du CNRS* 82: 174–6.

Rich, D. C. (1978) *Potential Models in Human Geography Concepts and Techniques in Modern Geography 26*, Norwich: University of East Anglia.

Rietveld, P. (1994) "Spatial economic impacts of transport infrastructure supply", *Transportation Research A* 28A(4): 329–41.

Rietveld, P. and Bruinsma, F. (1998) *Is Transport Infrastructure Effective? Transport Infrastructure and Accessibility: Impacts on the Space Economy*, Berlin: Springer-Verlag.

Schafer, A. and Victor, D. G. (2000) "The future mobility of the world population", *Transportation Research Part A* 34(3): 171–205.

Scheurer, J. and Curtis, C. (2008) *Spatial Network Analysis of Multimodal Transport Systems: Developing a Strategic Planning Tool to Assess the Congruence of Movement and Urban Structure: a Case Study of Perth Before and After the Perth-to-Mandurah Railway*. GAMUT, Australasian Centre for the Governance and Management of Urban Transport, University of Melbourne.

Scheurer, J. and Curtis, C. (2007) *Accessibility Measures: Overview and Practical Applications; Impacts of Transit Led Development in a New Rail Corridor*, Urbanet, Department of Urban and Regional Planning, Curtin University, Australia.

Sen, A. (ed.) (1973) *On Economic Inequality*, Oxford University Press.

Silva, J. (2005*) As Acessibilidades como Factor do Desenvolvimento de Regiões Periféricas*, O Caso da Beira Interior, Tese de Doutoramento, Lisboa, Universidade Técnica de Lisboa, Instituto Superior Técnico.

Song, S. (1996) Some tests of alternative accessibility measures: a population density approach. *Land Economics* 72 (4): 474–82.

Spandou, M. and Macário, R. (2011) "Decentralization as an institutional determinant for the performance of urban mobility systems", 12th Thredbo Conference, 11–15 September 2011, Durban, and VREF CoE Workshop 26–29 October 2011, Beijing.

Stanley, J. and Stanley, J. (2007) "Public transport and social policy goals", *Road & Transport Research*, March, 16(1): 20.

Stanley, J. and Vella-Brodrick, D. (2009) "The usefulness of social exclusion to inform social policy in transport", *Transport Policy* 16: 90–6.

Suárez, E. L. (2008) "Measuring regional cohesion effects of large-scale transport infrastructure investments: an accessibility approach", *European Planning Studies* 16(2): 277–301.

Van Wee, B., Hagoort M. and Annema, J. A. (2001) "Accessibility measures with competition", *Journal of Transport Geography* 9: 199–208.

Vickerman, R. W. (1974) "Accessibility, attraction, and potential: a review of some concepts and their use in determining mobility", *Environment and Planning A* 6: 675–91.

Vickerman, R. (ed.) (2000) "Transport and economic growth, in regional science association international", 6th World Congress of the RSAI, Lugano, RSAI.

Vickers, G. (1965) "The art of judgement", Chapman & Hall, London, re-printed in 1995 by Sage Publications.

Wachs, M. and Koenig, J. G. (1979) "Behavioral modeling, accessibility, mobility and travel needs", *Behavioural Travel Modelling* 698: 712.

Waddell, P. (2001) "Towards a behavioural integration of land use and transportation modelling", in Hensher, D. A. (ed.) *Travel Behaviour Research*, The Leading Edge, Pergamon, Amsterdam, pp. 65–95.

Weinstein, B. L. and Clower. T. L. (1999) "The initial economic impacts of the Dart Lrt system".

Chapter 5

Opportunities for transport financing through new technologies

State of the art and research needs

Jonas Eliasson

5.1 Introduction

Most cities around the world are likely to face a considerable rise in demand for transport financing in the future. More labour and production specialization means that the need (and willingness to pay) for accessibility to labour, workplaces and input goods will continue to rise, driving up demand for transport. The same trends will continue to increase urbanization, resulting in rising transport demand in urban regions where capacity problems are already severe.

On the other hand, climate problems, congestion, oil scarcity and land scarcity mean that road traffic needs to decrease. Hence, high-quality, high-capacity public transit is an important part of the solution to this conundrum. This means that cities need to find funding for both investment and operations, especially since transit often needs to be subsidized.

This funding will need to come from a variety of sources. A significant part will be raised from the usual sources such as taxes on income, revenue, sales, etc. Moreover, property taxation (ideally local taxation of increases in land value) is a particularly well-suited instrument for financing transport investment, since this is a way to recoup part of the increase in property values brought about by a transport investment.[1] Another way of such "value capture" is to buy land before making a transport improvement, and sell it afterwards at a profit. In addition, various forms of public-private partnerships (such as "build-operate-transfer"), while not strictly a new source of funding, may be a way to increase the cost efficiency of building and maintaining infrastructure, and solving liquidity problems.

However, a substantial part of the funding needs to come from within the transport system, from the benefits it creates for its users. The crucial question is how these benefits can be transformed into revenue sources, which can then be used for funding investments and operations. This discussion paper reviews how technological advances may help in enabling this. The main purpose is not to give a comprehensive state-of-the-art account of the related issues, but rather to highlight and explain how and why technological advances may have the potential to enable new sources of financing transport, and point out what I believe are the most important research areas in order for this potential to be realized.

When starting to write this chapter, I asked a few knowledgeable colleagues: "Will technological advances open new sources for transport financing?" Their spontaneous answer can be summarised as "No. New technology does not create more money. It may become more convenient to pay, and payment systems may become cheaper to operate, but as to new sources or some ability to extract more total revenues – no." This sobering answer should be kept in mind when discussing these issues. However, I believe that there are two different ways in which technological advances may in fact contribute to financing the transport system.

First, certain technological advances may create value that can subsequently be converted into revenue. One example is information services such as parking guidance, route guidance and incident information. Increasing the quality of public transport may of course also increase the willingness to pay (WTP) for its services, even possibly to the point where increased revenues may more than cover increased costs. The potential of increasing revenues through "value creation" by technical innovations is discussed in Section 5.2.

Second, a substantial part of transport funding needs to be covered by user fees. Technological advances may enable transport prices to be much more differentiated, without creating inefficient use of resources (in the form of so-called "deadweight losses"). In some cases, differentiated pricing instruments may even increase the efficiency of the transport system, for example by pricing out congestion. To maximize resource efficiency, transport prices should be equal to social marginal costs (they should include marginal external costs and benefits). But since marginal costs vary substantially across time and space, real-world transport prices are oversimplified for ease of collection. In the best case, they are set somewhere close to average marginal costs. But average marginal costs are often very low: the average marginal cost of an additional transit passenger, for example, is almost negligible. The corollary is that increased price differentiation means that revenues can often be raised while simultaneously increasing efficiency of resource use. One example of price differentiation that both generates revenues and increases efficiency is moving from fuel taxes as the sole way to price road transport to differentiated road user charging.

Greater price differentiation may also offer the potential to increase transport revenues in general, apart from any efficiency considerations. Long-distance operators (airlines and train operators) have used so-called "yield management strategies" for a long time. The general idea is to customize prices to different groups of users in order to extract a price as close to the maximum willingness to pay as possible. In general, this will also maximize resource use, since the strategy will aim to sell all available capacity as long as the price is above marginal cost (which is often negligible in the short run). This concept could be partly transferable to urban public transport.

It is also possible that differentiated increases in prices may be more acceptable than general price rises – and acceptability is a concern in a politically controlled setting such as the transport system. "User pays" is a principle that has widespread support in many, though not all, circumstances. Indeed, this principle is often met with greater acceptance than more "efficient" pricing principles such as marginal cost pricing or shadow pricing. If transport prices can be tied closer to the transport service provided, then it may be possible to get acceptance for extracting more revenue from transport users than if the same revenue were obtained by general "flat" increases.

But increasing transport prices has proved difficult for many reasons. Some of these difficulties may be alleviated through new technologies. However, there are also other difficulties, where new technology will not help. Several are connected to institutional settings and political considerations: public acceptability, political logic (such as vote-seeking), political governance issues (incomplete authority over revenues or price levels) and lack of financing incentives (for example if a regional body wants to persuade the national government to fund a transport investment).

Section 5.3 provides a brief overview of the relevant theory for efficient transport pricing. Section 5.4 reviews recent and emerging technical advances that are relevant for enabling transport financing. Section 5.5 summarizes areas where research is needed to realize these possibilities.

Finally, I should point out what this discussion paper does *not* cover. First, it does not discuss technical improvements of the transport system itself, although this may obviously increase the willingness to pay for transport services. Hence, promising innovations such as BRT-type systems and bus operations and control strategies are outside the scope of this chapter. In the survey of research areas, I have not included purely technical development of information and payment systems (such as communication technology or technical standards). Finally, I do not go into ways of reducing operational costs for public transport by, for example, using fleets and personnel more efficiently.[2]

5.2 New revenue sources

Some technological advances have the potential to open up new revenue sources within the transport system. In contrast to technologies merely making it possible to charge for transport services in new ways (for example road pricing systems), these technologies create value for users in various forms, some of which can be converted into revenue streams. In this section, three important and typical examples of existing or emerging technologies will be discussed. The focus is on how they could be converted into revenue streams – and perhaps more importantly, whether it would be a good idea.

5.2.1 Parking guidance

Finding a free parking spot is obviously a significant problem in congested situations. So-called "search traffic" can represent a considerable share of traffic in urban streets with studies reporting a figure of up to 30 per cent. Even if such figures may be exceptional, reducing search traffic may include a social benefit in addition to the individual benefit gained by the driver.

It is possible to install simple sensor equipment in the street surface to detect whether a parking spot is free or not. This can be communicated to a central server, which in turn provides parking guidance to smartphones or similar devices. This is a service where there is most likely a high WTP. Since most of the benefit would accrue to the user, a subscription service would be natural, and the service would generate revenue. While this service could in principle be provided by a private company, there are good reasons to retain it in the public sector. The fundamental source of the revenue – the scarce resource that generates a WTP – is not the comparatively simple software (which a private company can develop), but the street space itself, which would obviously need to be under public control. Hence, a company would be subject to the risk of the city changing its parking policies to the detriment of its revenue. Handling this risk would be costly and limit the city's freedom of action.

A parking guidance service provided by a government body raises a fundamental issue: whether services under public control should be priced (and supplied) to maximize aggregate social welfare, to maximize profits, or according to a "user pays" principle (which would require user fees to cover both fixed and variable costs). In the case of a parking guidance system, the fixed costs of installing the sensors and providing the software are relatively high while the marginal usage cost is very low. If the aim were to maximize total social benefits, it would be optimal to provide the service at marginal cost, i.e. almost free. The problem is that the revenues will not cover fixed costs, so they need to be covered with some other source of funding, usually general taxation.[3] This creates the problem, however, that the general public will fund a service that is used only by a subset of the population. A "user pays" principle would require fees to cover fixed costs as well; this could be viewed as "fair", but will, on the other hand, constitute an efficiency loss (fewer people will use the service). This clash between aggregate efficiency and fairness is inevitable as soon as marginal user cost is lower than average user cost. This problem is typical for transport pricing; the same issue crops up when discussing transit pricing and road pricing (especially when crowding and congestion is low).

If prices are set to maximize profits, on the other hand, revenues will usually[4] cover fixed costs. When analysing the two pricing policies, the potential for creating further benefits with this revenue stream should also be taken into account.

I am not aware of any large-scale parking guidance system currently in place (not counting simple parking garage applications), so it is difficult to calculate the potential revenue from such solutions. But considering cheap sensor technology, high smartphone penetration rates and the high willingness to pay for reducing search time, this could be an important revenue source. Integrating this into transit information provision also seems a natural idea.

5.2.2 Route guidance

GPS-based road navigation systems are ubiquitous. Traditionally, most of them have relied on static geoinformation – maps, essentially – with the possibility to include real-time alerts about roadworks, accidents etc., information which is typically provided by transport agencies. Recently, navigation system providers have introduced the possibility for users to provide travel-time information automatically, and this information is then used to adjust travel times in the network to better reflect reality. Currently, this information is sparse and needs to be aggregated over long time periods to be reliable. But once the market penetration is high enough, such information may even be reliable in real time, or at least it would be possible to disaggregate it with respect to aspects such as time-of-day and season, to deliver reliable information about average conditions based on historical information.

Unfortunately, this development can be viewed as a lost opportunity for public stakeholders, who could have played a larger part in this development, and perhaps even used it for generating profits. Public entities used to control all information about the transport system – geocoded information (street maps, destination data), and even some real-time data on travel times and incidents. Ten years ago, several countries had visions that their transport agencies would provide real-time transport data to commercial providers, thereby controlling the information and hence to some extent steering traffic, and maybe also generating revenue. However, the commercial providers have now tired of waiting for this to happen, and are instead developing their own (proprietary) data collection processes. Detailed static information is already collected by Google Maps – much more detailed and advanced (including 360-degree pictures of streetscapes) than any public entity thought about collecting. It seems unlikely that public agencies will now be able to convert the data monopoly they used to have into revenues.

On the other hand, there are actually arguments in favour of subsidizing navigation systems which provide real-time travel time information. Simulations have shown that users' imperfect information about travel times in the network causes considerable efficiency losses. (Travel times vary substantially from day to day, even when not affected by particular incidents and traffic volumes are similar between days.) Put differently, if users received real-time route guidance, overall travel times could be reduced considerably. But to realize this, a substantial proportion of road users need to provide travel time information to the central database, and use the navigation system for route choice. These external benefits are, in principle, an argument for subsidizing such navigation systems. So far, this suggestion has not been realized anywhere (as far as I am aware), but it is likely to crop up once more people realize the potential.

5.2.3 Transit information

Transit information provision has undergone vast improvements in many cities over the past decade. Real-time departure time and incident information is common at stations and bus stops, and route guidance systems through web pages and smartphone apps are increasingly well developed. This development will certainly continue, with applications becoming more user-friendly, reliable and better integrated with other information services. However, it is difficult to foresee any truly qualitative change in these information services – they will mostly do similar things but better and more conveniently. Consequently, this is likely to make public transport easier to use and hence more attractive (especially for new or infrequent users) – but from a financial perspective, they will not generate new revenue streams, beyond the increased customer base.

This is because the business model so far has been to provide all information for free, either because of hopes to recoup the cost through rising usage, or because transit agencies have viewed information provision as a core part of their task. Theoretically, this information could be converted into revenue by charging passengers for it. However, this is probably not a good idea. First, since setting up information has high fixed costs but low marginal costs, subsidies will be necessary (if it is accepted that the overall aim of public agencies is to maximize aggregate benefits rather than profits). Second, attractive public transit usually has high external (non-user) benefits, justifying the use of subsidies. One such subsidization scheme is the provision of information for free; it is preferable to recoup its costs in other ways.

5.2.4 Can information provision be used as a revenue source?

Parking guidance and transit information are just two examples of transport information services – the list could be made much longer. Generating revenue from information services has developed to a global multibillion industry over the past decade. However, development of transport information services has been slower than expected, and public stakeholders have not been a significant part of this development. There are several reasons for this, including fragmented ownership and unclear business models.

Most current business models for information services rely on advertisements as the revenue source, while few successful services are based on user charges. While it seems unlikely that revenue from transport information services will play an important part in financing transport investment, it may fund the information service operations and potentially generate a surplus for transport operations.

Why, then, is this development so slow? One reason might be that the public sector lacks the necessary funding or skills. It may also be unclear who will offer this service. Private sector investors might be cautious in investing due to the risk that the public sector will offer the service for free. This means that there may an opportunity for PPP initiatives to accelerate the establishment of new service providers. Research focusing on and piloting new business models in combination with public procurement legislations in Europe would be useful.

5.3 How should transport be priced?

More differentiated transport pricing, enabled by technological advances, will make it possible to extract more revenue from the users of the transport system without creating efficiency losses – in many cases, there are even efficiency improvements to be gained. As a background, it is useful to review some principles of how transport services should be priced in order to create maximum social benefits (or, in other words, the most efficient use of resources).

Aggregate social benefits are maximized by setting the price of transport services at their net marginal social cost, which equates to the difference between marginal social costs and marginal external benefits. Marginal costs of transport services are the sum of three types of costs. First, there is the marginal provision cost: the cost of accommodating a marginal user. This includes marginal capacity costs in public transport and marginal maintenance costs. These costs are often low, generally speaking. Second, there are costs imposed on other users of the same service, primarily road congestion and transit crowding, which are often substantial in urban areas. Third, there are costs that fall outside the specific transport service, primarily accidents, emissions and noise.

There may also be external benefits of travelling which can include network effects, labour market and urban agglomeration benefits. The size of the latter is an intensely debated issue, especially on the question of whether they are substantial for marginal improvements in relatively mature transport systems. Finally, if some modes are priced in a way that do not reflect their full social marginal costs (for example, if road congestion is unpriced), then prices of competing modes should take this into account through second-best corrections.

5.3.1 Road pricing

Road traffic is associated with a number of familiar external costs, with varying characteristics:

Carbon emissions

Carbon emissions only matter on a global scale, and are proportional to fuel consumption (with different emission rates depending on the fuel type). Hence, the social cost of carbon emissions does not vary with time, space or vehicle characteristics, and can be internalized by fuel tax alone.[5]

Other emissions

The cost of other emissions such as NO_x and particles varies mainly in space (local air quality is a more important concern in high-density areas) and to some extent with time and vehicle characteristics as well.

Noise costs

Noise costs vary considerably with space, time and vehicle characteristics. They differ from most other external costs in that the marginal cost falls rapidly with traffic volumes, since a slight increase in traffic volume hardly increases noise levels. This means that noise externalities are often most effectively internalized through policy measures which target vehicle characteristics rather than use.

Infrastructure costs

Infrastructure costs, the marginal wear and tear on roads, are primarily an issue for heavy traffic on small rural roads, such as timber transport from logging areas. Marginal costs obviously vary in space, but also according to vehicle characteristics such as weight (and weather conditions).

Accident costs

Accident costs vary with time and space, but also with vehicle characteristics and driver behaviour. Accident costs are mostly handled by regulations and legislation, e.g. speed limits and compulsory insurances, but there are two types of pricing instruments with great potential. First, vehicle taxes could be differentiated with respect to external vehicle-related accident costs. By choosing a heavy car, owners impose accident costs on other users, but gain safety themselves. This effectively leads to an "arms race" in terms of vehicle weight, and hence to an inefficiently heavy vehicle fleet. Second, insurance policies could encourage safe driving by discounting premiums for keeping speed limits which could be monitored by on-board equipment. Differentiating with respect to fixed vehicle characteristics requires no new technology, so lies outside the scope of this paper: innovative insurance policies which respond to driver behaviour (such as speeding), however, may be a very promising technical innovation.

Congestion

Congestion is mostly only relevant in urban traffic, where it is usually the most important externality. External congestion costs vary with space and time, and to some extent with vehicle type.

Some externalities, therefore, could be internalized through broad policy measures (such as fuel tax, legislated safety standards and environmental zones), whereas some require differentiation to be meaningful (such as external accident costs and congestion). It is the latter that offer a source of both efficiency gains and revenues if technological advances enable more finely tuned pricing systems.

5.3.2 Transit pricing

Efficient pricing of public transport is more complicated than for road traffic, mainly because calculating the marginal cost of public transport provision is complicated.[6] Public transport provision exhibits significant increasing returns to scale: once fixed costs of investments are paid, the short-run marginal passenger cost is negligible. Hence, the efficient price is near zero. Evidently, fixed costs will not be recovered from revenues, so a socially optimal pricing policy needs to cover fixed costs with another funding source, which is usually general taxation.

The problem is which costs should be considered fixed and which should be considered variable – or in other words, estimating the medium-term marginal capacity cost. Many capacity-related costs are fixed in the short run but variable in the long (sometimes very long) run. One additional passenger will most likely not necessitate the purchase of a new bus – but if the number of passengers increased further, more buses would eventually be necessary. For rail transport, capacity may need to be expanded. But note the words "necessary" and "need" here – what precisely do they mean? These decisions are policy choices, not automatic mechanisms. Is it evident that we should assume, when calculating transit fares, that additional demand must and will be covered by capacity expansion? In a case where expansion is prohibitively costly, is the marginal capacity cost zero or very high? This is not just a theoretical question: measures of marginal capacity costs are essential for transit planning. They crop up each time a transit agency considers extending a line or increasing its frequency. Calculating the cost associated with extensions is non-trivial, and different answers may be obtained depending on the time horizon. A common conclusion from analyses of marginal capacity costs is that they are considerably higher during peak hours when all available vehicles, personnel and infrastructure are in use than between peaks when there is spare capacity. The policy conclusion is that off peak prices should be set considerably lower than during peaks.

Another reason to have higher prices during peak hours are the external "crowding costs" – the loss of space for other passengers which an additional passenger uses.

An increase in demand does not only cause crowding and capacity costs but also attracts potential benefits. As long as capacity costs are low, additional passengers can create external scale benefits, since additional passengers on a bus route may make it financially viable to increase frequency on that bus line, a benefit that accrues to all existing passengers.

Extensions of a public transport system cause external network benefits. For example, each addition of a transit line also makes the existing lines better because they are connected to more destinations. External network benefits are one of the main reasons that it is efficient to have one main transit operator covering a whole urban region, rather than several independent operators. In general, this does not influence pricing policies as these benefits are internalized through a transit planning agency.

Road traffic in urban areas is usually underpriced, primarily because of high congestion costs. If transit and car trips are substitutes, then transit prices should include a second-best correction term – it should be subsidized to compensate for the underpricing of road trips. However, if road externalities are internalized through road pricing, or if externality levels are low, then this argument for transit subsidies vanishes.

Summing up, transit prices should be differentiated in time and space and consequently longer trips should usually be more expensive than short trips, and peak trips more expensive than off-peak trips. An efficient pricing system will depend on the specific cost structure of transit provision, unpriced road externalities and road/transit cross-elasticities. Of these factors, it is primarily the first where data is often scarce.

As was noted at the outset, socially efficient transit pricing will often mean that fare revenues will not cover fixed costs. Cities have chosen various strategies to cover fixed costs – usually a combination of "higher-than-optimal" transit prices and subsidies acquired through general taxation. How these sources should be combined is a political question: it depends on to what extent it is judged to be "fair" that users pay for a service that includes covering fixed costs.

5.3.3 External labour market benefits and agglomeration benefits

The external costs and benefits mentioned above are reasonably well quantified. But there are two additional external benefits, which have proved hard to quantify precisely: external commuting benefits and urban agglomeration benefits.

External commuting benefits arise because some of the worker's wage is paid in tax. The effect is even greater when a potential worker considers going from welfare to paid work. "Urban agglomeration benefits" refer to the fact that general productivity is usually higher in high-accessibility areas such as large cities. There is good evidence that accessibility improvements increase total production through higher employment, higher average labour productivity, and more worked hours – but it is difficult to make precise estimates of these effects. This is because the effects are heterogeneous and specific to the context. Even if it is obvious from cross-sectional data that the effect exists, calculating the effect of a marginal change in accessibility is very difficult.[7] The reason that transport policy needs to consider these effects is that they are external to the worker: since he does not perceive the full benefit of the labour (as some of it disappears in tax) or his own addition to agglomeration benefits, workers will work, commute and locate in large cities but not at a level that would be socially optimal. Hence, transport policy needs to encourage these activities to some extent.

External commuting benefits can be taken account of, to a large extent, by allowing travel costs to be deducted from taxable income. With deductible commuting costs, transport prices do not have to take external commuting benefits into account (even if the problem of quantifying such benefits still remains when undertaking social cost–benefit analysis of transport investments.

As to urban agglomeration benefits, they have proved even more elusive to quantify. While it is evident that they exist on a large scale – they are a primary reason for the existence of cities – it is an open question whether they are relevant when evaluating marginal or even major changes in the transport system. My own view is that standard CBA captures enough of the relevant costs and benefits that it allows a separation of the best proposals for transport improvements from the rest. Some benefits may be missing in the standard CBA framework, but there seems to be little reason to believe that it is not useful for ranking policies and investments.

5.4 Transport pricing technology

This section is a survey of new and emerging technical possibilities that may have potential for transport financing. As I have argued above, a general theme is that these technologies open up possibilities for more differentiated pricing policies, which in turn make it possible to extract more revenue from the transport system without creating efficiency losses (and in several cases there may even be efficiency gains).

5.4.1 Road user charging

Fuel taxes and flat distance charges

The traditional way to price road traffic is through fuel taxes. This was introduced mainly as a source of finance, motivated by the "user pays" logic, but has subsequently been reinterpreted as a way to partly internalize the external costs of road traffic. However, since external costs vary in time and place, fuel tax is a blunt instrument but nevertheless continues to be the most efficient way to price carbon emissions in the transport sector, since the social cost of such emissions is independent of time and place.

The "user pays" argument for fuel taxes will break down once the fuel efficiencies of cars varies widely between models, or when a significant proportion of vehicles use alternative sources of energy. This has motivated the replacement of fuel tax with flat distance-based taxes in some American states. The argument is that this is a fairer way to charge drivers in proportion to their use of roads. The intention is not to differentiate the distance-based tax so the technology can be made very simple: each vehicle just needs to keep track of the distance it has travelled, and report this at intervals (one idea is to use autonomous Bluetooth contact at gas stations). However in Oregon, the state does not want to charge drivers for distances they drive outside the state. This means that the system needs to be GPS-based, and hence require expensive equipment and installation in vehicles. With an ironic twist, the state is now considering differentiating the distance-based charge to encourage fuel efficiency and alternative fuels.

Passage and area charges

Just as with fuel taxes, toll roads were introduced according to the "user pays" logic. For almost 300 years, since the days of turnpikes, payments were cash-based and enforcement consisted of a physical barrier. In the late twentieth century, free-flow payment systems were introduced which opened the door for pricing schemes to reduce congestion in urban regions, by eliminating the need for large toll plazas and queuing at toll booths.

Passage-based tolls for financial or traffic management purposes are now commonplace. The most common technology is based on transponders (tag-and-beacon), where vehicles are identified through transponders linked to a bank account or to the identity of the vehicle owner. The Singapore system has a similar functionality but uses a different technology. The Swedish systems (Stockholm is operational since 2006 and Gothenburg starts in January 2013) identify vehicles through automatic number plate recognition (ANPR), but are similar to transponder-based systems from a design point of view. All of these systems allow differentiation with respect to time and place. The only restriction is that investment costs increase with the number of charging points, putting a limit on geographical differentiation. Note though that passage-based tolls do not need to come in the shape of cordons: any structure is possible in principle. Passage-based systems can also be differentiated with respect to vehicle characteristics, such as fuel type, provided that characteristics are noted in a vehicle register.

London's system identifies vehicles through ANPR, but is different from the passage-based systems in two respects. First, the vehicle is charged whenever it is anywhere inside a specified area, but regardless of the distance it travels or time it spends in the area. Making the charge area-based limits the ability to differentiate the charge across time. The second difference is that it is the vehicle owner who is responsible for keeping track of the charge and making sure it is paid, in advance of or soon after the trip. Most other systems use automatic payments or invoicing, so the driver is not responsible for calculating and keeping track of the charge. Making the driver responsible for keeping track of the amount to pay also limits differentiation. The main advantage of the London system is that vehicles need only be identified once, by one of the many cameras. This significantly decreases the demands on the ANPR identification rate. Despite this, the London system is very labour intensive, partly due to the low reliability of its ANPR system and, most significantly, because of the need for manual handling of payments.

Any free-flow system needs to be able to cope with enforcement – how to catch potential toll evaders, including innocent drivers who do not have a transponder. This is the main design constraint for any pricing system. Transponder-based systems usually use ANPR to identify vehicles without transponders; a high transponder penetration rate therefore tends to imply lower operations costs, since most ANPR systems are labour intensive (with Stockholm as an exception).

There are two aspects to enforcement: identifying the vehicle, and tracking the owners and making them pay. As a rule, the second part is more difficult since it presupposes a vehicle register linking vehicles to owners, and effective civil authorities able to collect payments. In fact, many developing countries do not have a reliable register. The second part of the enforcement chain may be an even larger problem in countries with weak institutions, or where there is considerable foreign traffic. A possible solution is an enforcement mechanism where accumulated debts are linked to the vehicle, and authorities have the power to seize the vehicle if they are not settled. This method is used for the German motorway toll system, especially targeting foreign trucks. The same principle could be used in urban settings. The only requirement is an efficient way to identify vehicles. This does not necessarily have to be a registration plate (which can be forged):

emerging image interpretation and identification technology have the potential to identify vehicles based on other characteristics.

Distance-based charging

Distance-based road user charging makes it possible to differentiate the pricing scheme even more and to cover a larger geographical area – a region or a country. There are various technologies already in place, usually using a combination of satellite positioning and odometers. Such systems are often termed *autonomous* systems, since they require very little contact with equipment outside the vehicle. While passage-based systems require investment in roadside equipment (and possibly transponders inside the vehicles, which are cheap and easy to produce and install), autonomous systems usually require very little roadside equipment, but instead require expensive and rather cumbersome installations in the vehicles. This means that distance-based systems tend to be more financially viable than passage-based systems when there is a relatively low number of vehicles and a large area to cover. Hence, autonomous systems have so far only been implemented for freight traffic, in national or regional schemes, especially to force foreign trucks to pay.

The Netherlands and Oregon have had[8] plans to implement autonomous systems covering all types of traffic, as a replacement for vehicle taxation (Netherlands) or fuel tax (Oregon). However, it is difficult to see how the benefits can outweigh installation costs. The case for large-scale autonomous systems generally assumes that satellite positioning equipment (and the necessary open interfaces) will soon be standard for all new vehicles. This has been an argument for more than a decade, but satellite positioning is still sold separately rather than as standard equipment on vehicles. Considering that vehicles are used for 15–20 years, relying on a scenario where all vehicles are equipped with satellite positioning seems dubious.

Just as with passage-based systems, enforcement is the most difficult design constraint and probably the main cost driver. If all vehicles have the necessary equipment, and it is tamper-proof and fool-proof, then there is no problem. Forcing all vehicles to have the necessary equipment installed is feasible for freight traffic: trucks are already subject to regulations such as compulsory tachographs, and the acceptability issue is not a problem especially if foreign traffic is targeted). Experience suggests that neither tampering with the equipment nor errors in charge calculations are a major problem, but a large-scale system may pose wider difficulties as it would encompass millions rather than thousands of vehicles.

Forcing all private vehicles to install the necessary equipment would be a very complicated and expensive task. Problems arise because most planned schemes rely on all vehicles having the necessary equipment. In passage-based systems, it is comparatively easy to take care of vehicles without transponders: identify them with ANPR when they pass the gantry, and send an invoice. In autonomous systems, enforcement and handling non-equipped vehicles become much harder. If a vehicle does not have working equipment installed, how is it caught when there are no specific charging points, and the area is very large? How can the correct charge be calculated if there is no equipment in the vehicle? For freight traffic, it may be acceptable to say that having working equipment is the driver's responsibility, and if the equipment is not installed or not working, then a maximum charge is levied. But doing this with private vehicles would be associated with enormous acceptability problems. Furthermore, catching vehicles without working equipment becomes very costly once the area or the number of vehicles is large.

Distance-based charges for heavy freight traffic are often motivated by infrastructure costs (wear and tear). These may be significant, especially for heavy traffic on small rural roads. To make such taxes efficiency-enhancing, they need to take into account the axle loads of the vehicles. I don't see any major technical problems with engineering such a solution, but I am not aware of any such systems in use.

5.4.2 Safety-differentiated car insurances

The road pricing systems discussed above allow for differentiated pricing with respect to time, place and vehicle characteristics. Given additional information about the specific situation such as weather conditions, congestion and roadworks, prices can be varied to take into account congestion, emissions and infrastructure costs.

Traffic safety, however, is intimately associated with driver behaviour, which road pricing schemes cannot take into account. However, insurance requirements could be used to encourage safe driving. Several attempts have been made to construct and test such systems, with encouraging results.[9] The general idea is to give drivers incentives to obey traffic rules in an opt-in system that checks that speed limits and similar regulations are followed. The technology is relatively simple: satellite positioning together with geocoded traffic rules. One of the advantages of the idea is that it does not rely on large-scale implementation to give benefits, in contrast to road pricing where virtually all vehicles need to be targeted: it can start at a small scale and involve voluntary participation. Equipment costs can be recouped by lowered accident costs.

5.4.3 Transit pricing

Technologies for public transport fare systems have improved significantly during the past decade. It is nowadays simple to differentiate fares with respect to origin–destination and time of day, and hence to travel distance and average load factors. The London Oyster card is a good example: travelers "tap in and tap out", and the correct fare is automatically drawn from the pre-charged card, which can also accommodate season tickets.

The Oyster technology is relatively expensive, however; this is a common problem for dedicated technical solutions which have to carry all overhead and development costs on a comparatively small revenue base. Experiments with replacing the Oyster card with standard credit cards therefore sound promising, since this allows the fare system to piggyback on an existing payment infrastructure, with back-office functions. A payment method for non-credit card holders would obviously have to be worked out, but this should be a minor problem: many credit cards have direct debit versions, where payments are drawn from an account, and hence have no credit function. Smartphone payments are also under development, offering similar possibilities in terms of price structures. These solutions point to the possibility of integrating transit fares into general payment solutions which could include parking pricing and road user charges. Smartphone-based systems can also incorporate information provision, integrating multimodal route guidance with pricing information and, finally, charging the correct total fare directly to a bank account.

These possibilities will make it simpler for travelers to navigate through transport systems, and more convenient to pay. But one should not be too optimistic about the potential to extract more revenue from the system: after all, current technology already allows for rather detailed price differentiation. It is possible that better and more convenient information and payment systems may increase travelling, but it is an open question whether this rise would be large enough to offset the investment in such systems.

Airlines and long-distance train operators use "yield management" strategies to maximize profits. The idea is to price-discriminate among customers, making those with high willingness to pay (WTP) actually pay more, and vice versa. In other words, the idea is to convert as much as possible of the consumer surplus (the difference between a customer's WTP and the actual price) into producer surplus (net profit). In order to do this, proxies are used to identify customers associated with high or low WTP, such as booking shortly before the trip (high WTP) or being willing to stay at the destination over the weekend (low WTP). Many of these proxies are difficult to transfer to an urban public transport setting: rescheduling restrictions, advance booking and payment, minimum stay rules, class systems. A crucial condition is that tickets are personal: otherwise a second-hand market would emerge. Some of these ideas, however, can be transferred to a transit setting, such as advance payment which is one reason for having discounted seasonal permits. Class systems used to be a method for price discrimination in urban public transport as well for longer distance travel, but would not be cost effective or accepted in the modern age. As well as price discrimination with respect to age which is common, it is conceivable that socioeconomic price discrimination could be driven further, and fares be differentiated with respect to income, employment status etc. This would require transit tickets to be personal and linked to socioeconomic status. The link to credit cards or cell phone accounts would facilitate this.

Price discrimination in the public transport system may prove hard to sell to the public. Some price discrimination could be motivated by equity concerns, but further differentiation with the express purpose of increasing revenues might not prove acceptable.

5.4.4 Parking

Parking pricing is already a potentially powerful policy instrument and important revenue source even though it is underused in many cities. Since it is already possible to differentiate parking prices, new technology cannot add much. However, actual price differentiation is often limited by the need to inform users about the price structure as otherwise the intended behavioural effect will not be achieved, and users will find it unfair if they cannot reasonably anticipate the price of the trip, including the parking charge. Information provision through smartphones may enable more flexible pricing since it can respond to events causing sudden hikes in parking demand. As mentioned above, parking information and payment can also be integrated with the transit system, making the trip more seamless. This may considerably increase the attractiveness of public transport, especially for infrequent users.

5.4.5 Better data sources

Electronic fare systems, especially personal tickets, have an important advantage over traditional ones for the operator and planner as they are a tremendous source of information about travelers and their trips. In order to construct efficient pricing schemes, one needs to know travel demand patterns and how they vary across times of days and seasons, and how travelers react to price or supply changes. Traditional travel surveys can only partly answer such questions: electronic ticket information allows for much more detailed information, pretty much in real time. This information should also be augmented with supply-side information, such as actual bus running times.

Put together, this data means that decisions about changes in price or supply can be evidence-based to a much greater extent than before. Current practice is usually to use a combination of data collection and gut feeling to obtain an *ex-ante* analysis of a suggested change in provision. If the *ex-ante* analysis is positive, the change is implemented, and in the best case, a limited evaluation is carried out a year or so later. However, with ubiquitous data, this whole culture could change. First, ex-ante analyses can be more precise. But more importantly, evaluation of changes becomes almost instantaneous and requires very little extra effort. A suggested change can be implemented, and if it does not produce the intended effects with respect to demand or revenues, it can be reversed. In this way, the whole public transport system can *evolve*, using experiments and evidence gleaned from them.

Real-time road traffic information also opens up the possibility of fine-tuned road pricing systems. Congestion pricing levels could be tied to congestion indices and adapted to reach certain target levels. This has been implemented in Singapore for over a decade, and Stockholm is considering a similar policy. In Singapore, the Land and Transport Authority adjusts the charge levels every three months to keep average speeds close to targets. The system currently considered in Stockholm would let charges follow a seasonal pattern (higher charges during the summer, when traffic volumes increase), and change base levels at longer intervals to allow drivers to anticipate and adapt more easily. Changes would be based on evaluation of past and anticipated congestion levels, much the same idea as in Singapore.

5.5 Research needs

This section is a brief outline of the most important areas in need of further research. Some are necessary in order to implement successfully the general concepts cited above, while others are related to understanding barriers to implementation. The second type may be the most vexing: several of the general concepts have been possible to implement for quite some time but have been introduced only in a very limited number of places or not at all.

5.5.1 Efficient road user charging

More efficient road user charging (RUC) has been on transport researchers' wish list for decades, but implementation has been very limited. Most of the implementation problems seem to be connected to public and political acceptability.

However, perhaps more surprisingly, the topic of designing charging schemes has received surprisingly little attention. Deciding where and how much to charge road users turns out to be a surprisingly tricky conundrum, mainly because of network externalities related to the fact that congestion on one link propagates onto others. Few large-scale transport models can handle this, and the simple economic principle of marginal cost pricing turns out to be difficult to put into operation. Moreover, perfect marginal cost pricing is impossible to implement, both for technical and cognitive reasons. How to construct RUC systems that can be implemented feasibly, with the inevitable compromise between benefits, implementation costs and cognitive load is an under-researched topic.[10] One of the main obstacles is the lack of large-scale transport models able to handle detailed representations of both transport demand and road congestion. Typically, most large-scale models focus on one or the other, which limits their ability to analyse the effects of RUC policies. Developing transport models to account for changes in departure time, heterogeneity of values of time, and severe congestion is necessary both to design efficient charging schemes, and to convince decision-makers and the public that road user charging is worth a try.

In principle, emission costs of road traffic are less subject to network effects and hence easier to calculate. The understanding of the link between emissions and health is still under debate in the medical literature: the current consensus seems to be that it is in the same general magnitude as accident costs but more precise numerical estimates remain scarce.

As to noise, the costs which are internalized are captured by property prices, and this effect is fairly well understood. However, there is a growing body of medical evidence linking residential noise exposure to a variety of health problems such as cardiovascular disease, which is an external part of the cost. Noise levels are only weakly linked to marginal changes of traffic levels, however, because the marginal increase in noise from a small increase in traffic volume is generally low once traffic volumes are above a certain level and therefore pricing road use is not a very efficient method of controlling it. Instead, pricing and regulation need to target vehicle characteristics. How to do this is an under-researched topic, and I am not aware of any country that has tried to introduce noise policies, such as differentiating taxes on tyres and vehicles according to noise.

Perhaps the most difficult topic, however, is the possible existence of external benefits of transport. While we understand the external costs of transport sufficiently to be able to provide robust numerical estimates, our understanding of the external benefits of transport is still poor. As was noted above, external benefits are created when there are external agglomeration benefits or external benefits of commuting resulting from tax collection. However, even though their existence is known, there is no robust numerical evidence. Clearly, it might – in principle – be a mistake to price transport in a way that takes all types of external costs into account without considering the external benefits. The extent of this problem is not understood. I am personally inclined, though, to believe that for the marginal changes in pricing policies we are discussing here, changes in agglomeration benefits are not a significant concern.

5.5.2 Efficient transit pricing

While several aspects of road pricing require further study, it is a comparatively well researched and well understood compared with transit pricing. There is a substantial theoretical body on transit pricing, but the empirical data is a lot scarcer, and more closely tied to the specific circumstances of each city and network.

The first requirement for efficient transit pricing is detailed information about the cost structure of provision: fixed costs, long-run marginal costs, short-run marginal costs, broken down on the network level. While some of this information is usually known to transit providers, it is less systematic than intuitively expected. There are numerous studies on aggregate cost structure, but the detailed information required for a differentiated pricing policy is a more complicated matter.

Network benefits also need to be considered. Their existence is uncontroversial – but numerical estimates are difficult to obtain, since they are linked both to cost structures and subsidy rules.

Crowding costs need to be taken into account and there is some recent research on this topic.[11] In particular, crowding effects on travel demand (including peak spread effects) is an important but under-researched topic. This is particularly relevant for time-differentiated pricing schemes: crowding-based pricing schemes could create substantial passenger benefits and revenues by redistributing passengers over time to reduce crowding.

If road traffic continues to be underpriced, transit prices need to take external costs of road traffic into account as well. This requires accurate estimates of marginal external costs of road traffic, which, as noted, is a rather thorny issue due to network congestion effects. Moreover, cross-elasticities between car and transit trips are required. Modern transport models are often fairly reliable in this respect, but it is important to realize that it will not be sufficient to use aggregate averages to capture efficiency gains from price differentiation.

The issue of external benefits of transport is perhaps even more important for transit provision than for road traffic. High-quality public transport is often credited with an ability to attract developers far more than can be explained by mere accessibility effects. There is consistent empirical evidence that this effect exists, even if its size is unclear. So in addition to the external benefits associated with commuting and agglomeration, there appears to be a structural effect on city attractiveness from public transport beyond its user values. This is, however, a topic of much controversy and wishful thinking where more research is warranted.

5.5.3 Benefits of price differentiation

Given access to better information, the next question is: how large are the potential social benefits of more efficient pricing? Are they worth the cost in terms of technology, cognitive load for the users and possible political difficulty in implementing changes? This is obviously different across cities, but perhaps surprisingly, there is very little evidence based on empirical data.

Road pricing benefits are usually based on theoretical studies or network models with limited capability of representing extreme congestion where network propagation effects become important.[12] The benefits of transit pricing are even less understood. One problem is that current transport models are not designed to handle differentiated pricing structures, and hence are ill equipped to design or evaluate transit pricing schemes, or convince decision-makers of the potential benefits.

In this context, it may be enlightening to try to understand why transit prices are currently so little differentiated. For example, most cities have various forms of flat-fare discount tickets targeted at regular customers. Despite substantial crowding during peaks, low marginal costs for off-peak travelling, and high costs for increases in peak capacity, peak pricing is surprisingly uncommon. Yet, aggregate social welfare could be increased with a more differentiated pricing structure, which would also be consistent with the "user pays" principle generally supported by the public.

So why are public transport prices so flat? Given the starting point of this chapter – the increased need to finance transport investment and operations – why do decision-makers pass up on the opportunity to employ the pricing structure that may simultaneously make the use of resources more efficient and increase revenues? There are several possible hypotheses.

- Fear of public reaction is one candidate – but that does not explain how the current flat price structure emerged. Moreover, low general public acceptability can hardly explain the absence of initiatives for differentiated pricing – certainly, some users would win from changes, which would be attractive politically.
- In many cities, transit subsidies emerged as a way to increase the amount of available land for development as a response to increasing population, but it is unclear how important this argument continues to be once land use structures are developed.
- Another argument is that complex price structures may put off potential travelers.[13] But this does not seem to prevent airlines, long-distance train operators or commercial toll road operators from introducing complex fare structures in order to maximize profits. Obviously, the potential negative effect is smaller than the increase in gross profits. It seems likely that similar considerations would be relevant for an operator wanting to maximize social benefits rather than profits.
- Indeed, it is a common assumption that simple and integrated fares will increase the number of travelers. But even if this were true in principle, claiming that total revenues, or total social benefits, increase from such fare structures is a much stronger statement. For that to be true, the increase in total demand needs to offset the reduction of net revenue per passenger. Moreover, flat fare structures generally mean that short trips

are overpriced, reducing demand for them and corresponding revenues and social benefits.
- The existence of external benefits in the form of extended labour and housing markets is a reason to subsidise commuting – but it does not seem to fully explain the very low differentiation levels, considering that the issue of external commuting benefits can be resolved by making commuting costs deductible.

My view is that transit agencies have not sufficiently considered the potential benefits of more differentiated pricing schemes. This, in turn, may have several explanations, including lack of competence. Overall, I have not seen many suggestions being put forward within transit agencies, and then been rejected after consideration. On the contrary, it seems few transit agencies are even considering the issue. This can be contrasted with congestion pricing which a host of cities around the world have at least considered, even though many have ultimately rejected the idea.

5.5.4 Cognitive load of differentiated prices

Optimal pricing structures can quickly become complicated, varying in both time and place. Are there cognitive limits on the price structures? How does the complexity of pricing structures affect users? Evidence from time-differentiated toll roads and distance-differentiated transit fares suggest that travelers are indeed able to respond to prices, even if the structure is complicated. But very little is known about whether price complexity *per se* deters users, and whether this can be offset by increased revenues or social benefits.

5.5.5 Acceptability

Public resistance has always been cited as one of the main barriers to implementing road user charges. The same is possibly true for changing transit fares – although this seems to be less of a problem, because it is harder to introduce a price for something that is initially free like road use.

There has been considerable research on the acceptability of road pricing, while relatively little is known about the analogous question for transit pricing. Factors affecting road pricing acceptability can be grouped into four types: self-interest (users' own expected costs and benefits), altruistic or social motives (perceived effects on environment, equity and other users), general attitude to pricing as an allocation method (compared with other methods such as queuing, rationing, administrative allocation or lotteries), and attitude to public interventions in general (in particular associated with general trust in the government). Finally, any change from the initial pricing policy is met with resistance, regardless of its potential benefits.

Perhaps not surprisingly, different scientific traditions have given varying weight to explanatory variables: economists to self-interest variables, political scientists to ideological motives, and psychologists to social motives and concern about change.

Attitudes to other types of transport pricing – vehicle taxation, insurance, transit pricing, fuel taxes – are less researched. The same types of explanatory factors are likely to be relevant for these issues as well, but the relative magnitudes are largely unknown.

5.6 Governance and institutional settings

Public acceptability is neither a necessary nor a sufficient condition for political acceptability. Questions over power are the key to the analysis and understanding of political support or resistance for transport pricing policy. Issues include decisions over the design of pricing schemes, the allocation of revenues, and the effect that the charges and their revenue stream will have on the funding of transport investment. In most countries, large transport investments are funded by national governments, often with co-funding by regional stakeholders and road and transit pricing schemes inevitably become issues in such negotiations. The analysis also needs to take into consideration that the accessibility generated by the transport system is reflected in land values and location decisions, which may be of crucial importance for municipal budgets in the long run.

For example, the fact that congestion charges are now politically accepted in Sweden is not only due to the higher level of public support. It is also because the charges have been integrated into the national transport investment planning process, and this has partly resolved power and negotiation issues between national and regional governments. In Norway, the ubiquity of road pricing systems can be attributed to the matching grants principle: if a regional government raises funds for a transport scheme through road pricing, the national government will match the revenues.

The institutional setting will have a huge effect on what types of transport pricing schemes are politically feasible. If the aim is to implement efficient pricing schemes that also generate sufficient revenues for operations and investment, then the institutional context needs to be set up in a way that makes this politically feasible. This means aligning political costs and credits, and reducing incentives to overspend on certain forms of expenditure. The Norwegian system, for example, has a tendency to encourage overspending on transport investment while simultaneously overpricing transport.

5.7 Legal issues

As the technology for transport pricing becomes more convenient to use, and less intrusive in the transport system, legal issues tend to emerge. The most prevalent example is what constitutes a legal proof-of-passage in a road pricing system. Is it enough to register that a transponder has been registered to pass a gantry, and that this transponder is registered with a certain owner? If that person then claims that he or she has not passed the gantry, what additional evidence does the toll operator need to produce? National legal systems demand different levels of evidence, often dependent on whether the payment is seen as a charge or a tax from a legal point of view.

The question of proof-of-passage emerged in road pricing schemes once free-flow systems were introduced. When the physical barrier preventing vehicles passing until they had paid was removed, the enforcement problem became the most important design constraint of any pricing scheme. Part of the enforcement problem is proving what a user would pay in the event of a dispute, which is as much a legal issue as a technical one.

This issue becomes even more complicated when moving to distance-based pricing, which mainly uses technology inside the vehicle. Enforcement may depend on registering sights of the vehicle at certain times and places, and then catching non-payers by proving that this evidence is inconsistent with the user's claims. The legal status of such ultimately statistical evidence is difficult to ascertain.

5.8 Integrity and privacy

Some technical schemes may be difficult to reconcile with personal integrity and may create a potential conflict with having legal proof-of-passage. If the law demands detailed evidence of vehicle movements, then privacy becomes an increasingly important issue. There are technical ways to solve such issues – for example, autonomous technology may be constructed to only report the charge that should be paid, but not the details of the vehicle's travel pattern – but the legal question remains.

It is unclear how strongly users feel about this issue in an age where many people voluntarily hand over sensitive personal information to multinational corporations and social media. But there is a difference between this and mobility information, in that credit card and internet information are in fact handed over voluntarily which makes it possible to opt out because of privacy concerns.[14] In contrast, certain transit pricing and road pricing technologies will collect detailed mobility information without any possibility to opt out.

5.9 Enforcement

The most important design constraint of pricing technology is how to catch potential non-payers. Enforcement is almost always the factor that limits a technology, and often the main cost driver. There is little research on the topic of efficient and effective enforcement in these fields, and how to set up cost-efficient enforcement structures while meeting legal requirements.

Technical issues are just part of the issue of enforcement. The administrative process is also vital: enforcing claims needs backing from courts and public agencies to be effective. Often, this chain is easier to establish if it can piggyback on an existing process, such as the tax system which is the case with road user charges in Sweden where legally, charges are "taxes". While this presents some problems relating to regional decision mandates, it makes available a formidably effective enforcement organization.

5.10 Efficient transit operations

Ubiquitous real-time information opens up new possibilities for efficient transit operations – operations and control strategies that adapt to demand, link loads, incidents and traffic in real-time. This has the potential to make public transport more attractive by reducing variability, delays and crowding, and to reduce costs of operations through more efficient fleet management.

5.11 Conclusion

The question posed in this chapter is: what can potential technological advances offer transport financing? As noted at the outset, hopes should not be set too high: the types of new technology discussed in these contexts seldom create more money. But there are certain cases where new technology may open new financing sources. Here is a summary of some of the most promising opportunities, together with outstanding research issues associated with them.

Looking at these potential areas, it is striking that there are many low-hanging fruits available even with current technology. Moreover, most of these opportunities do not depend on optimal implementation, which would require extensive data and high implementation costs; they would most likely deliver substantial benefits and revenues also in relatively crude designs. For example, even simple forms of urban congestion pricing, time-differentiated transit pricing and non-speeding insurance incentives would most likely bring considerable efficiency benefits and revenues.

So why are these policies not used more than they are? As to congestion pricing, there is actually a large literature on the subject, highlighting problems in terms of public acceptability and institutional barriers. But as to most of the other suggested policies on the list, it is more difficult to see what keeps decision-makers from using them. This might be the most important issue to research. Experiments and field trials would be a way forward.

Table 5.1 Opportunities for finance through new technology in urban transport

Opportunity	Major research needs
Road user charging, especially urban congestion pricing	Designing efficient congestion pricing schemes. Network simulation in hypercongestion. Demand models capturing heterogeneous responses to time-differentiated pricing. Cognitive limitations.
Differentiated transit pricing	Marginal costs of transit provision. Effects of time-differentiated fares on demand and link loads. Crowding costs and demand effects. Why isn't transit pricing more differentiated already? Effects on demand of fare complexity.
Differentiated vehicle taxation (or excise duty) with respect to external accident costs, noise and possible fuel efficiency	Effects of differentiated vehicle tax/excise on demand. Numerical estimates of external accident costs.
Better transit data for evaluation and customizing pricing schemes (and other policies)	Turning data into information. Changing transit agencies' cultures to encourage experiments, trials, evaluation, evidence.
Insurance premiums with incentives for safe driving behaviour (e.g. "pay-as-you-speed")	Effects on driver behaviour. Quantification of accident effects.
Seamless information/payment systems for transit/parking/route	Technical development. Effects on demand. Business models.
Parking guidance services	Technical development. Costs, benefits, willingness to pay. Business models.
Adaptive transit operations using real-time data	Bus control strategies for improved regularity. Fleet management. Demand-responsive supply strategies.

Acknowledgments

Thanks to Gunnar Johansson and Robert Paaswell for valuable contributions and ideas, in particular regarding business models for information services and the potentials of using real-time data for improved transit operations.

Notes

1   A central result from urban economics is the "Henry George theorem", that says that changes in accessibility will be capitalized in land rents. See Smith and Gihring (2006) for a literature survey and an argument that value capture should be used more to finance transport improvements.

2   Buehler and Pucher (2011) provide a good discussion of such potentials.
3   I tacitly assume that the marginal cost of public funds is lower than the dead-weight loss of pricing the use of the service.
4   This is not always true: there are cases where profit-maximizing prices will not recover fixed costs, but where aggregate social benefits with marginal cost pricing will be higher than fixed costs (meaning that the investment was "worth" its cost).
5   However, there is evidence in Green (2010) that the revealed WTP for fuel efficiency is inefficiently low, i.e. purchasers do not take fuel efficiency enough into account. This would be an argument for various forms of pricing and regulations that target vehicles directly, especially purchases of new vehicles.
6   A seminal reference is Mohring (1972), with several follow ups. A good recent contribution, providing a rather complete pricing framework and applying it to a few case studies is Parry and Small (2009).
7   Graham and van Dender (2011) show that agglomeration benefits are highly variable in many dimensions, and empirical estimates may therefore depend on the econometric method that is used.
8   The Dutch scheme has been scrapped but reborn several times; currently it is shelved. Oregon is currently proceeding with its planning.
9   See for example Hultkrantz and Lindberg (2011).
10 Reflections on the design of the Stockholm charging system can be found in Eliasson (2009a) and Eliasson (2008).
11 See Wardman and Whelan (2010) for a review and metaanalysis.
12 One exception is the CBA of the Stockholm congestion charges in Eliasson (2009b).
13 Hodson (2005) provides an overview of fare structures in European cities, comparing "integrated" tariffs (which are generally "flat" in structure) with "differentiated" tariffs (mainly with respect to travel distance).
14 A discussion about the right to be surveillance sensitive can be found in Hansson (2005).

References

Buehler, R. and Pucher, J. (2011) "Making public transport financially sustainable". *Transport Policy*, 18(1), 126–38.

Eliasson, J. (2008) "Lessons from the Stockholm congestion charging trial". *Transport Policy*, 15(6), 395–404.

Eliasson, J. (2009a) "Expected and unexpected in the Stockholm Trial", in A. Gullberg and K. Isaksson (eds) *Congestion taxes in city traffic: lessons learnt from the Stockholm trial*. Nordic Academic Press.

Eliasson, J. (2009b) "A cost–benefit analysis of the Stockholm congestion charging system", *Transportation Research Part A: Policy and Practice*, 43(4), 468–80.

Graham, D. J. and van Dender, K. (2011) "Estimating the agglomeration benefits of transport investments: some tests for stability", *Transportation*, 38(3), 409–26.

Green, D. (2010) *Why the market for new passenger cars generally undervalues fuel economy* (Discussion Paper No. 2010–6). Joint Transport Research Centre. International Transport Forum.

Hansson, S.-O. (2005) "The right to be surveillance sensitive". *Journal of Information, Communication and Ethics in Society*, 3, 13–14.

Hodson, P. (2005) "Price differentiation and fare integration in urban public transport". Proceedings of the European Transport Conference, Strasbourg.

Hultkrantz, L. and Lindberg, G. (2011) "Pay-as-you-speed: an economic field experiment", *Journal of Transport Economics and Policy (JTEP)*, 45(3), 415–36.

Mohring, H. (1972) "Optimization and scale economies in urban bus transportation". *The American Economic Review*, 62(4), 591–604.

Parry, I. W. H. and Small, K. A. (2009) "Should urban transit subsidies be reduced?" *The American Economic Review*, 99(3), 700–24.

Smith, J. J. and Gihring, T. A. (2006) "Financing transit systems through value capture", *American Journal of Economics and Sociology*, 65(3), 751–86.

Wardman, M. and Whelan, G. (2010) "Twenty years of rail crowding valuation studies: evidence and lessons from British experience", *Transport Reviews*, 31(3), 379–98.

Chapter 6

Assessing the diversity of schemes for financing urban access and mobility in preparation for a comparative study

José M. Viegas

6.1 Introduction

Urban agglomerations are complex systems in which access and mobility play a vital role. Urban access is a measure of the possibility of reaching various facilities or opportunities for work or leisure within a specified time threshold. It is therefore a measure of potential. Mobility is the process by which the displacement towards those facilities or opportunities actually occurs. It is thus a measure of work or energy. Through an aggregation process it is possible to compute the frequency distributions of these measures across an agglomeration, based on desired locations and through this to compare different urban areas.

Policy objectives in this area must always be designed in terms of access, although the constraints such as costs, congestion, emissions and land used by infrastructure are related to the mobility dimension.

Access and mobility are complementary ways of representing the distribution of activities across space and the effort required to join them. The provision of access starts with issues of land use, and then progresses towards layout and design of infrastructure and the organization and deployment of transport services. Mobility goes one step further by including travelers in the equation.

In terms of finance, access is related to the supply side (costs) and mobility is related to the demand side (revenues). It is impossible to have a good level of mobility if access is bad, but it is indeed possible to have excellent access with rather low levels of mobility if, for instance the land use mix is very rich and people do not have to go far to get where they want, or people do not have the money, the time or desire to go to some destinations.

Moreover, in the near future, it is very likely that the quality and ubiquity of telecoms will allow the provision of access to several types of functions without the need for any face-to-face encounter. This is already the case with routine medical check-ups in several parts of the world, and is increasingly the case with education.

Analysis of mobility does not make sense outside the framework defined by the prevailing conditions of access. This chapter uses the expression "financing of urban mobility", as this corresponds to the more usual expression, but always bearing in mind this dual nature of the challenge.

Access is provided by several transport modes, each of which has its own requirements in terms of infrastructure, either dedicated to a specific mode or shared with others. For each of the motorized modes there is the need for vehicles and drivers, some form of traffic signaling and control system, and significant consumption of energy. Even for those that have a public right of access, there is still the need for a professional organization planning and operating the services. In terms of administration there is normally a political agency establishing policy guidelines, a technical agency in charge of road traffic including on-street parking, an organizing authority in charge of public transport and a police force responsible for the enforcement of rules. All these help the system perform more efficiently but also generate costs.

Ideally, provision of mobility should be undertaken with a perfect fit to the access requirements of citizens. However, this is not possible because of the high variability of access requirements (within the day and across space, but also over longer time spans) and of the rigid nature of most of the components of the cost of providing access, namely infra- and supra-structure, rolling stock, organizations and operations staff. The only significant cost component with easy adjustment of quantity (and cost) to the access requirements is energy (fuel), which means that adequate provision to the majority of potential clients implies some idleness of production factors outside the demand peaks.

This difficulty of adjustment also occurs in many other service sectors of the economy, and managers have to be able to find the best way to incorporate the ensuing inefficiencies in the prices they charge their clients.

The major difference of urban mobility with respect to those other sectors is the recognition that easy access to a diversified range of facilities and opportunities is a powerful indicator of quality of urban life and thus a right that should be enjoyed by all citizens, irrespective of car ownership. This is frequently – but not always – translated in (explicit or implicit) specifications by a public authority of minimum levels of "access coverage" of the urban area by the public transport network, possibly with different service levels by day and night, which in turn implies that load factors are often insufficient to allow a full coverage of the corresponding costs of provision from the fare box. Using the terminology adopted by the European Commission (2007), public service obligations are defined when those services would not be produced and delivered under normal market conditions, without any form of protection from other operators or without public subsidy.

Financing, or "cost coverage", of urban mobility systems then easily becomes a problem when public authorities define generous levels of access coverage and the density of users of public transport is low, which may be caused by dispersed forms of land use, or by high levels of car ownership with little or no constraint on the use of private cars to use the denser parts of the agglomeration. The distribution of income (purchasing power) across the population can also be a critical factor, as this limits the prices than can be charged to those who have no alternative to public transport.

This need for a solid and stable financing framework of urban mobility is critical at a time in which the growth of cities and the increasing levels of car ownership require a brave response from public transport providers to increase their market share, especially as an ageing population means there is competition for public funds that would traditionally have been available for public transport.

The objective of this chapter is to provide a framework for the analysis of the options and the preparation of the launch of a comparative study of schemes of financing of urban mobility across the world.

A small pilot covering five or six cities in diverse cultural settings and with close monitoring by a team of experts could help to understand how the diverse competences are organized, how the survey questions are interpreted and how to mitigate risks of misinterpretation. Composition of this small set of cities should be based on willingness to cooperate, availability of good databases, a tradition of transparency in government, and diversity of administrative split of competencies. Following the pilot study, the scoping, budgeting and preparation of the terms of reference for a more ambitious comparative study could be developed.

Only passenger transport is under consideration in this paper. Some cross-influence with urban freight transport exists in the fluidity of traffic, but this is not significant enough to have a strong impact on the costs (and thus on financing) of passenger transport. Freight transport is by and large economically self-sufficient, in that it does not require any form of subsidy besides the right to use the infrastructure for which it does not pay directly.

6.2 Difficulties of financing urban mobility

The current situation concerning financing of urban mobility in developed countries is complex, with private car users generally (in Europe and elsewhere where fuel duties are high) paying more than the direct "visible" costs incurred to serve them, including infrastructure provision and maintenance, with the reverse situation in public transport, where the part of operating costs covered by fares frequently is somewhere between 30 per cent and 50 per cent, although with significant exceptions (Faivre d'Arcier, 2009; EMTA, 2010; Pucher and Bueler, 2005; Werner, 2011). Investment costs for public transport are almost always paid for out of public funds.

The immediately obvious problem is that the amount of public funds to subsidize urban public transport has been shrinking, and the situation is deteriorating further for three main reasons:

- While there has been some increase in patronage of public transport in a few large cities, mostly through increased frequencies of service and higher quality of vehicles, costs have risen faster than revenue. The UITP, the worldwide association of public transport operators, has a strategic goal of doubling the number of passengers by 2025 (UITP, 2009) but industry insiders recognize that this will only be possible by trebling the supply which would imply a bigger financial gap;
- Second, as urban sprawl grows, each additional kilometre of public transport services (no matter by which mode) has a lower cost coverage from fares than the average of the previous lines, so the average deteriorates with the expansion of networks, except when a new urban area of significant density is reached;
- Third, in Europe and Japan, and to a lesser extent in North America, the increasing proportion of older people will require greater resources for health care and assistance in general which will squeeze public transport subsidies.

Bearing in mind these factors, a new financing framework for public transport is needed, especially if the aim is to attract middle class users. However, if it is recognized that public and individual transport are not only competitors but also (functionally and financially) complementary, it makes sense to take a holistic view of the urban mobility system.

Essentially, revenues of the urban mobility system originate from a limited number of social groups: direct beneficiaries (the travelers); indirect beneficiaries enjoying the external benefits of an urban mobility system and of public transport in particular; and taxpayers.

The first sub-group of the indirect beneficiaries is constituted by the economic activities that receive added value from the improved access made possible through a performing transport system. When this added value is internalized in the land rents, then the indirect beneficiary is the tenant (paying for it through the higher rent thanks to that improved access) and the land owner who collects the higher rent but usually has not contributed to the investment that generated the improved access.

Another sub-group of indirect beneficiaries is the car travelers who enjoy a less congested road network than they would if there were no public transport. This external benefit should also be acknowledged, in parallel with the fiscal revenues to which this group contributes through taxes and charges.

Regarding taxpayers, some of which of course may also be public transport users, they may be in the present or in future generations through the exercise of public debt.

A coherent and stable framework must be found – taking into account demographic perspectives as well as the development of technologies and

changes in energy prices – to ensure economically, socially and environmentally sustainable mobility in cities, as a precondition for their success
and contribution to the welfare of society at large.

Different configurations of supply and charging regimes will generate a
spread of costs and revenues from the direct beneficiaries in the various
modes. Strategic decisions must be made on configurations of supply and
charges (from which modal splits and access levels to different destinations
will result), and the contributions required from indirect beneficiaries and
taxpayers to balance the accounts. On a more tactical level there are issues
about the mechanisms needed to channel the money flows from the various
sources to their points of spending.

A comparative study seems a good approach because different countries
have adopted a variety of schemes to start addressing the problem. A study
of these schemes will provide a sample of varied rationales and insights into
this very complex problem, and with it an improved capacity to devise more
intelligent solutions.

6.3 Challenges and pitfalls of an international
comparative study on financing of urban mobility

There are numerous challenges associated with any international comparative study, arising from different levels of purchasing power and equipment
available to households, contrasting ways of organizing social life, and
varying prices of inputs to the activities under study (Heston and Summers,
1996).

In particular, any comparison using prices or economic values has to be
undertaken carefully. The use of adimensional indicators is preferable
because they do not depend on measurement or currency, but the denomi-
nator of the fractions underlying those indicators must also be selected with
great care, as this is not a neutral choice: for instance, presenting values per
area unit or per inhabitant will produce different rankings depending on the
prevailing densities of the urban agglomerations being compared.
Productivity measures in particular have to be considered with great care
(van Ark et al., 1999).

In the field of urban mobility, there is another difficulty arising from
terminology differences: the same term has different meanings in different
countries, and different terms are used for identical meanings. This is not a
new problem. Previous comparative studies related to urban mobility by
international institutions, namely the ECMT in a study from 1992 to 2002
of urban travel and sustainable development. It included a survey covering
167 cities (ECMT, 2002), and the UITP "Mobility in Cities" database of
urban areas and associated public transport across the world (UITP, 2005).
In such cases a significant part of the workload is dedicated to data harmo-
nization.

The work published in (Pucher, 1995a) and (Pucher, 1995b) covers questions related to urban mobility and is based on a rich set of data sources, with special emphasis on an OECD study and emphasizes the need for a combination of data from multiple sources, as well as tabulations and data processing by the author.

Glossaries are always necessary in such endeavors. As an example, how does one define "trip"? Should it be as each leg of a journey, or each displacement? There are, too, issues around accounting: how is the passenger unit defined and computed: by each boarding or by every complete journey?

While the consensus is that the ideal choice is to consider complete journeys, the data collection systems in place imply that all public transport operators who do not have a sophisticated electronic fare collection system will only be capable of providing data for individual trips, and defining passengers per boarding. So, the definition that is adopted will be linked to the sample selected to conduct the comparative study, through the particular fare collection system.

The urban mobility system raises additional challenges for comparative studies:

1   Fragmentation of responsibilities for different transport modes (and sometimes even functions within the same mode) across different levels (national, regional, metropolitan, local) and public administration organizations, makes data collection and validation of its consistency very difficult even within the same urban agglomeration. This difficulty is compounded with international comparisons because the fragmentation varies from country to country, thus requiring a thorough understanding of how things are made in each country. Solutions to this problem are normally possible based on careful analysis of the available data, as long as access to relative fine levels of detailed classification is possible.

2   The geographical area relevant for the analysis of mobility frequently does not match any specific administrative authority or group of authorities. This creates situations in which the data sets related to land use and fiscal flows correspond to one set of municipalities, while the data sets related to transport flows, costs and revenues correspond to a subset of those municipalities plus a number of corridors with penetrations in other municipalities. This is a more complicated problem, normally requiring some modeling to produce estimates of all data for the same territorial space.

Depending on the level of maturity and sophistication of the statistical agencies in each country, it may also be useful to check the procedures used for production and validation of the basic statistical data. Normally satisfactory levels of rigor should be expected when the data is related to financial flows, but the same is not always true when dealing with flows of people and quality indicators.

Insufficient attention to these challenges creates significant risks of misrepresentation of the real situation on the ground. The resulting errors can result in protests from those misrepresented (even if it was their own data that was misleading), and the consequent loss of credibility and reputation of the study, its authors and sponsors. This is a major, very significant, pitfall of such studies.

At this stage, acknowledgement of such challenges is necessary so that adequate preparation for the data collection and compilation exercises can be made, and the corresponding time and money are made available. When carrying out the study, more detailed planning will be needed, as well as monitoring and reporting on risk management strategies.

6.4 How deep should we look?

As mentioned in Beaverstock *et al.*, 2000, "All measurement and data are the products of theory: from the vast realm of possible information on a topic, selections are made based on how a problem is theoretically conceptualized".

The study of financing schemes can be undertaken at different levels. The basic idea is simple: what are the best practices to bridge the gap between the revenues and costs of public transport?

The complexity of the urban mobility system is recognized. An interesting example of the breadth of analysis required is given in Barter (1999) where the author tried to make an assessment of the urban mobility situation (more from the point of view of quality of performance than financial flows) in a number of Asian cities, and was forced to consider a wide range of variables and to develop methods to make the data comparable. Similarly, in Faivre d'Arcier (2009) several sources of inefficiency in the French urban public transport systems were identified, at the operational and strategic levels of decision-making.

For the purpose of this paper four possible levels of depth of analysis have been identified:

1   We may take the level of access provided and the associated costs as fixed, and concentrate the analysis on the sources of revenues necessary to cover those costs, their relative weights and the mechanisms adopted for employing less traditional sources, discussing the effectiveness and acceptance of each one.
2   We may consider that it would be possibly easier (and also fairer) to bridge the financial gap if the costs of provision of access by public transport could be reduced, either by improving its efficiency or by

reducing the level of service in some parts of the territory. In that case, our field of attention should be extended so that it also covers the issues of productive efficiency of public transport and its quality of service. In such cases, the financial gap could be covered by revision of the access quality targets or by measures to improve operational efficiency.

3   It is also worth stressing that a much higher market share of public transport is required for high quality city life and that this would require attracting middle class passengers with features currently not generally offered in public transport. Such provision would certainly also require a different financing framework from the ones presently in place.

4   An even deeper look at the problem may be necessary to consider for cases in which a large financing deficit may result from the fact that good access is only possible with high levels of motorized mobility (based on public transport or on car use), because of inadequate land use patterns. In such cases, it will take far longer for (land use-based) solutions to be effective and interim measures at other levels would probably be needed.

While the existence of difficulties related to a significant financial gap is quite easy to recognize, the symptoms associated with problems at the two other levels are generally not obvious, and establishing their existence would require additional efforts in data collection and analysis.

It is difficult to know at the outset whether mobility financing problems of any specific agglomeration are simply a result of inadequate collection of revenues for costs that are justified (situation of type 1)) or they are aggravated by the problems described in situations 2) and 3). Similarly, it is very difficult to produce an immediate estimate of which cities have financing problems associated with each of these situations.

In some cases bridging the financial gap exclusively with measures related to revenue collection may generate solutions that are neither fair nor proportionate, which in the end increases the risk of opposition from local people.

The strategy adopted for the remainder of the chapter is to focus attention on the first level, with brief mentions of issues related to the other levels.

6.5 Examining the options and setting the data requirements for the comparative study of financing solutions

6.5.1 Revenue-based solutions

Staying exclusively within the financial dimension, another study design choice must be made: are we interested only in the issue of financing the budget gaps of public transport, or on going further towards the creation of a "satellite account" of the urban mobility system, similar to those currently undertaken for the road sector at national level in several countries?

In the former case, it should be possible to identify all the financial flows affecting the public transport system, but defining adequate levels of contribution by the different types of indirect beneficiaries would have a weaker foundation. In particular the information of the respective financial balances of all the agents in their transactions with the remainder of the urban mobility system will not be available. So, some degree of arbitrariness, with the corresponding risks of unfairness, in the allocation of those contributions across groups would be inevitable.

In the latter case, a much richer level of understanding of the financial inputs and outputs of all agents in the urban mobility system will be available, which would allow a more rigorous and transparent framework for the definition of the levels of contribution of indirect beneficiaries towards the revenues of the public transport components.

The choice is not obvious, because considerable more effort is required for the second option both on data acquisition and on its processing. So, we opt to treat the issue of bridging the financial gaps in urban public transport rather carefully, and then make a quick sketch into the second, looking at the whole financial flows of the urban mobility system.

As stated above, there are three large sets of possible contributors on the revenue side of urban public transport:

• travelers (direct beneficiaries);
• indirect beneficiaries;
• taxpayers.

To which a fourth smaller one must be added:

• ancillary revenues from advertising, charter services, etc.

As regards travelers, most cities have several types of tariffs which can be grouped in four sets:

• single journey tickets, possibly with different prices according to geographical attributes (distance thresholds or zones) and or to the time of travel (peak or off peak);
• a pack of identical tickets (carnet), with some quantity discount;
• a period pass of travel rights throughout the period, with durations from one day to a maximum of usually one month, but possibly up to one year;
• an electronic wallet, sold at a discount which will be discharged on a per journey basis, but possibly with price caps for predefined periods (day, week, month).

This range demonstrates that considerable efforts have been made towards reducing transaction costs as well as stimulating customer loyalty. However, the classic formula of carnets and the period passes have an imbedded assumption that people travel within the same geographical range every day.

Increasing revenue from travelers does not necessarily imply a general increase of ticket prices, and could instead be carried out through processes of market segmentation, through which products or services are differentiated and marketed according to the value they represent to clients, which can be measured by their willingness to pay. Price differentiation could be introduced according to speed of travel, peak demand management, advanced information and possibly seat availability and guarantee through reservation.

While many mature sectors of the economy use market segmentation extensively, urban public transport is an exception. This process – known as "yield management" – is now currently used in airlines and long distance railways where it has allowed simultaneous increases of revenues and of patronage.

The contributions of employers to the fares paid by their employees should be included as traveler related revenue. Such schemes are used in many countries, sometimes covering the whole value (Brazil), sometimes part of it (France, with 50 per cent).

The comparative study should examine not only the currently available transport titles (tickets and passes), their attributes and corresponding revenues, but also plans for market segmentation and in particular the use of individually targeted information on required services. The minimum quality offered by transport services should be good enough to encourage middle class users, but some extras could be the basis for additional revenue, like for instance, reserved seats and individually targeted information in the form of alerts via SMS to an approaching bus. It is also conceivable that intermediate modes like shared taxis could help attract travelers with higher incomes and correspondingly higher perceived value of time.

The second group to consider as a possible generator of revenue for public transport is indirect beneficiaries. This can be subdivided into two: a static set, for whom the benefits accrue due to the level of access to their location; and a dynamic set, for whom benefits are associated with lower congestion levels on the street network.

The first set is directly related to the differentiated market value of land in urban areas, of which quality of access is one of the most relevant factors. There are some greenfield development projects, in Japan in particular (Hayashi, 1989) in which the transport infrastructure investment is borne by the land developers as part of the conditions set by the public authorities to approve the project, and therefore the costs of the external benefits of good access are internalized. However, this is an exception. For the most part property owners do not pay anything towards transport infrastructure that increases the value of their property.

The idea of value capture is not that the State should recover all the value added to the property by the transport improvements, as this would create significant political opposition from all property owners affected. Partial capture of that value should be the aim, starting by explaining the concept and its fairness, and then proceeding with great transparency towards the property owners.

Even if it is agreed that the benefits from better access to a location are enjoyed on a daily basis (and are included in the rents paid by the tenants), and it is a fact that it has been shown to be possible to specify and calibrate econometric models that produce clear estimates of the differential contribution of good access to the property value (Martinez, 2010), the very few countries that apply value capture do it when infrastructure investment is carried out.

For instance, France introduced in 2010, in the framework of the Grenelle 2 law, the possibility to apply a surcharge on the value of property (land or building) when its value is increased by the construction of new infrastructure for public transport with a dedicated right-of-way (Certu, 2010). Although it applied to all property, this is collected only at the time of the investment, and the funds are to be used exclusively to help pay for the scheme.

In London, the Crossrail project has been in discussion for several decades and is now underway. Funding for the project has been secured from a multiplicity of sources, including a Business Rate Supplement charged to all non-residential properties in London valued above £55,000. This supplement will be charged for 24 years and has been securitised against a loan contracted at the beginning of the project (GLA, 2010).

Virtually all countries have some form of taxation on urban land, in which the tax is related to the value of the property, but making this revenue source available for financing public transport still requires a few steps: improved estimation of property values and of the part of that value derived from good access, and applying the legal mechanisms for the corresponding monetary value (or a part of it) to be made available for the urban mobility system.

A well known scheme of contribution by indirect beneficiaries is the French Versement Transport, created in 1973, by which all employers of at least nine people located within the conurbation served by public transport pay a levy of roughly between 1 per cent and 2.8 per cent of their payroll directly to the local transport organizing authority. The basis is that employers benefit from a much wider recruitment base because of the supply of public transport. In most French conurbations this represents roughly one third of the total revenue of public transport.

This has been a powerful contributor to the improvement and stability of public transport in French cities, but the scheme has limitations. It would be much fairer to consider benefits taking into account not only ease of attraction of workers but also of clients and, more critically, there are widely different levels of accessibility in different parts of the same conurbation – yet all employers pay the same percentage in each conurbation.

The Versement Transport should be seen as a proxy, which should be replaced by an instrument which more accurately reflects the benefits generated by public transport as it improves the access to every property, residential or commercial.

In this respect, the comparative study should look at schemes that capture land value related to location in favor of public transport, distinguishing contributions related only to the provision of infrastructural investment from those made towards operating costs. It should also identify the formulas for estimating the values captured, and of course the proportion of public transport costs than can be covered by this type of source.

Indirect beneficiaries also include road users, most of whom are private motorists. With other urban network-based utilities, like water or electricity, the consumer pays for access (a fixed monthly charge associated with the link to the network) and for actual consumption. In road transport a similar approach exists, although with some adaptation: in most countries an annual circulation tax is collected and the consumption-related component is collected through fuel duties.

For public transport there is virtually no fixed price component apart sometimes from a small charge for issuing the ID-card used to obtain frequent traveler discounts. This low fixed cost is a positive element in that it could otherwise constitute a barrier to access public transport, especially for the poor.

The external benefit generated by public transport of reduced congestion should be paid for by those who enjoy this cost reduction. Road traffic also generates negative externalities, which should be internalized. We are not dealing with that in this paper for the following reasons:

• Congestion is a within-group cost, so the fair treatment would be to charge for it to generate the corresponding behavioral adaptation and then redistribute it to the same group, possibly through investments that would reduce congestion;.

• The other externalities (emissions and accidents) are mostly related to society at large, and not to public transport in particular, and therefore it would at least be debatable whether the corresponding revenue should be allocated to public transport rather than other aspects of government spending such as health or education.

• There is a third type of externality, often not mentioned because it has a time lag between stimulus and response: expanding the road infrastructure has a direct impact on urban sprawl, and with it on lowering densities, increased difficulty of providing good access by public transport, and so – almost inevitably – creating high traffic volumes.

To solve the problem of financing urban public transport, it is preferable to charge motorists for the benefits they receive from public transport than for the costs they impose on society at large.

Using a sophisticated system for road charging like the one installed in Singapore (Chin, 2010) and collecting patronage data in public transport at the same time, it would be possible to produce accurate estimates of the level of congestion reduction – and the associated economic value deriving from the shorter travel times – generated by the fact that the passengers in public transport are not adding to road congestion. This could then be charged to each vehicle on the road, minute by minute.

Such a pricing policy would not only be fairer, but more resilient to the trends towards higher energy efficiency and shifting from fossil fuels to electricity. Although this would be a very accurate billing system – possibly as part of national schemes to replace indirect financing of road infrastructure through fuel duties by direct financing through user charges applied on a vehicle per kilometre basis – the technical sophistication and the perceived risks of privacy intrusion certainly make this a tough sell at present. The systematic difficulties of Dutch governments in bringing this type of scheme forward over the past decade are a clear demonstration of these political difficulties. The road pricing systems in place in London or Stockholm are much simpler, basically charging for the right to circulate within a certain area in each day. This is very far from any rigorous application of marginal social cost pricing principles, but at least establishes the principle of charging.

For reasons of public acceptance, these systems had to be simple at the outset, but now, after some years of operation, evolution is possible and desirable. Some basic principles could be established, like charging according to the distance travelled, modified by the level of saturation of the infrastructure used and the level of emissions of the vehicle. This would naturally allow a smooth geographic extension, as there would no longer be the price spike of crossing an arbitrary border.

But there would be another, very important, effect in that this would allow a direct comparison of the price to be paid for traveling a certain distance using a private car versus using public transport. Currently, in most cities, the cost of using the private car is already incurred and even in London and Stockholm, where there is an explicit price to be paid, people do not relate it to the distance traveled.

An interesting alternative, with lower technology requirements and no risk of privacy intrusion, although with loss of some rigor, would be to have a charge on parking dedicated to funding the public transport system, in which the level of the charge would vary according to the quality of access provided by public transport, which is easy to compute with the help of a geographical information system. This could be undertaken through a surcharge on all commercial parking transactions (both on-street and off-street) and a fixed monthly levy on each parking place made available by companies to their workers or clients. As an example in this direction, the Greater Vancouver Transportation Authority applies an annual levy on all non-residential parking sites and also a sales tax on off-street parking transactions (Transport Canada, 2011).

Some cities already use a part of the revenues from the parking systems they manage directly to fund public transport, but this is very partial, leaving out the private commercial undertakings and companies providing places for their employees and visitors. As such, it should not be considered as a charge on indirect beneficiaries, but rather as an internal money transfer.

When considering the general traffic as indirect beneficiaries, the comparative study must consider whether any scheme exists or is in preparation, the kind of activity that will serve as the basis for charging, potential developments, exemptions, and the proportion of the costs of public transport which can be covered from this source.

The third major source of revenue to cover operational costs is the taxpayer, mostly at local or metropolitan level, or more rarely at regional or national level. Under the clarifying framework defined in EU, 2007, these contributions may be of two kinds:

- compensation for concessionary fares, that is for lower than normal fares made available to some social groups;
- compensation for public service obligations, via a revenue supplement necessary to those services that are not economically viable in normal market conditions.

In a recent study for the ECMT/OECD (Viegas, 2008) it was found that concessionary fares, which are supposed to ensure the right of access of economically weaker population segments to public transport, exist in virtually all OECD countries, but the definition of those groups varies widely and the payments are hard to justify, clearly suggesting they may be the result of populist promises made during electoral campaigns.

A new EU regulation, which becomes applicable from December 2019, imposes strict conditions for the award of compensation for public services: the formulae and the parameters for establishing its value have to be published one year before the opening of the tender or the direct award of the contract, and no longer as a lump sum allocated for the operation as a whole, as currently happens in most systems.

In considering taxpayer contributions, the comparative study must scrutinize not only the values transferred to operators under each of these headings, and the relative weight given to total operating costs, but also, the basis for setting those values.

Taxis must be considered as a means of public transport which functions without any operational subsidy, although in many countries there is an investment subsidy in the form of purchase tax reductions. Also the informal sector made up of small operators with minibuses is a part of the public transport spectrum which mostly operates without subsidy.

The comparative study should collect information on these modes including their fares in relation to formal collective transport and subsidies, and consider their dynamics, as they often are the first to react to misfits between demand and supply.

Sometimes the public transport operator is allowed to run other operations like occasional non scheduled services – charters – which may also be a source of revenue. These ancillary revenues can represent 5 per cent, or even up to 10 per cent of total revenue. While this is not negligible, it is hard to imagine significant growth from this source.

The study should examine these ancillary revenues and their contribution, trying to highlight less common schemes to assess their potential for transfer into other urban areas. Particular care has to be taken with separation of accounts when there are transport activities beyond scheduled collective urban transport.

So far we have only been looking at operational results and options to bridge the gap between costs and revenues, but of course investment expenditure cannot be forgotten. With the exception of greenfield projects in which the developer pays for the transport infrastructure as a condition of approval for the project, virtually all investments in urban public transport are financed by grants or permission to borrow from government at various levels.

In fact, whereas in most countries financing the operations is a matter for local authorities, investment – particularly in rail bound modes – normally requires contributions from regional or national government. The local contribution is mostly financed through public debt, since the current accounts are generally negative or barely positive. But municipalities often also invest in the road infrastructure for public transport (bus lanes, stops, signaling).

Many investments – especially in rail bound modes – are made without proper consideration of their negative impacts on future operational results and consequently increasing losses in the overall system.

Sometimes the purchase of new buses is funded by operators, and included in the contract as operating costs. This is possible, not only because of the relatively short amortization period for buses, but also because there is a very sizeable second-hand market. Applying this to railway rolling stock is possible through leasing companies, but always implies longer contract durations for the amortization to take effect.

Another possibility for financing investment is recourse to private capital through public-private partnerships. In these cases, a private consortium and its banking syndicate support the initial investment and are paid back over the lifetime of the project, through a formula normally related to the performance of the system, with an adjustment associated with the level of demand. It is exceedingly rare that the fare box revenue is sufficient to cover operational costs plus amortization of the investment. Therefore, there is normally a significant level of public subsidy, covering part of the investment and the operational costs, or both.

The cost of PPP schemes may be higher or lower than entirely publicly financed schemes: the higher interest rate which the private consortium must pay is an increased cost while on the other hand the (supposedly) better project management skills and lifecycle appraisal of the project by the private sector tends to reduce costs. In any case, the investment must be paid back, so this is not a funding solution but rather a particular type of financing.

The study must, therefore, look at the investments in public transport from this double perspective: what are the sources of the necessary funds and their relative magnitude, and what kinds of precautions were taken to keep the future operational accounts under control? When part of the funding is from private sources the rationale and the legal (or equivalent) basis for that must be made clear.

There is a very wide set of other financial flows in urban mobility, mostly related to general traffic. Still on the public transport side, we should also account for costs associated with the planning, organizing, supervising and regulatory authorities.

These are normally part of the regular budgets of public agencies, and tend to be small in relation to the operating and investment budgets associated with transport itself. The services that perform these duties can be inserted at different levels of public administration, and may be part of larger public agencies which makes this part of the cost budget difficult to calculate.

The comparative study must also include an analysis of price competitiveness between public transport and the private car, which has a strong influence on the level of utilization and market share of public transport. Possible relevant indicators would be:

- (fare revenue/pax.km) / (fuel cost per pax.km in private car);
- daily revenue from parking (on-street and off-street), and number of such transactions. These should be obtained in absolute values and also in relation to the average daily operational deficit of public transport and the average daily number of boardings in public transport;
- market share of public transport in motorized modes.

To consider the financial flows associated with the general traffic, the most significant items will be:

- construction and maintenance of infrastructure (roads, streets, other public ways), normally paid for by the public sector;
- installation, operation and maintenance of the traffic control systems, also on the public side;
- costs of public agencies in charge of traffic management, parking control and enforcement, and of the traffic police;
- construction, operation and maintenance of off-street public parking facilities, in many cases with engagement of the public and the private sector;
- construction and maintenance of parking places in residential, office and commercial properties, supported by their promoters and then passed on to the occupants in various forms (sale, rental, and lease);
- vehicles acquired (through various forms of transaction) by families and companies, mostly in the private sector;
- insurance, maintenance, fuel and other consumables for those vehicles;
- costs incurred by the companies supplying the vehicles, insurance, maintenance, fuels and consumables;
- labor costs of professional drivers;
- special taxes applied to road transport vehicles, on purchase, annual road taxes, and fuel duties (VAT should be treated separately as it is not transport specific).

Organizing a satellite account of urban mobility would be possible, as all these costs are documented, but the effort required for achieving a good result would only be justified in case of a policy decision to make the urban mobility system function as a financially self-sustained unit.

For the purpose in this case it would probably still be interesting to collect the information related to the costs of owning and operating private road vehicles, as this could be important to put into perspective the charges that may be suggested on those vehicles as indirect beneficiaries of public transport.

6.5.2 Reducing cost of access through greater operational and tactical efficiency

Achieving a more sustainable financial framework for public transport is a very important objective, as this may help avoid its slow decay due to systematic financial gaps.

However, it is quite possible that in many cities, the most important single contribution towards financial sustainability is a concerted effort to reduce the costs of production of public transport, through gains in its operational efficiency. This is an exercise that must be undertaken for every operator in the conurbations being studied.

If the study is to address this dimension, a relatively small and simple set of indicators should be selected, bearing in mind that those indicators must keep their value in spite of the differences between countries. Two dimensions must be considered in the cause of simplicity: load factors and transport production costs/place.km, preferably with separate indicators in the latter group for each of the main cost items (labor, fuel/energy, rolling stock and other).

Besides operational efficiency, there may also be issues of tactical efficiency, namely relating the level of access provided by public transport to the citizens with the resources (vehicle.km) that are the direct result of choices on the design of the network and timetables.

There is no simple indicator for the evaluation of this kind of problem, but computer programs are available to produce optimal network designs for a given O/D matrix, allowing some diversity of political priorities, mathematically described as different objective functions (Zhao, 2006).

By their very nature, transport networks can be changed only slowly, which means they normally function at a sub-optimal level. While acknowledging that there can be different "optimal" designs depending on the objectives, running those computer programs allows an estimate of the degree of inefficiency, and its financial consequences, namely the difference and the ratio of real vs. optimal number of vehicle.kms to provide a given level of access.

The difference between these two values is an indicator of the order of magnitude of savings that could be achieved through a more efficient network design, while the ratio of the same two values is of special interest for the comparative study, allowing a comparison and ranking of the cities involved.

6.5.3 Increasing the market share of urban public transport within a sound financing framework

Increasing the market share of urban public transport is a very important objective for the industry, as reflected in the "PT x 2 by 2025" program (UITP, 2009).

As low frequency is one of the disadvantages of public transport, increasing the supply would be a natural remedy, but this is possibly not enough to attract new custom. Concerted marketing work is necessary to identify which service attributes could be more relevant to attract those new (mostly middle class) clients, and which would be the most economically efficient way of providing them: improving the basic service, making good use of the scale it provides, or adding extra features. In the latter case, two options seem interesting:

1   a "non-transport" add-on to the existing base service, like personalized
     information or a seat reservation, in which case it can be provided with-
     out any additional transport provision. Of course seat reservations are
     only possible when the passenger density on board is not so high as to
     make it physically and socially impossible;
2   a transport feature, like higher speed, which would require additional
     provision with differentiated means, for instance through intermediate
     modes with much lower density of stops (express minibuses) or door-
     to-door services (shared taxis).

In both cases, additional revenue could be collected to reduce the need for
subsidy. It should be easy to transfer from the basic level of service to any
of the superior levels of service, so that people could feel they had freedom
of choice within public transport. This may be as important to attract and
retain customers as the service specifications themselves.

6.5.4 Reducing the need for mobility through a more balanced
land use mix

The next dimension is the strategic level of decision-making which may lead
to solutions only in the long term: it is about the relationship between access
and mobility, or put in simple terms "how much transport is required to get
to where we want?" This certainly has to do with urban density, but that
indicator is not enough, because the spread of land uses throughout a
conurbation can have an impact at least as important as density. This refers
not only to averages: frequency and geographical distributions are also
important, because the same average may result from very different patterns
of inequity, and the locations of poor access must be identified. And indeed,
great levels of inequity in urban access can be found in many conurbations
and are by themselves a strong factor of social exclusion.

Fortunately, the development and market penetration of geographical
information systems are such that most municipalities in the developed
world have databases of their land uses on a very detailed level, with the
city block as the basic census unit.

The relevant synthetic information can help analysts (and through them
the political decision makers) understand the mean values and the statistical and geographical variability of the main indicators, so that a pattern of
appropriate interventions can be developed and subsequently tested with
simulation models. For clarity and ease of communication, the number of
indicators should be kept small.

The two basic concepts in this respect are:

•   Land use entropy, a measure of the degree of land use mixing within a
     development. Entropy values range from 0 to 1, with higher values for

more even mixes (Cervero and Kockelman, 1997). Entropy of a certain urban space is computed as follows:

$$Entropy = \frac{-\sum_{i=1}^{k}\left[Prop(i) \,^{*}\, In\big(Prop(i)\big)\right]}{In(k)} \qquad (1)$$

where

Prop(i) = proportion of built-up area in that space (or opportunities to interact with other people) related to use / function i;
k = number of use / function categories

• Willingness to move (walk, bike, ride public transport, drive), a measure of the proportion of people who are willing to walk (or bike) for a distance no bigger than x. This is normally captured by an inverted logistical (or Richard's) curve, with a shape as shown in Figure 6.1. Similar curves can be calibrated for the willingness to bike, ride public transport and drive, with different parameters resulting for each mode (de Vries et al., 2009) (Martinez et al., 2011).

Using these two concepts jointly and adopting a classification of land use types, it is possible to develop a scalar indicator of the level of synthetic accessibility enjoyed by each census unit b in its relation to the rest of the agglomeration with recourse to each mode, SAcc(b,m). Synthetic means that we consider different contributions from different types of land use, and then bring them all together in a single indicator, through the use of an entropy correction.

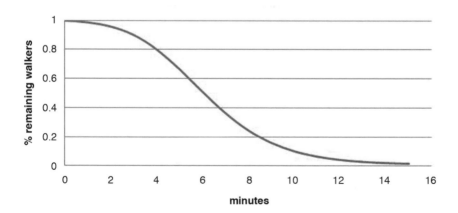

Figure 6.1 Inverted logistical (Richard's) curve for typical willingness to walk

Assuming the GIS for the selected cities has the capacity to compute travel times by mode between any two census units and for all modes, as well the primary data of land uses that allows the computation of masses for the different types of functions and for all census units (and this availability should be one of the basic criteria for eligibility), then the computation of these access indicators should be relatively straightforward. Depending on the level of intensity of use of bikes in a given city, there will be three or four such indicators for each census block: for the modes of walking, public transport, and private car in all cases, plus cycling.

The number of categories of land use to consider (k) will directly depend on the data available for each city, but where this exists in a systematic, digitally coded format, a value between eight and 12 should be expected.

The important information we obtain from these indicators is not in their absolute values but in their ratios, and in particular:

•   in the ratio between the lowest indicator for motorized transport (most frequently public transport) and the highest indicator for non-motorized transport (cycling when relevant, walking otherwise);
•   in the ratio between the indicator for the private car and the indicator for public transport.

In the former ratio, a high value means a great need to use motorized transport to get access to many useful destinations, whereas a low value means that in many cases such access can be obtained simply by walking or cycling. In the latter ratio, a high value implies that good access (within motorized transport) requires the use of the private car, whereas a low value means that public transport is competitive from the point of view of access provision.

These ratios can be computed for each census unit, and they will certainly show different values across the urban space of any given city, which provides valuable information for policy purposes. In this case, this information is meant as a reminder that these land use related aspects can have a strong influence on the need to provide motorized mobility and through it on the financial gap of public transport. For this reason it is probably enough to compute the average and possibly the quartiles of the distributions of the two ratios, and compare their values across cities in the sample.

6.5.5 Synthesis of the approaches to bridge the financial gap of public transport

This systematic analysis shows that, on the one hand, a coherent policy framework may be set out to pursue a much more ambitious treatment of the revenue side of the financial gap in public transport, and on the other hand, that the issues on the cost side can be dealt with through rigorous process, distinguishing the operational, tactical and strategic levels of decision-making.

Trying to solve the public transport financing gap solely by squeezing costs and developing new external sources of revenue is insufficient given that there can be the potential to improve its attractiveness to new segments of the population, not only enlarging its revenue basis but also attracting more advocates.

Ideas for increasing revenue have been presented through market segmentation initiatives or by obtaining payments from the indirect beneficiaries such as property owners and car drivers.

These various levels of decision-making reflect different types of interventions needed to improve results and different time horizons needed to obtain cost savings, but crucially the relative benefits can be easily assessed allowing decision makers to choose where to concentrate their efforts.

All the suggestions for sources of additional revenue and methods of cost reduction have been made with an explicit concern for easy transferability to help create an accepted methodology for the study but it will still face problems from the dialogue with stakeholders and data acquisition, largely deriving from locally entrenched traditions and vested interests.

6.6 General recommendations in preparation for the comparative study and its pilot study

As a result of the differences in fiscal traditions, concepts and terminology comparative studies in this field are complex and can be misleading if based solely on published information, as categories with the same name often have distinct meanings.

Therefore, an empirical effort is needed, which has to be based on a structured questionnaire covering both the logic of the financing scheme in each city and the numerical values corresponding to every cost and revenue item. Gathering information about recent organizational or technical innovations and about changes to the financing structure can be important to understand underlying tensions.

An additional difficulty for an empirical exercise is that organizational and financial responsibilities related to urban mobility are in most cases split among different entities, at various levels of administration, with different designations and definitions of competence domains. This means that it is far from obvious where to find the required information or to cross-check the values from the various sources.

Hopefully, a template will be developed from the pilot study, on the basis of which a categorization of existing schemes, the orders of magnitude of the contributions from each group of providers of funds, and their recent dynamics could be proposed. This, in combination with the information on performance, quality and innovation, should allow some interpretation of the framework conditions for each of the main schemes and of their potential contribution to good urban accessibility, as well as a clear idea of the topics to be covered in greater depth in the subsequent comparative study.

Another key consideration is to ensure that the price of public transport is not a barrier to access by the poor. The reduction in public transport costs must not be achieved by making it unaffordable to the poor. The pilot study should look at what can be done in this respect and try to assess the impacts of wider adoption of more pragmatic approaches to this problem.

The choice of cities for the pilot study is crucial, and should include both those in the developed and developing worlds. Given the potential significance of contributions from land value capture mechanisms, at least one city where this is applied should be included. Two well known cases are Hong-Kong and Singapore, but the specific circumstances of these city states makes such application less transferable, and examples from Japan should be sought.

A couple of cities with good public transport and very high car ownership would be interesting, such as one from Australia (perhaps Melbourne) and one from the United States or Canada (Chicago or Montreal)

From Europe, cities from Sweden or Denmark (high fiscal discipline, with a tradition for regulatory innovation), from Spain or Italy (growing need to control public expenditure, significant pressure from unemployment), and Poland or Hungary (relatively recent regime change, little tradition of subsidies to public transport since transfer to municipalities) would be the best candidates.

References

Barter, P. (1999) "An international comparative perspective on urban transport and urban form in Pacific Asia: the challenge of rapid motorisation in dense cities", PhD thesis, Murdoch University, Perth, Australia.

Beaverstock J. V., Smith R. G., Taylor P. J., Walker D. R. F. and Lorimer, H. (2000) "Globalization and world cities: some measurement methodologies", *Applied Geography* 20: 43–63.

Certu (2010) "Nouveaux modes de financement des transports", available at www.certu.fr/IMG/pdf/fiche-grenelle-transports.pdf (latest consultation 8 January 2012).

Cervero, R. and Kockelman, K. (1997) "Travel demand and the 3ds: density, diversity, and design", *Transportation Research-D*, 2(3): 199–219.

Chin, K. (2010) "The Singapore experience: the evolution of technologies, costs and benefits, and lessons learnt", prepared for the ITF/OECD Round Table of 4–5 February 2010 on Implementing Congestion Charging, OECD, Paris.

de Vries J., Nijkamp P. and Rietveld P. (2009) "Exponential or power distance-decay for commuting? An alternative specification", *Environment and Planning A* 41(26–27): 461–80.

European Conference of Ministers of Transport (ECMT) (2002) "Implementing sustainable urban travel policies – Final Report", Paris.

European Metropolitan Transport Authorities (EMTA) (2010) "Comparative study of the public transport financing and of the fare policy in different metropolitan areas of Europe", available at www.emta.com/article.php3?id_article=750 (latest consultation 8 January 2012).

European Union (2007) "Regulation (EC) No 1370/2007 of the European Parliament and of the Council of 23 October 2007 on public passenger transport services by rail and by road", Brussels.

Faivre d'Arcier, B. (2009) "How to improve the financial situation of urban public transport? The French case", presented at Thredbo 11th conference on competition and ownership in land passenger transport, Delft.

Greater London Authority (GLA) (2010) "Intention to levy a business rate supplement to finance the Greater London Authority's contribution to the Crossrail project – Final Prospectus", available at http://www.london.gov.uk/sites/default/files/finalprospectus.pdf (latest consultation on 8 January 2012).

Hayashi, Y. (1989) "Issues in financing urban rail transit projects and value captures", *Transportation Research*, 23A(1): 35–44.

Heston, A. and Summers, R. (1996) "International price and quantity comparisons: potentials and pitfalls", *The American Economic Review*, 86(2): 20–4.

Martinez, L. (2010) "Financing public transport infrastructure using the value capture concept", PhD thesis, Technical University of Lisbon, Portugal.

Martinez, L. M., Viegas, J. M. and Eiró, T. (2011) "A new approach to modeling distance-decay functions for accessibility and transport studies", presented at the World Symposium on Transport and Land Use Research, July 2011, Whistler.

Pucher, J. (1995a) "Urban passenger transport in the United States and Europe: a comparative analysis of public policies. Part 1. Travel behaviour, urban development and automobile use", *Transport Reviews*, 15(2): 99–117.

Pucher, J. (1995b) "Urban passenger transport in the United States and Europe: a comparative analysis of public policies. Part 2. Public transport, overall comparisons and recommendations", *Transport Reviews*, 15(3): 211–27.

Pucher, J. and Buehler, R. (2005) "Transport policy in post-Communist Europe", in Button and Hensher (eds) *Transport Strategy, Policy, and Institutions*, Elsevier Press, pp. 725–44.

Transport Canada (2011) "Tax mechanisms to promote sustainable transportation – overview", available at www.tc.gc.ca/eng/programs/environment-utsp-listofcasestudies-2596.htm (latest consultation on 8 Jan 2012).

Union Internationale des Transports Publics (UITP) (2005) "Mobility in cities" database, UITP, Brussels.

Union Internationale des Transports Publics (UITP) (2009) "Doubling the market share of public transport worldwide by 2025", available at www.ptx2uitp.org/content/ptx2-project (latest consultation on 8 January 2012).

van Ark, B., Monnikhof, E. and Mulder, N. (1999) "Productivity in services: an international comparative perspective", *Canadian Journal of Economics*, 32(2): 471–99.

Viegas, J. (2008) "Organization and financing of public transport", report prepared for the ECMT Working Group on "Implementing Sustainable Urban Travel Policies", Paris.

Werner, J. (2011) "Zukunft der ÖPNV-Finanzierung in Deutschland", presented at the workshop "Mit Bus und Bahn in die Zukunft?" at the Technische Universitaet Berlin, 7 June 2011, available at www.zewk.tu-berlin.de/fileadmin/f12/Downloads/koop/tagungen/Bus_und_Bahn/Werner_Finanzierung.pdf (latest consultation 8 January 2012).

Zhao, F. (2006) "Large-scale transit network optimization by minimizing user cost and transfers", *Journal of Public Transportation*, 9(2): 107–29.

Chapter 7

Public transport

The challenge of formal and informal systems[1]

Eduardo A. Vasconcellos

7.1 Introduction

This chapter provides a background to the discussion of proposals to better organize public transport in developing countries. It is based on the fact that current conditions are often inadequate, with unreliable, uncomfortable, expensive and unsafe services. The problem is becoming worse with the recent rapid increase in private motorization with motorcycles and, now, cars. One key aspect considered is the transition from an informal system to a more formalized one. An important related question is how efficiency and effectiveness of public transport systems could be improved through public policy.

7.2 Public transport in developing countries

7.2.1 The development of public transport supply

Public transport as an organised form of service supply in motorized societies appeared in the first decades of the twentieth century. In developing countries, uncontrolled urban growth increased average distances between home and work, creating huge pressures on public transport. In most societies, poor government institutional capacity, lower capital availability and poverty converged to generate low-quality public transport services.

Despite differences in social, technological and economic contexts, supply has been organized in several forms according to local circumstances. Such "evolving" processes are neither excluding nor linear, since in many cases different patterns co-exist and in others a pattern that had disappeared may reappear. There are numerous historical models and patterns:

- *The shift from private to public operation* There is a permanent tension between providing public transport by private or public means. Generally provision starts with individual private operation, which is eventually subject to regulation, then taken over by the public sector and finally returned to the private sector. This pattern has been experienced in a very similar way by both developed and developing countries; the starting point of the pattern varies according to each country or city.

Private operation types

- *The savage pattern* Individuals start operating vehicles in response to unmet demand and make profits that attract other individuals, generating an over-supply; average revenue per vehicle decreases and providers opt to cut costs by decreasing the level of service, such as not repairing vehicles, contracting illegal labour, avoiding vehicle taxes and labour rights. They compete fiercely on the street with other drivers; suppliers try to increase revenue by forming associations and cooperatives, excluding those who do not want to join the group and banning new individuals from entering the market. In some cases drivers are charged protection money under threat of violence. The result is that the market is divided into mafias who may or may not manage to coexist peacefully in the city. A public monopoly is replaced by private monopolies organised along routes or areas. This is the most common pattern all over the world and represents most of the systems in Africa, Latin America and poor Asian states.
- *The irresponsible pattern* which refers to the deterioration of a privately operated service under a regulated environment. Supply is organized by medium and large enterprises, with fixed routes and schedules and under fixed, pre-determined fares. Contracts give market exclusivity to private operators and illegal competition is eliminated or fiercely persecuted; profitability disparities among areas of operation, deficient enforcement and inflation-based tensions drive operators towards cost-lowering practices that severely harm the level of service, reliability and accessibility. The previous public monopoly evolves toward a private oligopoly. This is the Brazilian case.

Public operation types

- *The corporate pattern* is another form of irresponsibility, when a public company established to provide public transport organizes services with no reference to public needs; political pressures and lack of social control allow for a steady increase in the number of employees and the reduction of overall efficiency. Local political pressures increase supply of services in an irrational way, decreasing overall productivity; labour organisations increase wages and benefits without efficiency considerations; continuous decrease in performance and efficiency lead to sharp increases in operational deficits and to pressures for more subsidy. The system declines towards unsustainability; critical conditions and external pressures eventually lead to the dismantling of the public company and privatisation. This was the case, for example, with the Ruta Cien public bus company in México City and the CMTC public company in São Paulo, both operating with more than 10,000 buses, as well as with several African companies.

*   *The subsidized pattern* refers to systems that are regulated and subsidized, typical of wealthy societies such as in European and North America: public or private operators operate the services under strict rules and receive subsidies to cover costs not covered by fares.

In developed countries, savage patterns have been eliminated. Although in the USA public transport services were reduced to a minimum share of daily trips in face of the ubiquity of automobile ownership, in Europe most countries did not allow their public transport systems to deteriorate and most made efforts to rebuild and modernize them (Pucher and Lefèvre, 1996) and continued subsidizing them. In developing countries, although informal supply is often essential to vulnerable populations, most systems still fulfil the savage pattern model, operating in a highly unstable equilibrium. Some cities in developing countries have managed to incorporate both the savage and the corporate patterns simultaneously (such as Mexico City with informal transport operating at the same time as the *Ruta Cien* public company) and others had the savage and the irresponsible pattern at the same time (such as Brazil in the 1990s).

A few localized examples are useful. In the case of the savage pattern in South Africa the minibus taxi industry started small-scale operations in 1982 and was growing rapidly, when the government facilitated this kind of transport. Nowadays, it has a 65 per cent share of the market in the country (Walters, 2008). Due to the lack of proper regulation, 'the industry has been operating in a de facto deregulated environment. (leading) to over-supply, capital replacement issues and a lack of long term economic sustainability' (Walters, 2008: 105). He concludes that this situation led to high competition and rivalry on the streets between operators, resulting in violence to protect individual markets.

Georgia is an interesting case of an irresponsible pattern that evolved into a savage pattern and eventually into a fake, semi-regulated supply, with individuals forced to group into companies. The traditional bus system collapsed after the political changes in the 1990s and was gradually replaced by small bus operations, which were already responsible for 75 per cent of public transport demand in 2001. Operated in a chaotic way the minibuses led to increased congestion, pollution and accidents, forcing the government to impose controls. The attempt to reorganize the system resulted in the creation of shell companies that hired drivers and their vehicles but did not solve the problem.

Kazakhstan experienced a similar process to Georgia, with bus systems deteriorating rapidly following the political changes in the 1990s. However the outcome was different – a successful privatization. In 1996, a law introduced the opening of transport markets to the private sector and in 2003 further legislation established the basis for competitive tendering for urban passenger services, focused on overcoming the failings of the original liberalization law. The market was then formed by a combination of large bus enterprises and minibus services, spread throughout the country with varying market shares, and with apparently good results. Recently, the minibus industry has been hit by financial problems and changes may be necessary, in respect of vehicle size, scheduling of operations and creating demand responsive services.

In Ghana the private operators were replaced by a large public operator, which eventually collapsed and split into several types of organizations and transport technologies. In the late 1960s a large public enterprise (OSA) was formed grouping several private companies. In the 1970s the public company experienced a financial crisis that eventually resulted in a spiral of deterioration, loss of business, and collapse of both capacity and market. By 2000, OSA was bankrupt and had effectively ceased operation (Finn, 2008: 121). The services were then provided by imported second-hand minibuses and shared taxis, which spread throughout the country, operated by a mix of cooperatives, associations and bus companies leading to a concentration of organization and operation and the creation of a consistent and coherent service provision in urban areas throughout Ghana (Finn, 2008: 121).

In Sri Lanka, there were four phases: unregulated competition (1907–38); consolidation of regulated private monopolies (1939–57); expansion under a nationalized state monopoly (1958–78); regulated mixed competition (1979 to date). This example shows how economic and political changes may dramatically affect the way public transport is supplied and operated. From a deregulated environment in the beginning of the twentieth century – marked by hostile competition between individual providers – in the 1940s geographically-based private monopolies emerged, which generated both profitable and unprofitable bus companies (similar to the Brazilian case). In 1958 the system was nationalized, bringing a series of positive changes (improved working conditions, network integration and better operational management) and of negative consequences (overloading, unreliability, powerful workers unions' disruptive interventions). Finally, the system developed as a mix of public and private operators, working, however, under a deficient regulatory environment that led to worse deteriorating operating conditions.

7.2.2 Current characteristics of public transport supply in developing countries

Table 7.1 summarizes current public transport conditions in developing countries. While there are, of course, exceptions, by and large the transport provision can be divided into the following categories:

Table 7.1 Current prevalent characteristics of public transport supply in the developing countries

Economy level	Governance capability	Vehicles	Operation	Regulation	Financing	Fare system	Fare payment	Infrastructure	Road priority
Low (Tanzania)	Poor (Africa)	Bicycle / Tricycle / Moto-taxi / Van	Public / Private / Mixed	Unregulated	Self-financed	No integration	Cash	Unpaved roads / Paved roads / "Virtual" stops	No priority
Middle (Peru)	Medium (S. America)	Moto-taxi / Van / Microbus / Bus / Articulated bus / Train/metro	Public / Private / Mixed	Unregulated / Regulated	Self-financed / With subsidies	No integration / Integrated	Cash / Ticket	Unpaved roads / Paved roads / "Virtual" stops / "Pole" stops / Sheltered stops / Stations	No priority / Bus lane / Segregated
High (BRICs)	High (Asia)	Microbus / Bus / Articulated bus / Train/metro	Public / Private / Mixed	Regulated	Self-financed / With subsidies	No integration / Integrated	Cash / Ticket / Electronic	Unpaved roads / Paved roads / "Pole" stops / Sheltered stops / Stations	No priority / Bus lane / Segregated

1   Economic level: represents the existing income per capita in developing countries, in three levels – low, middle and high.
2   Government capability: meaning the state's capacity to plan, implement and monitor transport policies, which is related to its institutional capability and to the availability of human and administrative resources.
3   Vehicles: represents the type of vehicles that are most used to transport people, which is directly related to the country's economic level.
4   Operation: relates to whether public transport is operated by the state or the private sector (or both).
5   Regulation: relates to whether the system is unregulated or regulated.
6   Financing: relates to whether the system gets its revenues from passengers or also gets subsidies from other sources.
7   Fare system: divided into non integrated services and integrated services (which require a higher level of organization and management).
8   Fare payment: represents whether the service is paid in cash, with a special ticket (token) or through an electronic fare collection mechanism.
9   Infrastructure: represents whether transport uses unpaved or paved roads and what is the quality of the bus stops – virtual (no signs at all), pole, sheltered or station (with additional facilities).
10 Road priority: divided into no priority, bus lane (curb lane) or segregated lane (such as those in the BRTs).

Table 7.2, page 181 shows poor economic countries tend to be associated with low-level government capability. They have a transport system based on non-motorized means, moto-taxis and vans. The systems are unregulated or have very limited rules. Operation is self-financed, paid in cash and with no integration between modes. Vehicles use both paved and unpaved roads, with no priority and users have no designated bus stops.

Middle-level economic countries tend to be associated with middle-level government capability. They have a transport system based on motorized means, varying from moto-taxis to trains. The systems may be unregulated or regulated, the latter mostly in larger cities. Operation is mostly self-financed but some systems may receive subsidies (such as the metro in México City). Users may pay for trips in cash or using tickets and large cities may have integrated ticketing systems. Services may be integrated in large areas. Vehicles use both paved and unpaved roads, with few priority schemes in operation. Users have a large array of boarding points, from the virtual ones to large stations.

High-level economic countries may have either middle-level or high-level government capability. They have a transport system based on motorized means – in most cases varying from microbuses to trains. The systems are mostly regulated but unregulated or semi-regulated services may be found in small cities. Operation is mostly self-financed but some systems may receive subsidies (such as the bus system in São Paulo. Users may pay for trips in cash or using tickets and large cities may have electronic ticketing systems. Services may be integrated in large areas. Users have a large array of boarding points, from a simple pole to large stations.

7.3 Proposals

7.3.1 Main obstacles

The most important question for our purposes is how efficiency and effectiveness of public transport systems can be improved through public policy. A parallel question is how they could move towards more socially and environmentally sustainable systems. In order to address these challenges it is important to identify the key obstacles. There are three major ones:

The high number of actors and factors

The built environment and the mobility system result from a series of actions taken by public, private and individual actors, inside a complex chain of relationships. Understanding of how these actors are involved in the process is key to analysing how public transport supply in developing countries may be improved.

The most important public actor is the State, be it federal, regional or local (or a combination of these), which embodies all governmental agencies and institutions in charge of urban transport policies and related policies, such as urban land use, housing and health services. The second major element is the political and economic framework, representing the structural rules and codes that define and confine how people interact within society. This may range from western-style states based on a market economy and formal democratic political relationships – with a clear separation between civilian and religious power – and newly-democratised states such as those arising recently in several developing countries and to socialist states and those deeply influenced by religious or ethnic beliefs.

A third element is government policy, representing the way a country formulates and implements public policies, which depends on its internal structure and political nature. Major differences may be found among transport policies in developing countries. Most poor countries with a majority living in poverty have a small elite controlling almost every public policy decision. Some countries with higher average incomes still retain major social differences and are characterized by a powerful, well-educated elite working with civil servants seeking to modernise the country. Examples include Latin American countries such as Argentina, Brazil, Chile, Mexico and Uruguay and some Asian states such as China, South Korea, Thailand and Indonesia. Finally, there are also religious countries, where cultural beliefs and norms drive public action such as low-to-middle income Asian states and Islamic countries in general.

Five policies are particularly important to the discussion of public transport:

- *Urban development and land use policies* which define how urban space may be developed, organised and occupied, and what sort of land uses and densities are to be accepted which defines land values and people's access to land. Decisions concerning the spatial supply of public services – such as schools, hospitals, parks, public offices – are crucial as they determine people's accessibility to such services by public transport.
- *Transport policies* that define road and public transportation infrastructure, and determine the provision of services and access for users.
- *Housing and construction policies* that determine where people live.
- *Economic policies* that define rules related to fiscal and taxation measures, interest rates, labour relations and wage levels.
- *Traffic policy*, which determines access to vehicles and how available road space is used.

States may develop policies in different areas independently of each other or, more rarely, may try to implement them in a coordinated way. The level of skills among government officials varies widely, too.

A fourth factor is the level of external influence that may come from the private sector interested in being involved in policy decisions on transport issues. Pressure may also be exerted directly by local communities, transport-deprived groups, environmental organisations and the media.

A fifth element is *land* values and existing transport infrastructure. In most cities in the developing world, poor people are forced to live far away from jobs, medical care and educational opportunities. Transport supply and costs will directly affect travel possibilities.

A sixth factor is people's interests and needs which will also affect decisions concerning the use of space. Such decisions are taken within a complex mix of individual and family capabilities and constraints. Poor people will have to decide how to use the limited family budget and transport costs may put enormous pressure on this decision, preventing people from undertaking essential trips.

A seventh element is the variety of public and private agents with an interest in transport: the automotive industry whose interest is to sell motorised vehicles; the construction sector which seeks to make profits by building roads and public transport infrastructure; the real estate sector, which seeks to obtain land-based profits or rents, deriving from new investments on land use; the public transportation sector, divided into public and private interests which have potentially conflicting motives – while the interest of the public transport operators is to provide transport services as a public duty the private transport operators want to make profits and protect the industry from competition. In both cases, the interests of related workers unions or associations are relevant. The consultant sector which wants to provide services to public and private agencies in the formulation and implementation of public policies; such services may be linked to foreign industry sectors willing to sell specific products and services; finally, international lending institutions that are interested in obtaining financial returns from investments in transport infrastructure and services. Their particular conditions make them very powerful in influencing policy decisions and they may well seek to use equipment and services originating in the donor countries.

Finally, there are social forces, especially external and internal migratory processes, which profoundly impact on where people live and how they move around.

There is therefore a highly complex network of interests involved in these private investment operations. Every organization will be subject to a specific mix of structures dedicated to provide and support mobility. This mix will lead to a particular distribution of accessibility and will generate a pattern of travel that determines the shape of the transport system.

Weak democratic and citizenship development

Many new democracies are fragile, as they are subject to external and internal destabilisation pressures, which lead to threats of disruption of the political system; citizenship, as political consciousness of rights and duties is weakly developed, which is exacerbated by the deep social and political division between social groups and classes; public transport users are especially affected by these limitations and have enormous difficulties in fighting for their interests.

Public transport as a market issue

This view is widespread throughout the developing world and prevents any attempt to promote major changes once it is thought that provision must be addressed by the market: if the market does not see it as a problem, then there is no need for any action by policy makers.

High costs of running motorized public transport systems

The costs of organizing and operating motorized public transport systems are high in relation to the wealth of developing countries. Providing adequate roads, signing, terminals and good buses is expensive. Most countries do not have local vehicle industries and rely on locally adapted vehicles or on imported used vehicles. In a Latin-American city with 2 million people, existing roads cost US$2–3 billion dollars to build, which is higher than the annual city budget. The total cost of a fleet of buses would be between US$100 million in San Jose (1 million inhabitants) to US$8 billion in São Paulo (11 million inhabitants). A BRT costs US$10 million per kilometre, a rail line US$50m and a subway line US$100m. Currently, road assets per inhabitant in large cities in Latin America are worth an average US$1,000, the value of public transport vehicles per inhabitant is US$300 and total assets per inhabitant are US$2,318. This means that having a mostly paved road system and sophisticated public transport systems with motorized vehicles is unaffordable for most poor cities without a new approach to the issue of funding.

Unaffordable public transport fares

Public transport fares are unaffordable to a large part of society: monthly cost of public transport for the mostly poor in Mumbai varied between 9.3 and 14.7 per cent of their income, 12 per cent in Islamabad and 18 per cent in Delhi. Minimum one-way bus fares in large Latin-American cities other than in Brazil where fares were higher in 2007 were typically 38 US cents. Monthly costs would be US$19, which corresponds to 10 per cent of the average minimum salary.

Selective services

Public transport supply is often organized to cope with regular, peak working trips, neglecting other needs and disadvantaging women, children and the elderly.

Poor governance capability

The poor quality of policy planning and control, which is related to the governance capability. Most developing countries fail in this respect, mainly because public transport is seen as a market issue.

7.3.2 Policy issues

Four policies are essential to promote change.

The right to access

Access to space and to activities has a direct relationship to wealth. Poverty may prevent people from using transport to access convenient destinations (the same happens when there is a lack of transport); moreover, people are

Table 7.2 Main obstacles to improving public transport and major opportunities to overcome them

Obstacle	Main nature	Opportunities to change or improve	
		Within public transport domain	Outside public transport domain
Large number of stakeholders and interests	Several public and private actors interfere in the provision and operation of public transport	Strengthen relationships within the urban and transport network	Develop alliances with actors sharing same vision
Society vision	Public transport is a market issue or a public issue?	Implement model examples	Improve democracy, education and citizenship
		Build partnerships with health and environment sectors	Include issue in schools and public discussion activities
Cost of services	Services are costly in terms of roads, vehicles and human resources	Develop new transport technologies and systems, adapted to local industry and business environments. Improve roads and service reliability	Increase poor people's income
		Improve roads and running/stopping conditions for public transport	Reorganize use of space to reduce distances
		Define regulation to avoid on-street competition and to reward efficiency and environmental sustainability	Charge outside beneficiaries
		Reorganize suppliers into more structured and sustainable entities	Provide subsidies
		Improve service reliability	
Government capability	System may be low-quality and expensive if government capability is low	Implement capacity programs	Improve democracy and society control
		Strengthen links with agencies in charge of urban planning and public services such as education, health and leisure	

affected by not having access to desired destinations which can limit opportunities to work, study or use public services. Therefore, asking questions about who has access and under which conditions (equity audit) is crucial to uncovering inequitable conditions. Although solutions to structural poverty lie beyond transport policy, adequate transport planning and provision may minimise or eliminate some crucial barriers faced by the poor.

The key word to guide such proposals is 'accessibility', taken in its wider meaning – ensuring people have the opportunity to access space and services within their economic possibilities and under safe, convenient and comfortable conditions. To limit accessibility may threaten the continuity of the social system and severely harm the very notion of citizenship and the sense of belonging to a community or society. This can be especially serious for poor people. Investing in the wealthier sectors has proved inequitable, environmentally harmful and dubiously efficient. The organization of the automobile-based travelling environment and the recent growth of cities dominated by the middle classes demonstrates it very crudely. Space organized around car use results in large numbers of access-deprived people, destroys space for human interactivity, causes large numbers of deaths and injuries, results in high use of resources and severely damages the environment. Therefore, the main proposal is to target investment primarily on accessibility-deprived groups to decrease inequalities which the market will not resolve.

The right to access public transport

Accordingly, the discussion of the right to transport needs to consider access to public transport services. The first approach, with a liberal perspective, is that of access being limited to meeting demand. Such an approach underlies recent proposals to privatise and deregulate transport. The second approach postulates that transport conditions should be equally distributed, regardless of individual characteristics. Such an approach, while superficially suggesting equality, conveniently hides fundamental exclusion impacts, as does the myth of roads as democratic investments of public resources; further, such an approach ignores the potential to use transport investments to change inequitable accessibility. The third approach is that access should be provided according to needs. Such an approach is closer to the concept of equity but raises important questions of deciding what is a need and to what extent unsatisfied needs should be addressed.

For each of these three approaches, corresponding paradigms for public intervention in the transport sector may be devised. First, in the *laisser-faire* paradigm, that aims only to meet demand, provision is left to the market; second, the regulatory paradigm assesses both manifest and suppressed demand and defines rules for allocating public resources; third, the interventionist paradigm, which considers demand but also attempts to create a comprehensive intervention plan.

The most important consideration is that the prevailing market paradigm, which leaves all decisions to the market as a the best way of allocating resources, must be replaced by a social paradigm, in which transport is an essential tool for ensuring the right to access and bringing about broader social goals. The prevailing efficiency paradigm should be replaced by an equity paradigm, as a consequence of the commitment to reduce social problems. The proposal does not imply neglecting efficiency but rather approaching it through a different perspective, that of replacing the concept of economic efficiency with social efficiency to ensure the costs of providing social objectives are addressed. Some minimum general accessibility conditions may have already been devised for developing countries such as for access to work, school and medical services.

Table 7.3 provides a summary of these characteristics, which may help us in devising actions to improve public transport.

Table 7.3 Approaches to the right to transport

Political approach	Underlying paradigm	How transport supply is seen	Demand that is considered	Impacts
Liberal	Free market: *laisser-faire*	Only against payment of all costs	Manifested	Limited spatial accessibility; services limited to solvent demand; exclusion of large sectors; emphasis on economic efficiency
Regulatory	Regulation and definition of minimum conditions	Against payment of costs and also with few selected subsidies	Manifested and part suppressed	Higher accessibility; partial exclusion of users; higher average costs
Interventionist	Intervention to ensure social objectives	Against payment but considering economic capability and constraints	Manifested and mostly suppressed	Enlarged spatial accessibility; little or no exclusion of users; higher overall cost; emphasis on social efficiency

Source: adapted from Furniss and Tilton, 1977, and Hill and Bramley, 1986.

The right to use roads

The road system has to be viewed as a collective asset to be shared by all. No one has the right to circulate at will, regardless of others' needs and interests. No one can be allowed to misuse this collective asset, simply because of an alleged need to have access to motorised transport. The use of the traffic system should be defined with priority given to the most numerous and vulnerable users, which in developing countries are the pedestrian, the cyclist and the public transport passenger. This need not entail eliminating private transport, but will entail a road user hierarchy in which it is not prioritized. This does not presuppose an immobile society, but one where the required mobility can be achieved safely and conveniently by all, rather than solely by selected groups. Moreover, the mere provision of a traffic system does not mean that it can be used collectively as long distances in ever larger cities make it impossible to reach all destinations by walking. Thus if buses are not provided at affordable prices, streets become mere private means of consumption for those who have access to automobiles or motorcycles.

Although built with public resources roads are not necessarily available for collective consumption, as their access is defined by the social and economic characteristics of users. Unless car users pay the total cost of such private appropriation of public resources, the only way of minimising inequality is to provide an integrated public transport system, which mimics the spatial penetrability of private transport. This implies additional costs to the public transport system, which have to be covered by society.

The economic support to public transport

As a general principle, public transport operation should be financially self-sustaining through fares (coverage of infrastructure costs is a different issue). In practice, most bus systems in developing countries are economically sustainable. However, often such services offer a very low level of quality and safety and deprive millions of people from access to working and education opportunities. Therefore, current conditions deny both the right to public transport and the ability to use the road network. Two forms of support are necessary to ensure these rights: economic financing and support; and physical and operational integration, with adequate travelling conditions.

With a social approach, subsidies are justified as a way of providing services to the most needed who otherwise could not afford to pay for them. This could include the poor, women, the elderly, students, disabled people and geographically isolated people. Hence, subsidies have to be considered as an investment, provided they are targeted as a part of a specific program, reach the targeted groups and are not used to support inefficiency.

Service integration and providing adequate travelling conditions are other forms of supporting public transport.

7.3.3 Organizing better public transport systems

State organization and policies

Current conditions in developing countries pose enormous problems for overcoming the barriers to provide an equitable and efficient mobility system. Most of the problems derive from structural historical barriers not related to transport *per se*, such as poor education, unfair political representation, social exclusion and corruption and will take decades to overcome. They need high investments in education, democracy and citizenship strengthening and income distribution. At the social and economic level some of the potential ways to improve the situation are related to four actions:

1 recognizing public transport as a public issue and making this clear in the public policies and economic decisions;
2 reorganizing state agencies to allow them to fulfil their duties efficiently; competent local governance is critical;
3 striking agreements with other, more empowered social groups such as the health and environment movement;
4 organizing a large communication effort to unveil current myths and underpin real changes.

The first action requires a focus on governance rather than government and at the same time work with stakeholders to overcome the historic barriers to fair representation in the policy process. The second would require a reorganization of state human resources to place greater emphasis on the mobility system. The third change involves integrating environmental and equity considerations to ensure the needs of the majority of the population are met with an emphasis on equity. Finally, the fourth movement requires using the information available today to demonstrate how public assets and citizens' rights are catered for by mobility policies.

Public or private

There is no automatic relationship between private responsibility for transport and protection of public interests. By the same token, there is no direct relationship between public responsibility for public transport and protection of the public interest. What is at issue is not merely the old public versus private discussion but how social needs are met to achieve greater equity. Both approaches are questionable because public transport is a very special form of service and business. It takes place on public goods, such as streets and stations, and generates considerable externalities, such as air pollution, congestion and accidents. Therefore, the business of public transport cannot be analysed through neo-classical economics as a commodity that is offered to free consumers, in a free-market environment, and under optimum competitiveness, implying a "fair benefit for the risk implied". The consumers are not free, perfect competitiveness seldom exists and the risk is normally low. Hence, there is no basis for rewarding the service as a risky business. These conclusions do not mean that a state of *laissez faire* should prevail. Oversupply, congestion, inefficiency and violent conflicts are common consequences of deregulation. Moreover, there is no justification for eliminating all public oversight of the system. If private operators are called upon to provide most of the services, public regulation remains essential for three main reasons: transport uses public goods; it generates externalities that the market will not take care of; and it is an essential service for society and the economy.

Regulation of supply

According to neo-classical economics, regulation is acceptable only when market failures occur. These failures can be: the exploitation of market power to distort the market; the generation of externalities (pollution, congestion, accidents); and lack of transparency or information for consumers. The World Bank acknowledges that there are three reasons for retaining public regulation on the supply of transport: a) indivisible infrastructures (roads, railways) whose duplication would be wasteful or impractical; b) danger of duplication of schedules, excess capacity, dangerous operational practices (racing buses) and perceived losses in service stability and reliability; c) the requirement to provide for social needs when the unregulated market will not provide for them.

Hence, from a societal point of view, the nature of the provision and its urban, social and economic impacts require it to be seen as an essential public service. While regulation and monitoring by the public sector is inescapable, the question remains how to ensure they bring about social and economic efficiency. The key is that society has to realise that transport is a public service, not a market issue.

The most attractive solution is when the public regulatory role blends in with private operating and marketing efficiency. Historically closed markets that have entered the irresponsible pattern may require flexible regulation, while more open markets that have entered the savage pattern may require tougher regulation. Significant economic differences among social strata, as well as low density settlements may command special attention to ensure the provision of non-profitable services. In practice, regulation has to be defined in relation to factors such as transport conditions, existing provision, income of users in relation to average costs, government capability, the level of organisation of the private sector and its managerial skills level. The key issue is to ensure a good level of service by private operators through the creation of mechanisms to foster quality and productivity, to avoid collusion and to limit congestion, accidents and air pollution. There are basically three key mechanisms:

- The organisation of geographically defined areas, where operators have market exclusivity and are responsible for all services both profitable and unprofitable. This system produces an ordered supply by region, providing stability to the supplier and a close relation with local users; however, as seen in Brazil, it also creates large suppliers, with the potential to abuse their power in order to influence state agencies.
- The auctioning of routes in areas of high demand is a way of replacing the undesired street competition.
- Contracting services paid according to parameters such as distance or passenger numbers presents three principal positive results. First, there is a formal separation between the fare charged to the user and the payment to the operator, relieving the state of blame for fare increases to cope with inflation. Second, there is flexibility in allocating vehicles to routes, and in creating new or temporary services. Third, a flat fare system avoids the problems derived from profitability differences between routes, a permanent source of conflict between government and operators on low-profitability services. However, the system presents two main drawbacks. First, once a service is paid for by distance covered, the operator loses interest in enforcing fare collection, which leads to a decrease in revenue, unless specific controls are introduced. Secondly, operators tend to increase the distance they run in order to increase their payment. Both drawbacks drive the system towards financial instability, which prove disruptive. The system is viable, provided that rewards are also based on the number of passengers carried; if subsidies are needed, they must be delivered directly to users (as with the *vale transporte* in Brazil), the compensation mechanism must be managed by the operators, and the government must have efficient enforcement capability, supported by online mechanisms to verify the quality of the service, distances run and patronage.

In all cases only a strong public agency, capable of running the bid process for services, can prevent pressures from existing operators to avoid inefficiency and the adoption of irregular or illegal profit-seeking measures at the expense of service quality and reliability. Moreover, almost universally, subsidies will have to be considered. In addition, a transition process may be required when individual and competing operators are reorganized into small enterprises or cooperatives, to be able to operate a more structured and integrated public transport system. As stated by Sohail *et al.* (2006: 180), "A regulatory regime that encompasses both formal and informal transport providers is a key element when attempting to improve sustainable public transport services in developing countries".

This public responsibility proposal has to be tempered by reality. Many cities in developing countries are so poor that it is only possible to have a few unsafe and uncomfortable vehicles. To submit public transport to comprehensive public scrutiny in such poor social environments is unrealistic. Recently many efforts have been made to move systems from the savage pattern towards a more adequate one without dismantling the existing system completely. Efforts have been made to include existing operators in the new proposed systems, such as in the Transmilenio in Bogotá and the results have been favourable. However, this transition will occur slowly and will rely both on changes in the public perception of the value of public transport and in the economic and business environment.

In terms of supply, the search for the "best" mode and the encouragement of mode competition has to be replaced by the search for the best mix of modes. The differences in cost and performance of the modes vary and every mode has a role to play according to prevailing conditions. When analysing three important cases – Colombo (Sri Lanka), Faisalabad (Pakistan) and Dar es Salaam (Tanzania) – Sohail *et al.* (2006: 188) concluded that:

> The role of transport regulators is crucial. Regulators must ensure that the supply of public transport services is of sufficient quantity and quality (in terms of safety) to meet the perceived demand, and that the service is provided at an affordable price...(and to pay attention to the) critical importance of communication and co-ordination between stakeholders (defined here as transport users, providers and regulators) if regulation is to be effective.

This is based on the principle that to change urban transport conditions in developing countries, public transport has to be considered a public service and public control has to be seen as a superior form of guiding and protecting the public interest.

The virtuous pattern (Figure 7.1) shows the key characteristics of the proposed form of public responsibility for public transport. Its great advantage is to fit in a range of economic development and government capability situations. After government and society have defined the desired characteristics of the service (spatial accessibility, technology, cost, comfort) and incentives to productivity are outlined, the private sector is contracted to provide services under the watchful eye of both public agencies and society representatives. Such control leads to permanent reassessment and adaptation of services to improve performance and ensure economic sustainability in the light of available subsidies.

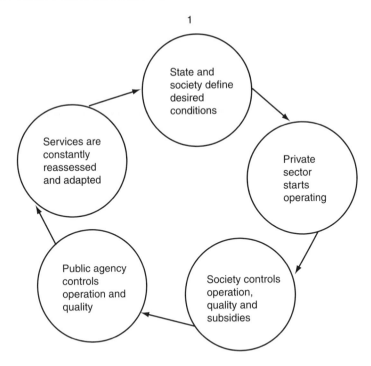

Figure 7.1 The public transport virtuous supply pattern

Financing

Once the concept of public transport as a public issue is understood, the first source of financing should be the public budget. An additional need is to clarify the cost structure of providing public transport, to better identify actions that may be taken. Charging part of transport costs from external sources is the second possible source. First, there are sectors benefiting from a good transport system – industrial, service and commercial – that can be charged, as happens with the French *versement transport*. In a more direct form, employers may be charged part of the transport costs of their employees, as with the Brazilian *vale transporte*. Finally, resources may be obtained by charging the surplus value to land owners benefiting from the increased accessibility provided by improved public transport systems.

In addition, there are users creating negative externalities to public transport. People using private modes that hamper public transport efficiency and productivity could be charged to use roads. The most promising ways are to increase parking costs and to charge for road use in defined areas or periods.

The establishment of new fare systems is a necessary complement to the financing of public transport. The fare system should consider social equity, meaning both that costs and benefits should be fairly distributed among users and non-users and that convenient transport should be available to those who need it. The collection of revenues must not be too costly, time consuming or inconvenient to either suppliers or consumers.

Integrated fare operation should be encouraged. Long trips requiring mode interchange are increasingly necessary in large towns. Any transfer implies economic and personal costs, which interfere with modal choice and demand. Hence, implementing system-wide integrated fares increases average speed and comfort. Recent developments in communications can greatly improve the speed and reliability of revenue control and reduce costs. However, there are two downsides. Electronic collectors may reduce employment opportunities and when the system is operated by a large number of firms, there are problems with revenue accountability and allocation between them.

Infrastructure supply and service operation

The change in public transport supply can be performed by linking three main policies regarding infrastructure.

- *Organizing the road system to better serve public transport needs.* Currently, public transport vehicles in the developing world use the streets with little regard to surface conditions, lighting, signs, signals, shelter or information. Buses also have to compete with other vehicles using the same space. For public transport operation to be efficient it is essential to ensure appropriate speeds and travelling smoothness.
- *Providing new infrastructure,* such as terminals, connected bikeways and pedestrian areas.
- *Organizing bus priority schemes* such as dedicated lanes to improve bus operation. At a higher level, it implies building bus corridors or BRTs. Such actions are more expensive and may only be worth undertaking if there is an appropriate level of passenger demand as well as the right institutional and regulatory environment and an efficient operational plan. The BRT has the potential to transform the public transport system, because it requires the complete reorganization of supply, involving the structuring of an enterprise-based system to replace the individual system. The new system has to be carefully designed and operated as a network, to be able to provide permanent, reliable and accountable services. This reorganization can engender opposition from existing operators who fear a decrease in revenues or the loss of their entire business. Even when the new system is organized, a large part of the traditional one may remain in operation, such as in Bogotá, and be

a permanent threat to the viability of the new system. Secondly, BRTs require extra resources to cover their higher costs. As the new enterprises that will run the BRT require profitability the new fares are inevitably higher – putting additional pressures on the poor.

Bus service organization

Service organization should be based on the expansion of the surface transport network using available streets, followed by efficient operation and effective control. This depends on an increased number of vehicles and crews, a better spatial and time coverage and the implementation of priority schemes. Services have to be diversified to cope with different demands, using the best tailored vehicle for each case. Users require high quality information which is now available at much lower costs due to technology developments in telecommunications. It also presupposes more comfortable vehicles and easier access points. Finally, it involves the organization of better transfer conditions between motorised public transport and non-motorised transport, especially the bicycle.

This reorganization relies on the integration of various transport modes operated either by public or private agents, with the objectives of equality, sustainability and efficiency. One of the greatest challenges is to make gender-sensitive projects that ensure better public transport supply for women, especially in respect to personal safety, ease of physical access and services tailored to their specific travel needs. Another challenge is to provide better access for people with disabilities.

Table 7.4 summarizes the main practical actions that may be considered according to the three levels of economic development.

Table 7.5 summarizes the most feasible changes that may apply to cities, according to the current level of public transport services.

Table 7.6 summarizes important characteristics and limitations of the main ideas. The proposed movements are split according to their political and economic costs, the time required to implement and the likely support and opposition.

7.4 Conclusions

Current public transport conditions in developing countries are mostly poor. Problems relate mainly to bad roads, signs and vehicles, and to lack of supply and low service quality. A large part of the population has limited or no access to services. Most governments have adopted conventional policies, which have been unable to improve services for the majority of the population.

There are numerous possibilities for changing current conditions. Different social, economic and political characteristics among developing

Table 7.4 Most important practical actions according to level of economic development

Objective	Action	Major needs and possibilities per economic level		
		Low	Middle	High
Governance	Legal environment and government capability	X	X	
Infrastructure	Road pavement and/or improvements	X		
	Bus stops	X		
	User information	X	X	X
	Proper sidewalks and pedestrian areas	X	X	X
	Bikeways	X	X	
Economic access	Fare discounts for the mostly poor	X	X	X
	Integrated fare systems		X	X
Financing	Fares partially paid by employers	X	X	X
	Vehicle financing by government	X	X	X
	Sector financing by enterprises		X	X
	Road and parking extra charges		X	X
	Charge for increased property values			X
Vehicle technologic improvements	Tricycles	X		
	Motorized three-wheelers	X		
	Vans and microbuses	X	X	X
	Standard buses	X	X	X
	High capacity buses		X	X
	Rail systems		X	X
Operation	Bus lanes	X	X	X
	Service integration		X	X
	Bus circulation		X	X
	Bus corridors		X	X
	"Executive" bus services			X
Urbanization	Link development to improved NMT	X	X	X
	Transit oriented development		X	X

countries mean that proposals can be tailored according to specific local conditions.

This paper presented a series of proposals, at the institutional, legal, economic and technical sides, which may be helpful to define a matrix of possibilities to be implemented according to local conditions and the level of government capability. While numerous changes have to be considered two are essential: to consider public transport as an essential public and not a market issue and to redirect all public actions related to transport policies accordingly. It must be stressed that prerequisites for moving to formal systems include institutional organization, service regulation, financing of infrastructure and vehicles and labour training.

Table 7.5 Typical feasible improvements

System level	Current characteristics	Most feasible opportunities
Very low	Unregulated services	Improve state governance
	Individual operators	Define minimum rules: frequency and routes
	Low-quality vehicles	Devlop local vehicle industry or fund vehicle quality improvement
	Low-quality roads/signs	Use budget to improve roads, stops, signing
	Financing via fare only	Transfer part of cost to employers + provide subsidies for the most needed
Low	Unregulated or semi-regulated services	Improve state governance
	Individual operators	Increase formalization and improve service coordination
	Low-quality vehicles	Develop local vehicle industry or fund vehicle quality improvement
	Low-quality roads/signs	Use budget to improve roads, stops, signing
	Financing via fare only	Transfer part of cost to employers + provide subsidies for the most needed
Medium	Semi or regulated services	Improve regulation and state governance
	Mixed enterprise and individuals	Increase formalization and improve service coordination
	Middle-quality vehicles	Develop local vehicle industry or fund vehicle quality improvement
	Middle-quality roads	Use budget to improve roads and provide priority
	Financing via fare only	Transfer part of cost to employers + provide subsidies for the most needed
		Restrict inadequate automobile use (middle to large cities)
High	Regulated	Improve regulation and state governance
	Enterprise operators	Improve service and coordination
	Middle-quality vehicles	Develop local vehicle industry or fund vehicle quality improvement
	Middle-quality roads	Use budget to improve roads and provide priority
	Financing via fare only	Transfer part of cost to employers + provide subsidies for the most needed
		Restrict inadequate automobile use (middle to large cities)

Note

1   Several concepts of this text were taken from Vasconcellos, 2001.

Table 7.6 Comprehensive actions, their costs and prospective alliances and opposition

Movement	Action	Cost		Term	Supporters	Opponents
		Political	Economic			
1	Recognize public transport as a public issue and make it clear in the public policies and economic decisions	Medium	Low	Large	Public transport users Environmentalists Citizenship movements	Automotive industry
2	Reorganize state agencies in charge of public transport to make them able to accomplish their duties; strengthen links with agencies in charge of urban planning and public services such as education, health and leisure	Low	Medium	Medium	State agencies and experts Health and environmental sectors	Liberal sectors
3	Organize road infrastructure and public transport boarding places, in connection to walking and cycling mobility; ensure quality and comfort in using public transport means; work to provide accessibility to desired destinations (and not only mobity) to all that need it	High	High	Medium	Public transport and users of non-motorized means Health and environmental sectors Consultants Lending institutions	Automobile users Middle class neighbourhoods High income commercial areas
4	Organized local transport supply using local means, under regulation that avoids competition on streets and rewards productivity and environmental quality	Medium	Medium	Medium	Investors interested in the new market Local vehicle industry Foreign vehicle industry	Traditional operators and associate workers Politicians with historica linkages to them Users (fares may increase)
5	If public transport cannot be sustained with user fares, devise extra financial sources to subsidize it; both budgetry or based on charging external beneficiaries or private modes that hamper public transport efficiency	High	High	Medium	Public transport users Environmentalists	Traditional economic sectors Policy leaders and stakeholders that may lose resources
6	Identify who generate and who endure the impacts of negative externalities related to local mobility; devise actions to minimize or eliminate such effects	High	Medium	Medium	Public transport users Environmentalists Citizenship movements	Automobile and motorcycle users Conservative politicians
7	If the use of private transport is too high develop actions that could make automobile and motorcycle users move to public transport means	High	Medium	Medium	Public transport users Environmentalists Citizenship movements	Automobile and motorcycle users Conservative politicians
8	Identify opportunities to change the way city space is occupied, in order to decrease average distances to be travelled	Low	High	High	Construction and real estate sectors, if profitability is high Lending institutions	People that will have to move

References

Finn, B. (2008) "Market ro le and regulation of extensive minibus services as large bus services capacity is restored: case studies from Ghana, Georgia and Kazakhstan", *Research in Transport Economics* 22, 118–25.

Furniss, N. and Tilton, T. (1977)*The case of the welfare state*, Indiana, IN: Indiana University Press.

Hill, M and Bramley, G. (1986) *Analysing Social Policy*, Edgar Elgar.

Pucher, J. and Lefèvre, C. (1996) *The Urban Transport Crisis in Europe and North America*, MacMillan Press.

Sohail, M., Maunder, D.A.C. and Cavill, S. (2006) "Effective regulation for sustainable public transport in developing countries", *Transport Policy* 13, 177–90.

Vasconcellos, E. A. (2001) *Urban Transport, Environment and Equity – the Case for Developing Countries*, Earthscan.

Walters, J. (2008) "Overview of public transport policy developments in South Africa", *Research in Transport Economics* 22, 98–108.

Chapter 8

Reflections on the usefulness of accessibility as a lens through which to consider the evaluation of transportation and land use policies and projects

Fred Salvucci

8.1 Introduction

This chapter discusses the policy and institutional context, particularly in the United States, for developing accessibility concepts as a lens through which to evaluate transportation and land use. It argues that change in evaluation technique alone will not be adequate to rein back a century of auto-dominated transportation and land use planning, and that current economy, equity, and environmental crises all require both institutional changes and major and sustained investment, particularly in transit infrastructure and services over the next several decades in order to achieve improved economic, equity, and environmental outcomes ("triple bottom line sustainability"). It proposes that accessibility-based analysis, as described in previous chapters, is needed to choose the most convincing approaches for this policy and institutional change and investment program, and that a focus particularly on employment accessibility in key "pioneer" cities, metropolitan areas, states, and at the national level, may be most effective to support decision-making with appropriate evaluation techniques in order to stay on course. When we consider the problem of providing increased housing and jobs for an expected 50 per cent increase in the driving-age population by 2050, while reducing greenhouse gas production from transportation to 25 per cent of current levels, the location of those jobs and housing will dramatically affect the ability to support growth with minimal congestion and pollution, and accessibility-based analysis should help to plan the transportation and land use strategies to succeed. Self-selection dynamics, whereby individuals and firms choose where to locate, can help produce improved outcomes. Moreover, the dynamics of how shifting significant purchasing power from the auto to other goods and services, enabled by high-quality public transport, can help stimulate the job growth needed for the increased population requires special consideration. While the focus is on the US institutional context, it suggests that a similar approach of adopting accessibility-based analysis, in combination with a new policy and institutional structure, and very significant and sustained investment, will likely be appropriate to support achieving triple bottom line sustainable transportation and land use in Europe and the rapidly-developing countries in Asia, Latin America and Africa as well.

8.2 Outline

"If you don't measure, you can't manage", but what if we measure the wrong things, or in the wrong way? Then our measurements and evaluations could actually lead us in the wrong direction. Prior chapters have suggested that mobility metrics may be leading us in the wrong direction, and that focusing upon accessibility as a primary objective of transportation and policy has important potential to make progress on the primary emerging problems of transportation and land use in metropolitan areas, and have reviewed a variety of methodologies to define accessibility. This chapter attempts to locate the discussion of accessibility in the policy and institutional context, particularly in the United States. Economic stagnation, inequitable outcomes, and environmental degradation at the metropolitan, national, and global scale are strongly influenced by dominant patterns of transportation and land use, which have emerged over the past century of ever rising primacy of the automobile and auto-related land use. It will take significant public transportation investment and operation and maintenance funding to change course in a manner that is conducive to increased economic opportunity, equitable access, and sustainable environmental quality. To help identify how to change the evaluation and implementation process to provide stronger emphasis on accessibility in the future, it argues that focusing particularly on employment accessibility, along with complementary changes in modeling and planning practice, cost–benefit analysis, and project selection are useful, but must be accompanied by changes in funding mechanisms and institutional structure, with substantial increased levels of reliable funding, especially for public transit, to successfully move our metropolitan and transportation systems towards improved sustainability from an economic-equity-environmental perspective. Moreover, these institutional policy concerns must be considered when discussing how to shift the focus to accessibility, and employment accessibility should be prioritized. The chapter goes on to use the following outline:

8.4   What problems are emerging from the current policies of primary reliance upon the auto to provide accessibility, and how can we develop a better approach?

8.5   How have we reached this point?

8.6   Where do our current methodologies of cost–benefit analysis and transportation demand modeling come from?

8.7   What are some key flaws, in current cost–benefit analysis practice and in the transportation and land use methodological approaches, which should be remediated in a revised approach?

8.8   How has institutional structure affected the current situation and the potential for change?

8.9   Reflections on the usefulness of accessibility as a lens through which to consider the evaluation of transportation and land use policies and projects

8.10 How should accessibility be measured?

8.11 How does government fiscal austerity affect these issues?

8.3 Synthesis and recommendations

Methodologies to conceptualize and analyse land use and transportation initiatives through the lens of accessibility appear to have the potential for a robust understanding of the performance of our metropolitan transportation and land use systems and developing insights into how to improve them. As described in previous chapters, accessibility metrics can be developed for different activities, and can provide improved insight into very important equity issues and the pressures that drive system dynamics affecting economic performance, and equity and environmental outcomes. Conflict among various constituencies can be clarified (not eliminated) through better understanding. But this improved understanding must be accompanied by sustained public investments, and institutional change, to accommodate population and job growth, and simultaneously reduce transportation greenhouse gas emissions, for progress to be made towards triple bottom line sustainability.

A priority activity for further work is to develop the analysis and arguments that will help to build the political will for institutional change, and sustained investments to lead to triple bottom line sustainability. Special focus on access to employment opportunities for individuals, and access to employees for businesses, both critical for economic growth to occur, is likely to have the best potential to develop the sustained political will which will be necessary to make progress.

8.4 What problems are emerging from the current policies of primary reliance upon the auto to provide accessibility, and how can we develop a better approach?

Greater concentration of population in metropolitan areas has been a continual characteristic of US economic growth. Accessibility of the entire population to opportunity has been a driving factor in improved well-being, but accessibility primarily by automobile is becoming self-limiting. Periodic and worsening economic, environmental, and equity crises, in both metropolitan areas and globally, appear to be related to the excessive reliance on the automobile to provide accessibility. Congestion effects, where use exceeds reasonable capacity, are found in many areas. The visible traffic gridlock in which individual pursuit of accessibility leads to congestion and loss of system capacity and reduced accessibility for all, is only the most tangible of these. Air and water pollution, energy shortfalls, financial and spatial constraints, and climate change are all exacerbated by automotive pressure to use scarce resources beyond limits of capacity. The alarming reversal in recent years of the previous growth of well-being of the American middle-class since World War II is a wake up call that the current trajectory is indeed a "Tragedy of the Commons."[1]

Up until now, gasoline consumption and greenhouse gas production has continued to rise long after it has become clear that both were already excessive, at the time of the 1997 Kyoto meetings. Today there is a general consensus among climate change experts[2] that the United States has an ethical obligation to lower its greenhouse gas emission from transportation by at least 75 per cent by the year 2050, even with an expected 50 per cent increase in driving-age population. But up to this point, improvements in vehicle technology have been overwhelmed by growth in population, growth in the number of vehicles per capita, and growth in vehicle miles traveled per vehicle. For greenhouse gas generation to shrink with population growth, vehicles per capita and VMT per vehicle must go down substantially, threatening accessibility, economic growth, and living standards. For greenhouse gases to fall while the economy grows, and incomes rise throughout the population, dramatic improvements in accessibility through proximity and public transportation appear necessary, in addition to substantial improvements in vehicle fuel efficiency.[3]

If there is no policy plan other than incremental growth, the degeneration of the environment, economy, and equity will continue. Housing for the 50 per cent increase in the driving-age population will occur through incremental sprawl, congestion will increase, accessibility will diminish, and employment growth will be adversely affected. What employment growth occurs will be through incremental sprawl and the least accessible housing will be occupied by the least affluent people; a lose–lose–lose option.

To achieve a good outcome in the face of a significant increase in driving-age population, with reduced vehicles per capita and reduced VMT per vehicle, but increased accessibility and economic growth and improved equity will require a robust new policy and plan for where the growth in population and jobs should occur, and for significantly improved public transportation to support growth without gridlock.

Improving accessibility with less reliance on the automobile seems both compatible with, and conducive to economic growth not just in newly developing countries and in unique cities such as Hong Kong, Singapore, or Shanghai, but in highly successful developed world cities such as London and Zurich, and hotspots such as Kendall Square in Cambridge, and perhaps more broadly in the centers of metropolitan areas that form the backbone of the American economy. Higher density appears to support increased economic productivity, but densification of land use beyond modest levels requires greater use of public transportation and walking, and less reliance on the auto. With greater use of public transportation, accessibility for people can support much higher density than the limits of accessibility for automobiles.

Higher density for all is not popular. Yet paradoxically, since it is feasible through public transportation to support higher densities in metropolitan areas, this allows other areas to retain lower densities and more open spaces (potentially a win–win scenario). The physical density limits of primary reliance on the automobile require growth to occur through sprawl, but shifting to higher use of public transit can permit higher density in some places, and lower densities in others, allowing people and businesses and institutions more choice to self select among locations with characteristics they prefer. Greater availability of public transportation allows larger numbers of people to choose to opt out of automobile congestion and the cost of auto ownership. This physical model of facilitating greater choice in land use density through greater levels of public transportation and land use density can simultaneously relieve the pressure of excessive auto use on environmental resources, reduce pressure on open space and clean air within the metropolitan area, and lead to reduced greenhouse gases at the global level. If we want larger numbers of people to enjoy higher quality of life through economic growth, while avoiding the environmental and spatial limits of automobile growth, substantial increases in public transportation capacity, quality, and use are essential to accommodate economic growth. As we consider the likely 50 per cent increase in driving-age population by 2050, if those households live and work in transit accessible areas, it will be much more feasible to achieve sustainable outcomes, within moderate levels of congestion and pollution. Moreover if more and more people can achieve adequate accessibility through expanded public transportation, they can divert considerable expenditures associated with ownership of multiple autos per household toward purchases of other goods and services, improving both their own well-being, and the local economy. Increased spending on expanded public transportation itself generates higher regional income, since most metropolitan areas do not produce petroleum or automobiles, but operating public transportation requires significant local labor, contributing to the local economy.

8.5 How have we reached this point?

The preconditions that ensured the automobile system would become the primary means of metropolitan accessibility in the United States began over 150 years ago, even before there were automobiles. American cities were growing rapidly as the nation industrialized, and millions of rural workers from the United States and Europe moved to US cities, seeking opportunities for themselves and their families, and providing the labor to support economic growth. Accessibility to employment was by walking from nearby housing, which became incredibly crowded as employment grew, with major community stress on water supply and sanitation, health, and education as well. Vehicular transportation was primarily for goods movement, pulled by horses and on increasingly congested streets; a major source of air pollution and disease was from the excrement of animals pulverized by the heavy traffic. The rural immigrants generally had not previously lived in large cities, and many were illiterate or didn't speak English, and were of different religions. There were two primary ways cities responded to these challenges: one was a very high level of investment in infrastructure to provide increased capacity for sewer, water, and transportation systems. The other was suburbanization. As new commuter rail and streetcar services made it possible to live further from workplaces where new housing could be built, native-born and more affluent workers could move away from the problems of the old city into newer and more spacious housing, often with higher levels of open space and city services. Electrification improved the reliability and speed of the streetcars and made the older employment centers acceptably accessible from the new suburbs, while access to open space, more spacious housing, better schools and more compatible neighbors were attractive. (See Sam Bass Warner's "Streetcar Suburbs").[4] This system worked to improve and expand the city. While suburbanization introduced some tension in the equity of access to the better schools, parks and city services of the suburbs, the steady improvement of conditions in the city center, resulting partly from the reduced crowding facilitated by the suburban expansion, partly from reform movements to improve education and public services throughout the city, and partly because of the voting power of the urban workers, made the outcome one of steady improvement throughout much of the urbanized area, albeit without full equality.

As technology and production improvements began to make the automobile a viable alternative to public transportation for commuting, the accessibility fault line between the city and streetcar suburb was compounded. For those who could afford a car, the choices of housing and job locations increased, the disutility of travel in your own car became significantly lower than that of riding the often-crowded public transportation, and the range of choices of access to amenities expanded. As autos used the same streets as the streetcars, the rising numbers of automobiles increased congestion, the quality of public transportation service went down, and the cost of providing the service went up, creating a "Tragedy of the Commons" on the street.

But there was an explicit philosophical pattern break that accompanied this change. Perhaps best summarized in the quote attributed to Henry Ford, "We will solve the problems of the cities by leaving them behind." Up to that point (approximately 1920) the American city had been the engine for the innovation that led the US to become a world leader in production. "Leaving the cities behind" seems astoundingly rash for the nation, even if it might be seen as good for a producer of automobiles. But the 1920s saw the introduction of Euclidian zoning throughout much of the US, with setbacks and minimum off-street parking requirements to enhance accessibility by the automobile, requiring land use densities too low to serve effectively with public transportation. In addition, the auto traffic generation of the increasingly auto-oriented housing often exceeded the roadway capacity on the main streets. Automobiles circulated on public streets, usually provided by cities with some financial support from streetcar companies, and hampered the movement of streetcars. But the petroleum and automobile interests succeeded in ensuring states "dedicate" gasoline taxes to road construction and maintenance. These dedication provisions were written into many state constitutions, establishing a "user pays" mythology that ignores any external support given to the automobile system (such as the use of city streets) and any external adverse effects of the use of the roadway on other road users or of the burning of fuel on public health. The use of lead as an anti-knock agent for high compression engines was propagated and defended by a corporate strategy to deny the adverse impact of lead on children's brains and public health for over 50 years. Increasing vehicle speed limits eroded safety, especially for pedestrians, and was worsened by the building of new highways to more auto-oriented standards.

The auto was winning larger and larger mode share in competition with public transportation. Despite that, some auto and petroleum interests pursued destructive competition strategies to buy out streetcar lines, dismantling the systems and converting remaining lines to bus service, and increasing the auto capacity of the streets, just to administer the *coup de grace* to destroy the extensive public transportation systems that once served many United States cities. Intellectuals such as Le Corbusier and Frank Lloyd Wright joined in the advocacy and celebration of the automobile and dismantling of traditional city fabric. During the Great Depression, Roosevelt's Work's Progress Administration (WPA) stimulus funds went into road expenditures to create jobs, since it seemed reasonable for public Federal funds to support public roads, but the transit systems were then mostly privately owned, publicly regulated monopolies and not seen as appropriate to receive Federal funds. After World War II, public funding for roadways increased, while bankrupt and near bankrupt private railroads and public transportation systems dismantled infrastructure to avoid maintenance costs, and sold off key facilities for their real estate value.

In 1956 President Eisenhower secured congressional approval for the Interstate Highway Program, a concept in discussion since at least the 1930s, with a dedicated funding stream primarily from gasoline taxes to provide a 90 per cent Federal subsidy to build a new and substantially expanded highway system. The implementation strategy was to use the existing State Highway Department's institutional structure to implement the new highway network. Setting aside the question of whether one agrees with the policy of placing such priority on the construction of the interstate network, the implementation strategy was extremely effective. The significant amount of money available, and modest (10 per cent) matching state share made the interstate program very attractive and very stable over the decades, and strongly resistant to policy change notwithstanding very significant statutory change which occurred over the next several decades:

- In 1962, statutory requirements for transportation planning were introduced.
- In 1964, the Urban Mass Transit Administration was established, providing for the first time Federal funding to some transit projects.
- In 1964 title VI civil rights statutes were enacted.
- In 1966 Federal Highway Administration was placed under the Secretary of Transportation in a unified Department of Transportation. This placed public transportation, and transportation funding, under the same cabinet secretary, with some expectation of creating a multimodal attitude.
- Also in 1966, in the same statute, Section 4(f) provided very strong parkland protection from acquisition or damage by roadway and other transportation purposes.
- In 1970 the National Environmental Policy Act was passed, requiring that for projects using Federal funding, alternatives had to be developed and considered, information had to be available to the public, for public hearings and comment. Any adverse environmental impacts were required to be disclosed, and were expected, but not required, to be "mitigated".
- Also in 1970 the Clean Air Act was passed, regulating air pollution, much of which was generated by the automobile.
- In 1973, "Interstate Transfer" provisions were introduced, to allow states that did not wish to complete Interstate Highway segments to cancel them and receive equal amounts of funding for transit projects. In addition, states were given the flexibility to use other highway funds for transit, and for the first time significant Federal funding was provided for transit operation.

- In 1983, the gasoline tax was increased by 5¢, 4¢ for highway and 1¢ for transit, the product of a multi-modal coalition forged by the Secretary of Transportation.
- In 1990 revisions to the Clean Air Act required that transportation plans conform to clean air plans and that states which violated their clean air plans were to be subjected to loss of 10 per cent of their Federal highway funds.
- In 1990 the Americans with Disabilities Act (ADA) required public facilities, including buses and transit systems, to be accessible to people with physical constraints, and required door-to-door service for disabled and elderly people with wheelchair-accessible vehicles.
- In 1991 the Intermodal Surface Transportation Efficiency Act (ISTEA) legislation strengthened metropolitan land use and multimodal trans- portation planning, established more transparency, and emphasis was placed on increasing focus on maintenance and roadway congestion with the requirements that states prepare plans for both maintenance management and congestion management. Provisions to allow states to use "highway" funds for transit were strengthened.

These statutory reforms were brought about through active citizen organi- zations, often in coalitions with intellectuals and academics, and mayors and governors, with strong resistance from the "highway lobby". It has, unfortunately, been the case that even after successful efforts to secure legislative change, citizen lawsuits which are difficult for citizens to initiate and fund have been required to force states to comply with most of the post-1956 statutes. Because the agencies that control the funding and the implementation procedures continued to be the Federal Highway Administration and State highway departments, the actual outcome of the statutory reforms was substantially undercut. By continuing to interpret the 1956 statute as defining their core mission, and subsuming the subsequent legislation within that mission, the highway agencies have been largely able to encapsulate the later statutory requirements within opaque procedures, with the Federal Highway Administration as the ultimate decision-maker.

8.6 Where do our current methodologies of cost–benefit analysis and transportation demand modeling come from?

The requirements for transportation planning were enacted after the 1956 law establishing the policy and primary mission of the Federal Highway Administration (FHWA), and the 90 per cent Federal funding that made the prioritization and construction of new interstate highways so attractive. Implementation of the new planning requirements tended to pursue two tracks: first, procedural requirements, to allow more transparency, such as requiring two public hearings, one at the conceptual and one at the detailed design of highway project phase, and secondly, the establishment of a "continuous cooperative coordinated" process in collaboration with municipalities and other layers of government with land use and sewer and water responsibilities, with the state highway departments (through which all Federal highway funds flow), primarily in charge of the process. Transportation demand modeling was developed largely to determine the size of traffic flow that should be anticipated on the new facilities to help design them, so path choice models, based upon travel time and cost were developed as methods that met the planning needs as perceived by the Federal Highway Administration. Significant development of procedure, methodology, and substantial data collection followed.

When in 1966 the unified Department of Transport (DOT) was formed it seemed to make sense that the available methods and processes developed for the dominant highway mode would be applied to the presumably multi-modal DOT. When the 1970 National Environmental Policy Act (NEPA) required environmental impact statements for all major highway and transit investments, the same highway related methodologies became the basis for performance prediction of major investments. While cost–benefit studies were not required for highway projects, planning studies often included them, not to compare projects to each other and choose the best options, but to demonstrate that the benefits exceeded costs. In the Federal transit program, which had to consider large capital grant proposals from many cities, far in excess of the available funding, cost-effectiveness measures based on travel time savings came to be used to evaluate and rank transit projects from very different cities and urban contexts.

8.7 What are some key flaws, in current cost–benefit analysis practice and in the transportation and land use methodological approaches, which should be remediated in a revised approach?

1   Benefit–cost analysis is not a significant factor in choosing highway projects in the programming process. If used at all, it is used to build political support by demonstrating that present value of benefits exceeds costs.

2   The social discount rate used to determine the present net value of costs and benefits is key. Philosophically it expresses the value we place on the next generation's well-being vis-à-vis our own. A high discount rate will bias choices towards quick to implement, quick pay-off investments, even if growing congestion makes investments useless over the long-term, while large investments in long-term, long implementation projects, with growing long-term benefits over long periods of time, will seem unattractive. A low discount rate effectively does the opposite, and would place higher value on long-range projects even if

construction periods are long, and benefits long-term. Since there is unlikely to be consensus about the appropriate discount rate, doing a sensitivity analysis using both a high and a low rate for comparison, could at least make this issue visible and conscious rather than hidden, but this is not normal practice.

3   Inherently short-term travel time savings methods appropriate to determine path choice are used inappropriately in a long-range context. But values are likely to change among different metropolitan areas, among sub-areas within metropolitan areas, and over time, making evaluation with assumed stable and equal values less appropriate. Again using sensitivity analysis testing, considering how the appropriate choice may change if values vary or change could help to make this issue visible and explicit, but is not usually done.

4   History and social networks affect land use distribution and trip choices, but they are not usually dealt with except through obscure "K" factors in the models, making the issue non-visible, and unintelligible.

5   Transportation demand models currently in use often have difficulty dealing with capacity constraints on key links and parking availability. It is common practice to allow volume to exceed capacity, and use this information to make the case that capacity should be expanded to avoid congestion, which serves the interests of the project proponents. But this can make planning a tautology, promoting sprawl to "avoid congestion". However, more sophisticated models now available can allow us to embrace the obvious fact that use cannot exceed capacity, and can help us understand how behavior may change in response to constraint. As an alternative to sprawl, densification of downtowns, greater use of transit and walking, increased mixed land use requiring maximum parking limits rather than minimum parking requirements, are strategies that may result in resolving the predicted overuse. Constraining auto-generating development in order not to exceed infrastructure capacity, through urban growth ordinances or other constraints such as constraints on auto ownership to not exceed roadway capacity, are more aggressive strategies being used in some rapidly-growing Asian cities such as Singapore and Shanghai.

6   The "tip of the iceberg" flaw leads to comparisons of highway and transit investments based on only the public investment involved, ignoring that individuals must spend about ten dollars on fuel and auto ownership costs for every one dollar spent by the government on highways, while transit investments by the public include the cost of the vehicles and the operating costs as part of the public costs. But this flaw obscures the major savings that accrue to the commuter, who avoids auto expenditure by using transit as a primary mode for access to employment, and the benefits to the local economy of the increased disposable income of those commuters.

8.8 How has institutional structure affected the current situation and the potential for change?

The decades-old practice of using the State Highway Department as the designated recipient of Federal highway funding, and the huge amounts of money involved, particularly in the Interstate program, have helped to make the highway agencies "culturally" dominant players.

8.8.1 Strength through political power

By 1956, the state Highway Departments had already developed significant political power. In some States, highway commissioners and chief engineers (such as Moses in New York, and Callahan of Massachusetts) remained in office much longer, and were often more powerful than governors, as they controlled large amounts of spending on the design and construction of highways, with linkages to very influential real estate interests, contractors, and construction worker unions, as well as legislators and Congressional representatives. The State highway departments shared a "highway culture" with the Federal Highway Administration.

8.8.2 Exploiting Federal funding

In the US, many types of roadway investment are eligible for 80 per cent Federal funding, with highway agencies perceiving themselves as servicing the construction community and local governments by maximizing the dollar volume of construction. Faced with a constrained amount of local funding and staff, the agencies prioritize their limited funding to projects that can benefit from 80 per cent Federal funding, often to the detriment of proper maintenance. This problem is exacerbated by the ability to use Federal "capital" funding to rebuild facilities and vehicles that have not been properly maintained, which causes a perverse incentive to under-maintain, and then use Federal funds for major rebuilding, justified by the reasonable-sounding slogan, "Fix it First". The much longer process time for complex projects (which require more complicated environmental evaluation), and bridge replacements (which require more engineering attention), and faster process time for simpler, less complex (quite possibly also less important) projects means that there is a systemic bias in the portfolio of projects based not on any prioritization by evaluation, but on the "tyranny of small decisions." The newly-passed transportation bill worsens this problem by exempting many rebuild projects from environmental process requirements.

In considering the potential benefit of introducing accessibility as a significant factor in project development and evaluation in the US, it is essential to be mindful of the current institutional context, and modify systemic flaws or problems in current practice. As discussed above, the modal silo institutional structure, which is a legacy of the 1950s interstate era, has been strongly resistant to policy change, notwithstanding fundamental statutory changes over five decades, and growing recognition of the need to strengthen focus on maintenance of existing facilities and dealing with congestion as a serious and growing problem. The "tyranny of the pipeline", an institutional predisposition in highway agencies to conceptualize planning as a first-in, first-out process with a prioritization of maintaining a steady flow of construction projects, has tended to overwhelm several significant efforts to advance other priorities, or prioritize investments based on evaluation. This dominant institutional imperative (the pipeline) results in perverse outcomes. Staffing and expertise problems within public agencies exacerbate this tendency.

The dominance of highway "cultural" values on the planning and design process is strengthened by the practice within the implementation of the National Environmental Policy Act of defining the "purpose and need" of a project narrowly, and prior to environmental and socioeconomic analysis. This practice makes it likely that alternatives considered are substantially constrained to those which are consistent with the core highway mission of the agency. In the case of transit proposals, the purpose and needs practice similarly constrains the options considered prior to analysis.

The institutional structure of transit organization at both the metropolitan and national levels also constrains the implementation of policy based on expanding accessibility. At the metropolitan level, transit agencies have often evolved from the publicly-regulated private-monopoly electric street railways of a century ago into the public monopolies of today, but without the regulatory oversight monopoly power usually requires. As metropolitan areas have grown over time, overwhelmingly through substantial growth in suburban housing and jobs at low density that are difficult to efficiently serve with public transportation, service has often remained concentrated in the traditional central areas even though the service districts (and the taxes to support public transportation) are often metropolitan. This "lumpiness" problem creates tension among communities within the taxation district. Since the metropolitan areas with transit service generally encompass only part of the state, state political support of transit is weak in comparison to state support of highways, which are more ubiquitous. If there was recognition that accessibility problems of key constituencies such as suburban, elderly, and teens are caused by auto-centric land use, and if these accessibility problems are mitigated by expansion of suburban local distribution services, lumpiness would be reduced, and the political will to fund transit might expand. Of course, the cost of the transit deficit would increase if accessibility to currently marginalized groups is addressed, and the share of the national funding received by the traditional transit providers would decrease, but the national constituency for transit would be strengthened, and the likelihood of long-run success in achieving triple bottom line sustainability would improve.

Because the dominant Federal role in US transportation is the relationship between the Federal Highway Administration and the State highway agency, the evolution to multimodal policy has been constrained by a lack of symmetry between the relatively ubiquitous roadway services, and the relatively lumpy transit service. While FHWA takes a passive attitude regarding the State responsibility to fund maintenance, the Federal Transit Administration refuses to process applications for capital funding unless the proponent agency can demonstrate the financial capacity to fund operations and maintenance for decades. Again, the asymmetry of treatment biases expenditure towards highways, rather than transit.

Moreover, as much Federal support for transit has been justified by the need to provide accessibility services to disabled and aging populations, which are not traditional core services of public transportation organizations, tensions have built up within many public transportation organizations who have not yet evolved to see themselves as accessibility providers, and continue to focus on delivery of traditional bus and rail services to relatively small, high-density areas within the metropolitan areas. In addition, the view that the dominant role of the Federal government is to provide capital, makes the FTA "New Starts" funding program a particular focus of Federal transit policy. This has embraced a cost–benefit evaluation approach to a much greater degree than the Federal Highway program, but this has been a very mixed blessing for many reasons:

1   The FTA New Starts process is not used to evaluate alternative transit investments within metropolitan areas. In fact, FTA practice actively discourages consideration of more than one New Start proposal per metropolitan area at any given time.
2   There is no significant comparison of transit and highway investments.
3   FTA is extremely resistant to using Federal funds to cover cost increases due to changed conditions after a grant is awarded, while FHWA routinely provides Federal funding for cost overruns.
4   FTA has strict rules requiring demonstration of financial capacity to maintain; FHWA does not.
5   Notwithstanding the very time-consuming New Starts process, there is not significant encouragement for project proponents to integrate land use planning with transportation by changing zoning to permit increased density or reduced parking to foster transit-oriented development.
6   Transit projects are subject to a greater level of time-consuming cost-effectiveness scrutiny, and typically are required to provide higher levels of local matching funds (50 per cent), while highway projects have no cost-effectiveness requirement and usually require only a 20 per cent local match. The fact that there are many transit initiatives in the face of these disincentives, even in metropolitan areas not considered to be transit-oriented, is indicative of significant latent support for transit.

7   Pressure for geographical distribution of projects is embedded in government institutions. Election to State legislative bodies and the Congress is by district, which produces extremely strong pressure to distribute projects, whatever the technical evaluation process might indicate. The recent tendency for ballot initiatives to support transportation funding produces even stronger pressure for geographic distribution of capital expenditures, while tending to ignore adequate funding of operation and maintenance costs. The FTA New Starts process does evaluate competing projects among different metropolitan areas, but in any event, Congress has to approve the result, causing a strong pressure for geographic distribution of investments regardless of cost-effectiveness.

8   Pressure from Congress and project proponents has led to some modifications of procedure, but substantial criticism persists, particularly because stimulation of economic development, which is often the primary motivation of transit proponents, is not believed to be fairly weighted. Current Secretary Lahood has frequently talked of the need to introduce "livability" into the process, but FTA procedures have not yet significantly changed.

9   The Metropolitan Planning Organizations (MPOs), which are supposed to oversee the multimodal planning process, typically have policy boards composed of members selected from municipal and county officials with direct highway responsibility, and who view their responsibility as advocating for the roadway projects in their jurisdiction. The staff of the MPO often relies on the modal silo organization for funding, and is politically weak in comparison to the modal agency. As a consequence, the MPO, a reform intended to remedy problems of silo mentality within project funding choices, is inhibited by its own institutional structure. Almost certainly project choices have become more transparent, but are still strongly influenced by decisions of the State highway agency as to which projects will be prioritized to get through the environmental process to become "shovel ready", and by the local roadway responsibilities of many MPO members.

A further conceptual constraint of the US situation is the sheer size of the existing network, and the very large number of new projects at any given time. Both these factors reinforce the desirability of shifting to an accessibility basis of evaluation.

First, the size of the existing network means that even very large individual projects have only minimal impact on total system performance. This factor, in combination with the difficulty of dealing with congestion phenomena, means that travel time savings benefit prediction creates a false sense of precision. In systems with or approaching congestion, we don't really know if travel time savings predictions for a specific project will be

offset by causing increased congestion elsewhere, beyond the project boundaries, or whether any travel time savings actually achieved will be durable
in the face of rising congestion. Because of the widespread practice of allowing volume to exceed capacity of transportation links and parking supply, it
is often unclear if projected travel time savings are accurate, or exist at all,
even within the project boundaries.

Second, because of the large number of new projects under consideration
at any given time, it is logistically difficult to develop consistent evaluation.
Large numbers of model runs, and the kind of scenario planning and sensitivity analysis desirable to understand the reliability of projections, are
complicated. Nor is it realistic to expect that the institutions will really care
about the evaluation-based prioritization. Long analysis times make the
current metropolitan level transportation investment prioritization process
strongly conditional to a first-in, first-out linear process that avoids prioritization among projects, and makes the process susceptible to systematically
prioritizing simpler rather than more complex projects.

The typical "silo" highway agency has a dominant culture of processing
and engineering enough construction projects each year to satisfy the
construction industry. Such an agency cannot be expected to care if a different use of the same funds for a transit project (which would employ
different kinds of contractors) might be projected to produce larger benefits. If, after investing a decade in producing conceptual plans,
Environmental Impact Studies, and detailed engineering, new information
indicates that a substitute project that is not ready to go might be substantially better, it must be expected that the agency will view this as a severe
threat. Given the imprecision in the practical use of the modeling tools
available, there will be enormous pressure to "reverse engineer" the evaluation process to justify those projects that the agency has ready to go.
Recognizing this institutional context, it is important to introduce evaluation not of individual projects, but of scenarios, and programming of
projects.

Given this institutional context, the question is, would a shift in emphasis from travel time savings to accessibility for evaluation actually change
outcomes, or just modify the technique of reverse engineering?

In short, assuming that it is possible to develop evaluation techniques
based upon accessibility methods, will it matter, if the role of evaluation for
deciding among projects is not significant anyway? The purpose of raising
this concern is not to discourage the development of better techniques, but
to stress the importance of understanding the institutional decision-making
context, and the need to include considerations of process and policy when
deciding how to strengthen the improvement in accessibility as an outcome
of transportation investment programs.

8.9 Reflections on the usefulness of accessibility as a lens through which to consider the evaluation of transportation and land use policies and projects

Previous chapters have made the case that focusing on accessibility as a principal objective of transportation and policy has the potential to make progress on the primary emerging problems of transportation and land use in metropolitan areas. The belief that accessibility is a superior basis of evaluation of transportation benefit has been encouraged by recent experience in London, where economic research at Imperial College by Dan Graham developed a methodology to measure "agglomeration benefits" related to accessibility, associated with the £15 billion investment in the rail tunnel connecting West to East London (Crossrail).[5] Graham's detailed economic analysis of the improvements in economic efficiency of certain industries, particularly financial services, demonstrated substantial "external benefit", additional to those identified in the traditional cost–benefit analysis based upon user time savings. This was an important factor in convincing the UK government to proceed with the mega-project, which had been under discussion for a half-century. But, even more significant for general evaluation of transportation policy, it also demonstrated a flaw in the previous belief that travel time savings can measure the entire benefit of transportation investment, and demonstrates the possibility that "wider economic benefits" exist and are associated with some other transportation projects.

Analysis and evaluation of transportation investment and operations have long relied on travel time savings as a primary metric. Substantial intellectual and financial resources have been invested in this approach, with sophisticated modeling and evaluation techniques and massive collection of data on transportation and land use characteristics now available. It is desirable to develop new methodologies and evaluation techniques that can build upon these resources, but without thereby being captured within the old paradigms. Current practice is reasonably useful in predicting short-term behavior. It is much less useful for understanding the longer-term system dynamics of change, and substantially flawed as the basis for evaluation of outcomes. Because these current approaches were developed to support the decision making of transportation institutions (almost always highway focused), which viewed the land use context as a given, they are not well-suited to understand, predict, or influence the interaction with other transportation modes and land use and activity distribution. Because they are largely rooted in the presumption that the distribution of income is either acceptable or "someone else's" job, they tend to ignore equity issues. Except for identification of direct adverse impact such as destruction of housing for infrastructure, or air and noise pollution impacts at local and metropolitan levels, they are not developed to identify and evaluate environmental outcomes (especially congestion phenomena, when the volume of traffic approaches capacity of roadways, parking supply, and land), nor excessive levels of pollution. It is believed that by shifting the focus from travel time to accessibility, better tools can be developed that will help to integrate transportation and land use, and economic, equity, and environmental concerns.

But particularly in the US, the current UK approach to considering agglomeration benefits, while interesting, is of limited value because the very sophisticated approach used by Graham, which analyses different degrees of agglomeration benefit among different industries, relies on a level of finer specific economic information not readily available in the US.

It is tempting to simply add a factor for wider economic benefits to traditional user cost saving based cost–benefit analysis, in order to avoid the intensive and complex estimation of agglomeration benefits for individual projects used by Graham. This might prove helpful in increasing the political will to invest in infrastructure, but falls very short of the opportunity to reconsider the evaluation process through the lens of accessibility, since simply adding a uniform factor for wider economic benefits will not affect the relative priority among alternative investments. More fundamentally, Graham's analysis shows differing agglomeration benefits associated with different types of economic activity, so a simple proportional increase in benefits is inconsistent with his research.

In order to develop a more broadly applicable theory of wider economic benefits, it is important to consider how the questions of land use density intensification relate to wider economic benefits and transportation. Research by Jeff Zupan of RPA identified density ceilings above which the reliance on auto mobility breaks down unless public transportation allows more density to be supported. If density has constant proportional value, using transit to increase potential land use density can increase economic activity on that land. If high density causes more than a proportional value increase, because of wider economic benefits, the argument for density becomes more widely shared. Density intensification requires increased transit accessibility and reduced parking, if congestion is to be avoided. But existing land use patterns of modest density and high-value tend to develop strong resistance to further densification, and advocates often use zoning codes and citizen pressure to resist densification, inhibiting the achievement of the highest theoretical value. It is usually more feasible to find opportunities for significantly higher density in degraded areas such as abandoned industrial sites or rail yards (for example the London Docklands). If provided with improved accessibility, these can be redeveloped at much higher density more readily then already healthy economic zones. Alternatively, replacement of parking with active buildings can dramatically increase value and transit ridership in existing areas of modest density with adequate transit. As more active square footage becomes available, the growth pattern may be compounded as (with transit accessibility) more people per square foot can work in those same buildings. But this virtuous cycle requires a public transportation system able to respond to increased ridership demand with increased frequency and capacity. If the public transportation system is unwilling or financially unable to provide improved service, passenger growth will result in crowding and degraded service.

The breakthrough of Graham's research, in identifying the existence of agglomeration benefits in addition to the time saving benefits of traditional cost–benefit analysis may be just the beginning of identification of other "wider economic benefits" that should be researched. Several areas of interesting speculation come to mind. For example:

- The potential for large projects to restructure economic geography and urban design may be significant. The cost of redeveloping urban real estate in healthy cities, to achieve greater density, is high. A developer needs to acquire expensive buildings; relocate existing viable business tenants; and forego rents for the duration of redevelopment; spend money to demolish good buildings; secure zoning permission for higher density; often in the face of significant opposition from historic or neighborhood advocates; build the new buildings at today's high construction cost; and attract new tenants or bring back old ones, all in the ever volatile real estate market. If, instead, new accessibility is provided to obsolete industrial areas, or areas of marginal use such as remote parking, equipment storage, and obsolete rail yards, often available near traditional downtowns, then it may be possible to rehabilitate solid old buildings, or build new space on essentially vacant land, with less up-front cost, less risk of community opposition, and avoid many of the extra-high costs of redeveloping downtown. Typical FTA procedures will not allow the potential benefits of such redevelopment, and the associated ridership to be included in cost-effectiveness evaluation, even though the potential benefits are huge. (Think, for example, of the Jubilee Line Extension and Canary Wharf in London.)
- It is likely that using excessively high social discount rates, to develop net present value, not only under-estimates the true value of future benefits with long lead times, but actually changes the relative predicted value of alternate investments, favoring smaller initiatives with short-term benefits over large projects with long lead times, and mid- and long-term benefits.
- It is likely that construction costs using local labor may generate jobs for otherwise unemployed workers generating net revenue to taxing authorities, savings in unemployment and welfare costs, creating new tax revenue and social benefits, is not normally factored in.
- Increased transit-oriented development could result in reduced auto ownership and use, shifting purchasing power to more locally-produced products.

If benefit calculations are to be modified to focus on accessibility benefits, it may be timely to correct the benefits assessment methodology to capture these other wider economic benefits at the same time.

8.10 How should accessibility be measured?

If you don't measure, you can't manage, but what if we measure the wrong thing, or in the wrong way? Then our measurements and evaluation could actually lead us in the wrong direction. If the actual process of setting policy and choosing strategies and projects doesn't actually use evaluation techniques to make decisions, but to justify decisions already made through other "political" decision making, improving our measurement and evaluation tools will not matter. But if we hope to shift the course of transportation towards a triple bottom line, sustainable approach, we will need to build the political will for a massive, sustained effort over decades, a challenge at least equal to that of the Interstate system, so we will need to develop better tools to make the case for such an effort, and we will need to demonstrate that we have the tools to stay on course in a transparent process. The pursuit of accessibility measures should be in part based on the motivation to be able to justify major investments on something more convincing than saving millions of motorists a few minutes each and summing it up. The travel time savings-based methodologies that convincingly explain short-term path choice-type behavior fall far short as a justification for major expenditures. The travel time savings-based approach to evaluation has survived largely because it has not been visible to the public, but if we are to propose convincingly major sustained investment, we need something much more credible. Substantial effort has gone into developing accessibility measures, discussed in prior chapters, which provide a more convincing rationale, and a superior guide for decision-making. These are generally based on the number of opportunities for a desired activity, such as employment, that can be fit to data. It is very important that these research activities continue to develop tools that will be robust, understandable, and credible. To help inform this ongoing process, it is useful to consider how these measures might look from the perspective of individuals, individual firms, a public agency evaluation, judging transport investments or land use densification, and from a system dynamics perspective. Access to many different opportunities, such as education, health, safe environment, and open space are all important and factors that help to shape urban growth, and which deserve analysis as described in prior chapters. But, given the economic crisis that has focused attention on the issue of jobs, it may be more convincing to stay focused on the issue of access to jobs for individuals, and access to employees for firms, as primary evaluation criteria.

In most of the US, any measure of accessibility to jobs by individuals will indicate that, all else being equal, the individual will have access to more job opportunities within a reasonable travel time budget by auto, than by transit. With individuals in competition for an inadequate number of jobs, auto ownership confers a competitive advantage by providing access to a wider area for job searching, and thus there is a powerful incentive to acquire an automobile. But all else isn't equal. It costs an estimated US$5000 per year to own and operate an auto, and especially in a multi-job holder household, the possibility of saving $5000 per year makes it attractive to voluntarily become partially transit-captive. The first car in the household represents access to a broad range of opportunities for the family including (besides employment), shopping, health care, recreation and education, and thus is difficult to forego. But in a household with at least one employed member, it is reasonable to view the second car in the household as an intermediate good, of no intrinsic value other than to access job opportunities. This brings us to the question of "satisficing" accessibility in the face of the high cost of owning an incremental auto. If 5,000 jobs are reasonably accessible by transit, and 10,000 reasonably accessible by auto, is it really worth $5,000 per year to gain that increment of accessibility, of 5,000 jobs, of which I want only one, sufficient for my well-being? For the substantial number of people who use transit for the journey to work, it clearly makes sense to find an acceptable job within the transit-accessible range. If an adequate supply of housing has transit accessibility, the worker saves the money, spending it on other goods and services, increasing their own well-being. Because auto costs leave the local economy (especially petroleum), saving those expenditures and spending them on other goods and services again stimulates the local economy. If the market for transit-accessible housing is tight, causing gentrification, part of the auto savings goes into extra expenditure for housing, but this still provides local economic stimulus.

Viewed from the perspective of the employer's need to access a reasonable mix of employees, a similar logic ensues. Auto accessibility may reach a larger pool of employees than will transit, but how much accessibility is enough? If, in order to locate in a site that provides the employer with agglomeration benefits, densities exceed the capacity of the street system for total reliance on the auto, and the cost of providing parking needs to include the cost of building structures, employee access by transit will increase, to avoid both the disutility of auto congestion and of the increased cost of parking, in addition to saving the "normal" cost of owning and operating the automobile. Depending on how tight the job market is, part of this benefit will rebound to the employer, rather than the employee, resulting in lower labor cost, and stronger, greater profitability and job growth. Either way, the benefits are likely to be local.

The Brookings Institute has done an analysis of transit accessibility of jobs in US metropolitan areas,[6] and estimates that 70 per cent of jobs in these areas are "transit accessible", defined as a 90-minute maximum trip length each way. It is an interesting beginning of the kind of metric that might be applied. One could imagine a policy purpose such as, "Achieve transit-accessibility to jobs of no more than 90 minutes for 90 per cent of the population, 55 minutes for 70 per cent of the metropolitan population, or 30 minutes for 50 per cent of the population", as measures that could add policy context. Such indices could be calculated annually to track progress, to form a basis to pursue goal achievement within a 15-year horizon, similar to the Interstate Highway "cost to complete" policy achievement mechanism adopted in 1956, which proved quite successful. The legal requirement that EPA promulgate a rule for the reduction of greenhouse gas production could provide a new context for explicit consideration of maintenance and improvement of accessibility, while reducing vehicle miles of auto travel. This could provide a significant opportunity for institutional change and significant stable funding.

A cautionary tale to remember is the reduced effectiveness of the Clean Air Act State Implementation Plans (SIPs) and the maintenance management and congestion management mandates of the 1991 ISTEA statute, which had similar effectiveness objectives, but have been less successful than the Interstate cost to complete. The key principle may be that when receipt of additional Federal dollars is conditional upon implementing a new policy, and the institution controlling the funding is actually committed to the policy, results follow. But when Federal funding is "flexible" for local decision-making, or when Federal regulation on policy is not required as a condition of funding, or the funding agency culture does not support the policy, not much response results. Targeting funding to measured improvements in accessibility, along with oversight by an agency committed to the policy goal, might provide the combination of funding conditional on goal achievement for accessibility, similar to the process that worked so well to incentivize completion of the Interstate Highway System.

8.10.1 System dynamics

It is clear that a better understanding of system dynamics under changing circumstances would be useful. As reported in a recent conference convened by Urban Land Institute (ULI), there are density growth spots in the US economy, where the number, density, and transit orientation of jobs are growing. These are often characterized by heavy land use coverage, limited amounts of parking, and high land value. As they grow, four phenomena seem to be occurring simultaneously:

1   The number of employees per square foot of building space is increasing significantly, requiring increased transit mode share because of an inflexible parking supply.

2   New, high-density buildings are added, often displacing existing park-
    ing, and usually providing limited (if any) parking, relying on still
    greater transit capacity and transit mode share.
3   "Self-selection" occurs, attracting those firms that place the highest
    value on agglomeration benefits, and which find adequately deep pools
    of qualified potential employees who are transit accessible.
4   Frequency of transit service increases to achieve higher capacity, but
    also simultaneously improves transit quality and convenience, estab-
    lishing a virtuous cycle (in a situation with an adequately funded and
    well-run transit system).

Graham's measurement of agglomeration benefits relies upon a sophisticated analysis of individual industries, and requires very detailed input of
specific information. But an accessibility approach may not need to estimate
agglomeration benefits – the individual firms do that to make their self-
selection decision. The accessibility approach assumes that there are
agglomeration benefits in enough industries to create urban growth, a
process that has been going on for centuries, and attempts to measure the
accessibility to labor pools by transit and auto, to support the design of
adequate improvements in transit supply and quality, and employment
density, to capture higher transit mode share, which permits economic
growth without a proportional increase in parking.

One can imagine many different scenarios for transit-oriented growth,
from "lumpy" expansion, improved service to the historic center, to a more
universal improvement in transit accessibility throughout the metropolitan
areas. Different metro areas might try different scenarios that promise to
achieve the transit-oriented triple bottom line sustainability. "Jobs–housing
balance" might be compared to a re-centralization of employment strategy,
on the theory that as the likelihood of individuals changing jobs over time
goes up, because of economic turbulence and technology changes, it
becomes strategically more important to concentrate jobs so that people can
adjust to changes in place of employment without needing to buy an added
auto or change residence.

Analysis of economic accessibility from the perspective of neighbors or
social classes may help to quantify and inform equity considerations. In
short, I believe that if we design the over-arching institutional architecture
and policy goal to reach defined triple bottom line sustainable accessibility
in a defined timeline, refined, useful accessibility measures can help to prioritize efforts to improve transportation and land use. While this discussion
has been focused primarily on the US institutional context, with which I am
most familiar, I suspect the observations and approach can be useful in the
European and international settings, where consideration of existing institutional context and embedded flaws, developing a modified institutional
context designed to achieve a triple bottom line in the accessibility system,

can help inform the development and refinement of useful ways to measure accessibility, and methods with which to apply them.

8.11 How does government fiscal austerity affect these issues?

Since before the automobile era began government austerity has undermined the accessibility benefits of growth in urban density. "Stadt Luft macht frei" ("city air makes you free") expresses the long-held aspiration leading to the migration of rural population to the cities. In the progressive era, significant investments in sewer and water system capacity, public transportation, education and professionalization of fire and police protection services, mitigated the negative externalities associated with urban density to maintain the attractiveness of urban life essential to successful densification. Whenever government austerity has inhibited the delivery of these services, the result is a destructive and expensive segregation through partial privatization, as a more affluent part of the population seeks separation, and strategies to provide reasonable quality services only to the more affluent, reinforcing the pressure on the lower middle-class to escape the city, and systematically removing from the city both the financial resources and the civic leadership necessary to improve living conditions for all. As the automobile became technically adequate to support commuting in the 1920s, the pressure to opt out of the city became stronger as the quicker path to improved services for many became buying a car and a suburban home to achieve improved levels of education and public safety much quicker than the time required for reform and upgrading services in larger urban areas. As the public transportation systems became dependent upon never adequate public subsidy, pressure to shift to the automobile increased. In the current period, strong public policy concerns regarding economic growth, equity, and environmental quality provide reasons to prioritize a shift toward greater use of public transportation. But the lack of adequate funding to support an expanded, high-quality public transportation service and the investment required to increase public transportation capacity is a primary obstacle to the improvement in accessibility needed for progress. Further exacerbating this problem is the Baumol effect. Providing public transportation and other public services is highly reliant on local labor with little of the import substitution that is available to other goods and service production. This means that in relative terms, the cost of public transport, like healthcare, education, and other public services, rises faster than the general rate of inflation, leading to recurring budget crises. The fact that public transportation reliance is practised by less than half of the population in most metropolitan areas makes securing adequate funds politically problematic. In the United States Federal system, Federal funding has been helpful to allow local costs to be adequately mitigated in order to support growth in service.

The recent breakdown of comity in the US Congress may be the result of the difficulty of dealing with sum-zero politics within a "no new taxes" austerity constraint. Within the failed effort to get a six-year extension of transportation funding, traditionally a bipartisan, nearly 100 per cent consensus, the House proposed zero funding for transit, undercutting the 4¢ for roads and 1¢ for transit tax increase brokered by the Reagan administration. With austerity ignoring the Baumol effects inherent in US public services, it is impossible to deliver the improved public services necessary to make urban densification viable.

When there is Federal austerity, problems become disproportionately worse for public transportation. The automobile system absorbs the financial inadequacy caused by austerity through inadequate maintenance of infrastructure, with impacts that become visible more slowly. To make major gains in shifting accessibility toward public transportation it is essential to deal with government austerity.

Notes

1   Hardin, G. (1968) "The Tragedy of the Commons". *Science*, 162 (3859): 1243–8.
2   Presented by John Deutch, MIT (12 September 2012).
3   Greenhouse gas production and fuel per VMT can be substantially reduced through technological improvement, but for vehicles/population and VMT/vehicle to decline without reducing accessibility, substantial improvements in transit and land use density are required.
4   Warner, S. B. (1978) *Streetcar Suburbs: The Process of Growth in Boston, 1870–1900*, 133, Harvard University Press.
5   Graham, D. J, and Melo, P. C. (2011) "Assessment of Wider Economic Impacts of High-Speed Rail for Great Britain", *Transportation Research Record-Series*, 2261: 15–24.
6   Tomer, A., Kneebone, E., Puentes, R. and Berube, A. (2011) *Missed Opportunity: Transit and Jobs in Metropolitan America*. Brookings Institution.

Accessibility and transportation funding

Fred Salvucci

9.1 Introduction

Greater investment in public transportation is essential if transit mode share is to increase. This chapter explores the idea of using value capture techniques to support transportation investment. It argues that while a national effort to significantly increase funding for public transportation in a sustained way is needed, and should ideally be funded based on a carbon tax or a petroleum excise tax, national governments are often slow to act – particularly to fund programs perceived as useful primarily to big cities. It is likely that national action will need to be preceded by action in pioneer metropolitan areas. The recent example from London, with adequate segments of the business community supporting an increase in the business levy to provide a portion of the cost of the £15bn Crossrail scheme provides an interesting case of capturing part of the value of the economic growth expected to be generated by transportation investment to help leverage the willingness of the national government to financially support the project. This experience suggests that value capture taxes might be an interesting option in some pioneer cases. In addition, recognizing the long tradition of requirement for state and local matching funds to secure federal funding, it suggests that there is opportunity for testing alternative methods of beneficiary taxation at the state and metropolitan levels.

This chapter includes cautionary observations about pitfalls in badly structured value capture approaches, and risks that might occur from over-reliance on the technique. In particular, it raises the concern of perverse differential impact if these techniques are used for transit but not highway investments, or for high-density but not low-density land uses, which could disincentivise the high-density transit-oriented development that is often one of the purposes of the transportation investment. In arguing for the need for national sources of funding that will be adequate and stable over a sustained period, it briefly discusses most frequently suggested mechanisms, and differentiates those which are more appropriate for national or state application. The chapter also highlights potential opportunities to develop more robust funding mechanisms, and opportunities for institutional change that may arise in the next few years, including the possible desirability of developing transportation institutions at the metropolitan level along the lines of a publicly regulated utility.

9.2 Alternative methods of funding transportation

Financing transportation has traditionally been based on direct user beneficiary payments, for example car drivers pay for the cost of owning, maintaining, insuring and fueling their auto. Transit riders pay fares, which cover at least part of the operating costs. Government typically pays for capital investment in infrastructure, and some maintenance and operating costs.

Financing the government share of the cost of transportation is sometimes based upon general taxation, that is, income taxes, sales taxes, and property taxes. The philosophical basis is that there are external benefits of transportation and accessibility that are distributed broadly throughout the society and conducive to economic growth, and that financing transportation investment, maintenance and operation is a general purpose of government. The pragmatic advantage of this approach is that in a growing economy, the yield of broad-based taxes will tend to rise, and that rising amounts of money will be available, provided that sufficient political support for transportation can be generated in the budgetary process to claim adequate levels of funding.

It is also important to consider the need for political support not only to initiate funding streams, but also to maintain support for a stable, reliable and growing source of funding over decades when there is likely to be periodic anti-tax assaults on government funding. Transportation is vulnerable to such assaults for many reasons, but three deserve special attention.

1   Paying for operation and especially maintenance of transportation systems is always vulnerable to shortsighted attack. Securing political support to get something new is difficult but often achievable. Developing support to maintain something that people already use is paradoxically more difficult because the consequences of inadequate maintenance are visible only years later. This makes claims that public agencies should "do more with less," and "be more efficient" sound plausible and difficult to rebut.

2   The cost of maintaining transportation infrastructure constantly increases at greater than the average rate of inflation. This is because it costs more to maintain something older than something new. It is further worsened by the "Baumol effect" – that is, the propensity for cost inflation of activities that must be locally produced, with less exposure to the competition of lower-cost imported substitutes to be persistently higher than inflation in the general economy.

3   The public sector nature of such infrastructure in the context of regular elections means that there are likely to be periodic attacks on the
difficult-to-explain cost increases by those not in power. Whereas
private-sector activity is subjected to continuous marketplace competition of multiple providers with customers who must pay the market
price resulting from this competition or forgo their purchase, public-
sector production competition takes the form of attempts to replace the
current government by candidates who say, and may even believe, that
they can do more with less.

The desirable characteristics of funding streams for sustained improvement
in accessibility are:

1   an adequate amount of money to achieve the mission;
2   sources of taxation that cause either no distortion of decision-making
or provide benign incentives;
3   strong potential for political support.

The practical problems associated with securing the appropriation of
adequate funding include the need to document the amount of funding
required, its benefits in relation to cost, and geographical and modal distribution. In addition, because capital investment is so "lumpy" in both time
and space, achieving political support in the appropriations process for an
individual investment that only benefits one area over several years in the
future is not easy. It often requires coalition building with beneficiaries of
other projects and with producer interests such as contractors, construction
worker unions and suppliers. For these producer interests, it doesn't matter
much what gets built, or where, so long as there is steady investment, and
therefore these groups develop special expertise in lobbying. But
if government revenues fall because of recession, the competition for
general taxation revenue with other public purposes becomes more intense.
Even if the share of funding for transportation can be maintained, the
amount of funding available falls. This results in a persistent problem of
under-investment and instability in transportation funding, which in turn
has generated the standard strategic responses.

9.2.1 Strategic responses to limited funding

One way of stabilizing the amount of funding for transportation investments over the long term has been through national funding for a large
share of capital investment, typically 50 per cent or more, with a requirement for state or local matching funds. Because the state governments value
the economic stimulus of federal funds, they will generally provide the
necessary matching funds. In this manner the long term federal funding

provides a stabilizing factor for higher capital investment than would otherwise occur. Moreover, states often fear increasing tax rates to levels higher than their neighbors. The federal government has more flexibility to set rates on the merit of the need, providing a higher total rate of investment.

One controversy concerning federal funding is the donor–donee problem. Any federal program is likely to affect various states and regions differently; revenues from gasoline taxes are perceived as being higher from rural areas, and quite often, urban areas contribute proportionately more in income tax revenues and receive proportionately less than suburban and rural areas. But these controversies ignore the fact that the "donor" states are still receiving higher distributions than the lower yield they would achieve from state or local taxation. Contrary to "devolution" theories that smaller jurisdictions will invest more in infrastructure, because of the political desire to claim credit for lower tax rates, and the fear of establishing tax rates higher than that of adjacent jurisdictions, local and state governments tend to tax at levels lower than their needs. Stated differently, even if national funding favors non-urbanized areas disproportionately, it is still likely that urban areas receive more funding than they would in a purely state and local taxation system. There is often animated debate about regional equity as everyone seeks to increase their share, but usually the resolution is high majority support to continue the federal program because the state and local jurisdictions generally believe that even the "losers/donors" are better off with the federal program than they would be on their own.

Bonding to provide capital is a second important strategy. This typically requires a supermajority vote of 60 or 67 per cent in the legislature, or approval of a voter referendum. Bonding also allows the efficient programming of funds to support construction and implementation over a long construction period and allows a given flow of funds to support a much larger portfolio of investments in comparison to a pay-as-you-go process. Capital investments are also recognized as providing benefits over the lifetime of the assets, and especially at the state and local levels are often paid for by bonding for this reason. That is, from an equity perspective, an asset that will provide benefits over a 30-year period or longer is paid for over time by the beneficiaries of the investment. Finally, since the investment is expected to generate a stream of economic benefit, achieving those benefits earlier has added value.

Funding for capital investment is also pragmatically useful because of both inflation and economic growth. Higher than average inflation in the cost of construction makes it advantageous to invest sooner at lower construction costs. Economic growth results in higher tax yields in future years so paying off bonds when tax yields are higher is convenient. Current political officials prefer to take credit now for visionary investment, but spread the financial responsibility to future governments. This combination of theoretical and pragmatic arguments justifies the interest costs inherent in bonds and results in bonding as a common practice in most state and local jurisdictions of the United States.

The use of bonding to reduce the instability of annual appropriations does not apply to maintenance and operating costs, and these activities lack the political support of outside producer interest lobbies. Therefore, maintenance and operating funds often lack predictability and tend to fall below levels required for preventative maintenance and achieving state-of-good-repair.

Dedication, or "hypothecation" is another way of creating more stable funding. Revenue streams from income and sales taxes are subject to vigorous competition among many public expenditures, in a very confusing appropriation process, and are subject to political attack by anti-tax forces. This has led to a strategy of dedication, or "hypothecation", of taxes for a specific purpose in order to increase reliable levels of funding for particular projects and develop a stronger base of political support.

Often the key to obtaining approval for a dedicated new tax is to develop support among transport advocates because of increased certainty and size of the new funds, while receiving support of advocates of other public services who benefit from the withdrawal of transportation from the competition for general funds, as well as support from anti-tax constituencies who see the hypothecation as limiting the access to tax funds by other constituencies. While dedication of funds need not have any functional relationship to transportation (for example, sales taxes are often dedicated to public transportation) there is sometimes a user-pays theory attached to the dedication, as when gasoline taxes are limited to use for highway purposes, making the analogy to a payment for service to strengthen the political defense against the funds being used for non-highway purposes. Of course the analogy to a price is flawed. The gasoline tax has to be paid whether or not the motorist uses the new roads that the gasoline tax will pay for. Tolls on specific facilities are closer to a price (although tolls are sometimes used to pay for other roads as well). While any tax can be hypothecated the pattern has been to dedicate funds from a specific revenue stream, that often has a political and procedural connection to the investment.

9.2.2 User-pays finance

The primary source of transportation finance historically has been through payment by the direct users of the transportation service, who benefit most directly from the accessibility provided. For roadway finance, the substantial share of the cost is paid by the individual, who pays up to 90 per cent of total costs in the form of automobile purchase and its maintenance, insurance, and fuel. The cost of parking, an essential component of the auto system that is substantially under-researched, is usually bundled into land use and building development costs. Approximately 10 per cent of overall cost is the road construction and maintenance, financed in part by government, especially at the state level, but primarily by gasoline taxes that are seen as a reasonable proxy for the use of the road for the individual driver. To the degree that additional gasoline taxes would be used to pay for additional preventative maintenance, which would result in both more timely and cost-effective maintenance of infrastructure, and more timely action to replace seriously deficient structures (and therefore resulting in reduced wear and tear on automobiles and trucks, and reduced congestion), this source of finance is very consistent with the beneficiary principle. To the degree that funds are used to expand the highway network, the user finance theory can be an exaggeration, as there is no certainty that the driver who pays the gasoline tax wants to or will use the new roads. If the road system is congested, the user-pays theory is further strained. If the expanded network generates more traffic on the existing already congested network, there may be a valid argument that investment in new or expanded transit capacity designed to provide substitute accessibility may be a better and more appropriate use of the funding. There are several, frequently-mentioned potential sources of user-pays funding:

Increased fuel taxes

Fuel taxes are usually accepted and have good potential to generate large sums of money. There has been a tendency to fail to increase the rate of taxation to reflect inflation cost and the improvement in fuel economy in automobiles, with the result that instead of periodic, gradual, modest adjustments, crises tend to build up until much larger increases are required. Fuel taxes are also vulnerable to the "user finance" rhetorical attacks arguing against any use of gasoline taxes for transit, or against the differential contribution and receipts from fuel taxes by various states ("donor–donee" conflicts among states). Increased fuel taxes are at least directionally correct in providing an incentive for more fuel-efficient cars, and to encourage the use of transit or walking for at least some trip purposes, because they internalize part of the external cost of the auto. There are many advantages to this existing system, and therefore gradually increasing fuel taxes to provide adequate funding levels may be seen as the default option by accessibility advocates and producer constituencies. The problem today is that federal (and most state) gasoline taxes have not been increased in 20 years, which means that even merely adjusting for inflation in this current economic downturn is politically difficult.

Vehicle-miles traveled taxation

This has become the periodic "flavor of the month", but the viability of the idea is dubious. It requires a complicated new collection system, which raises perceived privacy concerns that guarantees the kind of political controversy that anti-government forces exploit. It would be very vulnerable to the "user pays" claim that all the revenue "belongs to the road users" (and none for public transportation). It would increase the relative cost of travel on uncongested roads where fuel efficiency is higher. In the name of "fairness", the more extreme advocates of VMT taxation propose the elimination of existing gasoline taxes, which would reduce the incentive to buy more expensive, fuel-efficient cars, and give windfall profits to petroleum companies. This sum-zero taxation proposal ignores the fact that the transportation system needs *more* revenue, not the same amount.

There is, however, one experiment underway that is very promising. It is the payment of automobile insurance on a voluntary basis as a variable cost per mile rather than an annual payment. This option is now available in many states. In urban areas, auto insurance costs are often more than half the annual fuel bill, and therefore, converting auto insurance into a variable cost per mile could have a very interesting effect on usage. Additionally, if insurance costs became variable per mile, the relative size of the gasoline tax becomes smaller as a proportion of total variable vehicle costs, and the political feasibility of increasing the gasoline tax rate may go up. Of course, similar beneficial effects might occur if insurance payments were to be partially funded through increased gasoline taxes, with payment to the insurance company chosen by the individual. In short, while replacing the gasoline tax with a universal VMT tax is a bad idea, it may be interesting to monitor the experiment with auto insurance payment. If the privacy concerns with VMT taxation can be dealt with in the context of auto insurance, it might become possible to consider it in the future as a complement to the gasoline tax, particularly at the state level.

Congestion charging

This continues to be discussed as a way to improve mobility for those willing to pay, generate supplemental funding, and use the revenue to expand capacity. Core ideas go back to papers written by Vickrey of Columbia University in the late 1950s,[1] but very few applications have occurred because of the political difficulty in implementation and the technical complexity of collecting the tolls. But as discussed in previous chapters, new technology is making this toll collection problem much more tractable, leaving politics as the most significant impediment.

Often congestion charging is presented as a demand restraint technique, aimed at forcing enough drivers off of the road, at least during congested periods, to improve the quality of flow and mobility for those willing to pay. By avoiding the unstable flow that occurs as volume of traffic approaches capacity, throughput may actually increase. But the political optics of this are that users of the roads are often angry at paying for what they used to get for free, so this works better when it is applied to additional capacity such as the so-called HOT lanes where only new roadway capacity is subjected to the tolls. This produces free rider benefits on the "untolled" parallel roads and reduces the relative attractiveness of the so-called HOT lane but may generate enough winners and few enough losers to be politically feasible. But only in limited locations does physical space allow for added lanes, and the new capacity may generate additional congestion elsewhere on the network. But beyond the anti-government reactions ("someone promised me a free road and you are changing the rules, so I am angry"), some of those who pay the toll are actually winners because their perceived value of time is high enough that the payment of the toll is worth it, while others might have preferred the untolled, congested situation. However, because the political system is often much more sensitive to the anger of losers than to the silent support of winners, this is a difficult problem, especially during the debate prior to action when uncertainty and what McFadden[2] calls "economic agoraphobia" leads to the perception that magnifies the negatives and undervalues the positives. The private sector can deal with this asymmetry of expectation by strategies such as a money back guarantee to relieve the tension that inhibits the buyer from purchasing something that they may not value enough to pay the price for. A technique to mimic this strategy of the private sector is to use a trial period with the commitment of reversibility based on a referendum. This can be successful (as it was in Stockholm) but it is clumsy and politically risky. If the referendum requires removing the toll collection equipment, then the cost of the trial may be described as a waste, and the proponents of the trial can be politically damaged.

To understand the opposition to congestion charging and potential strategies to remedy these concerns which underlie the opposition it is important to consider the impact of congestion charging on not only those who pay the toll (the "tolled"), but also those who are not willing to pay the toll (the "tolled off"), and those who use parallel auto or transit routes and remain "untolled".[3] Pure demand restraint, unmitigated, destroys the accessibility of those who are "tolled off". This is likely to be a smaller number than those who pay the toll (the diversion of only a modest number of vehicles from peak flow is usually adequate to ease congestion on the tolled facility), but the negative impact on the accessibility of this group who are likely to be of lower income is an important issue which contributes to the political opposition. Viewing tolling from the perspective of the observations by Zahavi, and further work by Metz,[4] that daily travel time averages are similar across cultures, there is an inherent strange democracy in congestion. Drivers feel they are all in it together, and have the same 24 hours in each day. Auto congestion often contributes to the political will to expand capacity directly or through complementary transit expansion. Allowing the willingness to pay to determine who gets access to the limited roadway capacity undermines this "democracy of congestion". Higher income people are also likely to have more control of their work hours and more ability to avoid paying peak charges, contributing further to the sense of unfairness.

The other major constituency whose interests need to be considered is the "untolled", those who were using parallel routes or transit prior to the congestion charge, but who experience more congestion or crowding because the "tolled off" have now joined them. These are likely to be much more numerous than the "tolled off". The number who are "tolled off" of the toll facility in order to create free flow through congestion charging, when displaced onto parallel facilities, are likely to be large enough to cause worsening of congestion and crowding for much larger numbers of "untolled" travelers, damaging their accessibility. From an equity perspective, the benefit achieved by the toll payers comes at the expense of the "tolled off" and the "untolled" (who should be at least fully compensated by improved transit mobility).

The most dramatically successful examples of congestion charging are London, Stockholm and Singapore. In London, the toll payers are a small number of largely high income drivers who are probably winners because of their perceived high value of their time, and who in any case were never going to vote for the mayor, "Red Ken" Livingstone who introduced the charge soon after his election in 2000. In fact, very few people drive into the centre of London anyway, with private cars only having an 8 per cent mode share. The mayor put all the revenue from congestion charging, and much more, into increased public transportation services introduced concurrently with the congestion charge to improve an already high-quality transit system. In a sense, the mayor restructured the plan so that the drivers who benefit from the reduced congestion "purchased" this from the drivers who were forced off the road, by means of funding improved public transportation. This improved, rather than degraded, conditions for the large numbers of "untolled" travelers, many of whom were the basis of the Mayor's political support. The more modest numbers of "tolled off" travelers were most likely to be unhappy, but at least found somewhat improved public transport (though much of this was in outer London which was unaffected by the toll). Some may have ceased to travel to central London but because of the strong centrality of the London economy, the mayor appeared not to be concerned with the possible loss of business to outlying areas. The effort succeeded, the mayor won the ensuing election in 2004, which he claimed served as a referendum. Congestion charging and increased public transportation that were funded partly from toll revenues and partly because of the political will generated by the overall approach, have been sustained by the subsequent Tory mayor who succeeded Livingstone (although he did remove the western extension of the original zone added by Livingstone in his second term). In fact, congestion charging of the central area is no longer a political issue in London. The key to this success is that accessibility improved for almost everyone (that is to say, most of the tolled, all of the untolled, and even some of the tolled-off). This political stability, of the relatively crude and simple-to-understand London system, does not guarantee similar success for extending the principle to the entire network, a much more daunting technical and political challenge.

In Stockholm, the congestion-charging trial followed by an approval referendum was preceded by a significant increase in bus service, and the revenue is partly being used to fund a new ring road. This is a success politically because accessibility has been improved for most groups, although funding the new road raises concerns because it reinforces the belief that road revenues belong to motorists, which is problematic in the long run, and reinforces auto-oriented sprawl patterns.

In Singapore, a comprehensive system of charging not only for road use but also collecting extremely high taxes for permission to own an automobile ("certificate of entitlement") has successfully captured significant amounts of money and dramatically reduced congestion, with high quality and expanding public transportation increasing accessibility for all groups. Singapore is often dismissed as not having the same political constraints as Western Europe or the US, but a similar certificate of entitlement program for auto ownership in Shanghai seem to be working with recent research indicating public support. Even in such more autocratic situations with greater acceptance of government decisions, the "consent of the governed" is important to the stability of the government, and the broad set of beneficiaries contributes to public acceptance.

The most recent dramatic congestion pricing political failure, in New York City where Mayor Bloomberg failed to get the legislative support to implement London-style congestion charging to pay for increased funding for transit may provide important insights. The failure is often ascribed to suburban political opposition, but this implies more rationality on the part of the opposition than may be appropriate. Much of the opposition was orchestrated by legislators from a district in Manhattan whose constituency was actually favorable to the plan. The institutional political weakness in the mayor's position was that, in contrast to Livingstone, Bloomberg needed the approval of the legislature, and does not control the Metropolitan Transportation Authority (MTA). Advisers to the mayor suggested an alternative to congestion tolling which would have involved collecting a new fee from parking lot and garage owners, avoiding the need for legislation. This would have been very interesting as it would have been in the nature of a windfall profit tax on free riders (that is, the owners of parking facilities) rather than a user fee. It still would have suffered from the questionable ability of the mayor to increase accessibility by improving transit service, because he does not control the MTA, but New York may yet put together an interesting approach. In Britain, despite London's success, referendums in Manchester and Edinburgh to introduce congestion charging both lost heavily, partly due to the strong opposition of the local media.

Overall, London congestion charging is an interesting technique to create value and capture some of it to fund transportation, but its potential appears limited to a modest number of metropolitan areas. Applying congestion charging to a network raises much more complex technical, understandability, and political challenges, and tends to capture value from the high-value portions of the network and distribute it elsewhere, raising significant policy questions about further encouraging sprawl.

Other quasi-congestion phenomena, and "sin" taxes

The underlying aspect of the congestion charging idea is the opportunity to take a politically unpopular deadweight economic loss – congestion – and convert it into a source of revenue to improve accessibility for all (a sort of alchemist's dream of urban planning). But traffic congestion is only one aspect of urban transportation that is exceeding capacity constraints, causing exponentially escalating deadweight costs, with air pollution at the metropolitan level and greenhouse gases at the global level being particularly relevant.

Experience with the Clean Air Act suggests that when transportation control measures are perceived to reduce accessibility they are strongly resisted. Therefore, mitigating any negative impact on accessibility through concurrent visible action to improve access through transit and other initiatives is key. Two examples are worth mentioning. A carbon tax, with proceeds dedicated to expanding public transportation and the "hardening" of vulnerable facilities threatened by increasing flooding anticipated from climate change, might be seen as the infrastructure equivalent of using cigarette taxes to fund public health "no smoking" campaigns and cancer research. Taxing a "bad" to fund a "good" is superior, as opposed to viewing the gasoline tax, or carbon tax, as a user fee, whose proceeds belong to the polluters. A particularly interesting subset of this idea is the proposal to fund infrastructure by an excise fee on the petroleum companies, which is not likely to be transferred to the drivers.[5] The proceeds would be dedicated to improving less carbon-intensive accessibility such as transit and high-density development. This might seem similar to an increased gasoline tax, but it attempts to capture part of the value now gained by petroleum companies from motorists, rather than from the motorists themselves. These could be interesting national strategies to provide stable funding for accessibility expansion, which would be borne by the petroleum companies as beneficiaries, rather than the drivers, but will be greatly resisted by the petroleum companies.

9.3 Taxation of non-direct user beneficiaries of accessibility

9.3.1 Accessibility and transportation funding

The enthusiasm for shifting the focus of transportation planning and evaluation to accessibility has led to renewed interest in seeking sources of funding for transportation through "value capture" strategies; that is, in capturing the economic benefits received by non-rider beneficiaries of transportation, particularly landowners, who are viewed as capturing windfall benefits for free on the transportation investment. This interest is understandable. Transportation investment will require huge amounts of public funding in the decades ahead and the current anti-tax political climate makes it difficult to see where the money will come from. The recent successful effort in the UK to convince the Tory-Lib Dem national coalition government to proceed with the £15 billion Crossrail initiative was based in part on strong support from the London business interests to finance part of the cost of Crossrail through an increase in the business rate, a value capture type of tax.

Nonetheless there are significant potential problems with the value capture concept. First, the free rider beneficiaries of the transportation investment are a primary source of the political support required to overcome the anti-tax environment in order to achieve the transportation investment in the first place. If the financial mechanism is based excessively upon value capture, those business interests could see the effort as confiscatory, and join the anti-tax elements opposing the investment, or at least divide the business constituency and weaken support. Second, developing the economic potential of the improved access in the form of high-density transit-oriented development is not exactly a "free ride". Substantial effort is required in the always-risky real estate environment to assemble land parcels, relocate tenants, market development opportunities, and build larger buildings, in order to achieve higher density. Therefore, excessive rates of value capture finance could substantially discourage the creation of the high-density accessibility that is the objective. Third, other than in extremely rapid growth environments now found in China, India, and Brazil, the lag between transportation investment and land use densification can be at least a decade after project completion, while funding is required prior to the start of construction. Fourth, value capture is more often discussed in the context of funding transit than highways, but anything that adversely affects transit, and the densification of urban real estate *vis-à-vis* auto oriented development is directly counterproductive to the objective of improved accessibility with less auto travel. Finally, narrowly-focused value capture is likely to be counterproductive. Efforts to capture value within a few blocks of a transit station are likely to stimulate density just outside the value-capture zone. Efforts to force developers to build a station may engage a thoughtful partner in proper facility design, but risk a narrow, privatized view of the station. More fundamentally, the appreciation in value is likely to be long-term and area-wide. The London example got it right by increasing the business rate over a long term and over a large area, capturing both the appropriately broad zone and timescale, but the London business interests exhibited an unusual enlightened, self-interest attitude in rising to the challenge. Moreover, the business support developed only after decades of delay of Crossrail convinced some of the business constituency to support the increased rate, a very inefficient, and not unanimous process. It was also important to recognize the extremely energetic and persistent support of Mayor Livingstone for Crossrail. Without that leadership, it is doubtful that the London business community would have spontaneously agreed to the business rate surcharge.

In effect, it was recognized in London that trips have destination beneficiaries as well as origin beneficiaries, so in addition to a capital contribution based on anticipated fares from riders, the business beneficiaries supported the contribution based on an increased business levy, and the two "local match" commitments helped convince the UK national government to provide funding to construct the project. This breakthrough in London begs the questions, "Why not use a similar logic for roadway expenditures in the US?" "If it is reasonable to impose a gasoline tax on the driver, why is it not reasonable to impose a parking tax on the commercial beneficiary of the trip?"

Recognizing that accessibility by auto is greater than accessibility by transit throughout most of the United States, a tax or access fee on the owners of all non-residential parking as an access fee for the value created by the highway system could have three positive characteristics:

- First, it would collect money from the huge number of existing free rider beneficiaries and represent a substantial revenue stream.
- Second, it would make owners of existing real estate much more sensitive to the traffic generation which their parking facilities help cause, and provide an ongoing incentive to decrease parking and auto dependency and encourage transit use.
- Third, it would incentivize transit-oriented locations for new development.

But such enlightened self-interest has historically been difficult to achieve in the US (or anywhere else). The US Interstate Highway system, initiated in 1956, created substantially new value nationally but the funding base that financed its construction was pay-as-you-go – the initial four cents per gallon collected from drivers on existing roads. As a political strategy it was called a user fee-based system, but the new auto-based land value it produced, and the benefits to new users, were largely free riders on the financial base of the pre-existing drivers. The level of capital required to develop new transit capacity and rebuild aging highway infrastructure is of the same order of magnitude as the interstate program, and therefore it is important to consider the possibility that the value capture concept would be of little use in generating political support to fund a major infrastructure initiative in advance of the program when the political support is most needed. Indeed, it risks becoming an ongoing source of political friction and even opposition to the use of the funding for the investment essential to expand the accessibility system. Looking back, it seems incredible that the trucking interests who gained so much from the Interstate Highway program were opponents of the program in 1956 because they objected to the fuel taxes required to fund it. However, this becomes easier to understand when it is recognized that the fuel tax was levied on the pre-existing fuel consumption of users, particularly the truckers, who had yet to see any benefit from the new Interstate highways. Finally the user fee political rhetoric, once the financing system was set up, has now become the rationale for motorists to oppose the use of fuel taxes to support transit investment, and the source of endless conflict between "donor" and "donee" states. A similar counter-intuitive opposition from beneficiaries sometimes occurs with proposals to expand urban rail networks. Existing riders may prefer lower fares or taxes, or an improved level of service on the existing network rather than an expanded service that they believe they may well never use. Therefore the decision to expand a highway system or complement it with transit is a policy- and political-, rather than market-based decision. The need for a stable funding base for the construction, operation, and maintenance of a system of the scale of the Interstate program requires stability and reliability. But in the light of the concerns raised above, it is often the practice to see the "free rider" beneficiary of the access system as a source of political support to obtain other funding, rather than as the source of funding that risks turning them into adversaries.

In short, the financing requirements to improve accessibility through a combination of transport investment and land use densification needs a well-thought out political strategy, and well-developed communication strategy, to convince beneficiaries that a "free lunch" is unlikely to occur, and if beneficiaries want to see investment increase, they will need to contribute. Therefore, the potential to capture some of the value which accessibility creates should be considered very carefully from the perspective of both potential inadequacy of scale and possible perverse incentives, as well as the risk of generating political opposition.

9.3.2 Property taxes and parking fees

The traditional property tax is based on a theory of value capture, but it taxes the increased real estate values, which grow long after the actual infrastructure investment has been made. This is an important source of revenue, but there are three problems associated with making it a source of funding for infrastructure investment. First, precisely because the increased real estate value occurs after the investments are made, it is difficult to use to fund the infrastructure. Second, since property taxes are an important source of revenue for municipal and county government, they will likely oppose attempts by other claimants to capture part of the revenue. Third, real estate interests have become expert at fighting property taxes with tactics such as an anti-property tax referenda (for example Proposition 13[6]), making it difficult to sustain high levels of property taxation to pay for infrastructure once it has been built. Linking the proceeds of property taxes to operations and maintenance costs might increase the feasibility of the approach, in that those costs are continuous, not historic, and real estate interests may understand the importance of proper operations and mainte- nance to their property value. An access fee charged not to the users of parking, but to the owners, based on the number of parking spaces they provide, as the basic measure of the access benefit could be a robust source of income and force a contribution from all institutions, including non- profit organizations that are tax exempt and which benefit from roadway accessibility. Since the infrastructure for collecting such fees already exists at the level of property tax jurisdictions this might best be seen as a part- nership with other property tax collecting levels of government, which would require agreement to share increased revenues, as in tax increment financing techniques.

9.4 Opportunities to increase funding for metropolitan public transportation

The redevelopment of the American metropolitan landscape based on auto- mobile accessibility has been underway for almost a century, with the support of major automobile and petroleum industries, and is embedded in land-use regulations and transportation practice. Changing the focus of policy to an accessibility basis can improve understanding, but automobile accessibility will continue to be dominant over transit and walking, even at higher density, and even with some recentralization of jobs. The large investment in low-density housing, and the roadway infrastructure which supports its continued growth, will not disappear because we change eval- uation techniques; in fact, accessibility-based analysis will make clear that auto accessibility will continue to be dominant over transit and walking in most of the metropolitan area. It is likely to indicate that density and some re-centralization of jobs is more important than the jobs–housing balance in improving the relative accessibility of transit *vis-à-vis* the automobile. But only if the environmental and economic constraints are introduced, and the quality and quantity of transit improves, does transit become competitive.

The landmark Interstate Highway legislation of 1956 was introduced in the name of national defense by a popular president who was a war hero, after at least a decade of discussion within government, industry, the Congress, and the public, and with the support of automobile and petroleum industries and over a half-century of auto-oriented land use and transportation momentum. To change the direction of this auto dominant trajectory, even if its momentum now appears to be stalled because of congestion, a roadway maintenance backlog, and rising gasoline prices, will take major effort and is not likely to come about in one dramatic piece of legislation directly from Washington DC. "All politics is local", as former Speaker of the House Tip O'Neill famously noted.[7] Washington is more likely to follow the lead of several pioneer states and metropolitan areas, after the pioneers proof the ideas and show them to be robust.

9.4.1 State and metropolitan area approaches

The funding crises affecting public transportation in every US metropolitan area must be addressed at the state and local level, at least initially. This is urgent, as the current reality threatens to reduce the quantity and quality of public transportation, when the societal need is to increase accessibility by transit. In dealing with the extensive problems at the metropolitan level, it is useful to consider five aspects of the crises: how to

- safeguard against making things worse;
- develop adequate financial support to invest in expansion, to provide local matching funds when national funding becomes available, and to provide 100 per cent state and local funding for expansion needs that are likely to exceed available federal funding;
- develop new institutional capacity to take advantage of loan opportunities such as the Transport Infrastructure Finance and Innovation Act (TIFIA), public-private finance, and value capture;
- build alliances with other states and metropolitan areas to expand and restructure the federal program;
- pay for the operating subsidies to support increased levels of service.

While recognizing that it is difficult to generalize about the challenges facing the diverse metropolitan areas across the country, there are some common themes that should be considered.

Increased public transport fares

Increasing farebox contribution to transit finance may be essential to deal with the transit crisis. For a long time, transit agencies have maintained low fare strategies to attract more riders, and have often supported these strategies based on arguments of equity and affordability. However, most transit systems are now eliminating routes and reducing off-peak frequency, and continuing to underserve many parts of metropolitan areas. This service erosion often imposes worse damage to the accessibility of transit dependent customers than the financial impact of fare hikes necessary to avoid the cuts. In public hearings, when confronted with the choice between service cuts or fare increases, the main public response is that service cuts are worse than fare increases. This public response is reflecting an underlying reality that the ongoing damage to accessibility caused by inadequate quantity and quality of service, and the damage caused by the shock of service cuts (damage to both the accessibility of the customers affected, and also the political will to support transit as the customer base is diminished) is far worse than the problems caused by fare increases. If fare increases are needed to avoid worsening already poor levels of service, it makes sense to consider raising fares in order to provide better levels of service. Simultaneously, aggressively pursuing expansion of employer-based transit passes, on a pre-tax basis and with employer subsidy, can ease the pressure of the fare increases and broaden the financial base of the system. At the same time, it is important to recognize that fare increases to avoid service cuts and to expand services are viable only where an extensive service exists. The feasibility to charge higher fares is much greater in a very extensive system such as London, Paris, or New York, than in Boston or Chicago, and more feasible in Boston than in Phoenix, so the value proposition is essential. If the system creates value, it may be possible to capture some value. If the value isn't there, such an effort will fail. It is reasonable to expect that a low fare/high subsidy service will continue to be essential to build ridership in small starter systems and suburban services.

Long-term value capture approaches

Broad-based value capture approaches, such as property tax contribution to transit (whereby some of the increase in property value generated by transit supports the service that creates the value) should be considered. These long-range annual assessment approaches should be distinguished from the short-term "quick hit" developer contributions, which often lack transparency and provide only short-term support.

Access fees on non-residential parking

Assessment of access fees upon the owners of non-residential parking, to recognize and end the "free ride" that the owners of parking enjoy could be promising. An annual assessment per space could calculate a contribution to transportation maintenance costs. This could at least ease the cost of maintaining roadways, but it might also be a legitimate source of transit finance that recognizes the relief that transit provides to both the roadway system and the air quality of the metropolitan area. A surcharge on parking fees in congested areas, dedicated to increasing transit, may be a more politically viable method of introducing congestion charging than imposing tolls on traditionally free roadways.

Universal transit passes

"Universal" transit passes, which provide marginal-cost access to transit for the entire affinity group, but charge the institution only for actual use, are now technically feasible. This opens the possibility of capturing from only those institutions that actually achieve value from the service.

Exploit heightened awareness

Planners should use the visibility that fare increases cause to discuss broadening and increasing the taxpayer support for improved public transportation, to complement the increased fare payer contribution.

Planners should engage in multi-modal alternatives analysis when considering how to replace physically deteriorated roadway infrastructure. There are extensive elevated viaducts in most metropolitan areas that have outlived their useful physical life and must be rebuilt or replaced. Often they are simply rebuilt at greater cost and with substantial construction disruption, without considering the possibility of simply removing the deficient structure and increasing a transit service to maintain accessibility. In many situations this can be a cost-effective strategy, and one that can mitigate construction disruptions to motorists.

9.4.2 Federal reauthorization of transportation funding

Historically, transportation and public works funding has enjoyed a strong bipartisan consensus, with nearly unanimous Congressional votes from both Democrats and Republicans. Ronald Reagan increased the gasoline tax by 5¢, one cent for transit and four for roadways. In this dynamic, the only way to get more money for transit was to support much greater amounts of increased funding for roadway construction.

In 2013, there could be a major initiative to reauthorize transportation funding on a deficit finance basis. If there is any policy for which federal deficit spending should be embraced, it is for infrastructure investment. Almost every American homeowner purchased their home through mortgage financing. Every city and state uses debt finance and bonds to invest in infrastructure that will have useful lives of 20 or more years. Only the federal government uses pay-as-you-go finance for capital investment. With interest rates low, deficit finance of infrastructure investment is prudent and rational as an investment strategy, and simultaneously provides economic stimulus to important sectors.

It could also be the opportune time to recognize that the road system is now so extensive that the addition of new links or beltways is meaningless, and that improving the level of maintenance on the extensive existing roadway system is much more important than adding new roadway links. The national priority should be renewing and maintaining the existing system, and complementing it with improvements in public transportation. Freed of the user finance myth, it should be possible to shift to a more appropriate policy, while continuing to distribute enough funding geographically for roadway maintenance to satisfy the political demands of the substantial auto-oriented districts.

A new, multi-year transportation authorization could be the occasion to aggressively refocus the federal program to renewing, reconceptualizing, and, in many cases, downsizing the roadway network, and increasing transit net investment to bring it into closer conformity with financial as well as environmental sustainability. A new reauthorization could be the statutory opportunity to require accessibility-based analysis on all federal investment on a multi-modal basis, ending the current silo approach that applies inconsistent evaluation criteria to highway and transit investment. New initiatives to safeguard infrastructure from climate change stresses and acquiring open space and development rights to improve accessibility might provide new public policy rationale and allies.

A deficit funding strategy could liberate the transportation reauthorization from the "user pays" mythology that holds transit funding far below levels of funding justified by the large volume of reasonably cost-effective proposals in excess of authorized levels, the propensity for earmarking, and highway investments that proceed with no evaluation, and the incessant donor–donee discussion. (While urbanized areas are often "donees" when considering only gasoline taxes, they are usually "donors" of income and other taxes.) With freedom from the "user pays" mythology of the gasoline tax, funding could be distributed to governors, mayors, and MPOs, rather than highway departments, easing the current silo mentality.

As an alternative to deficit finance, a petroleum company excise tax, or a carbon tax could eventually fund a reconstituted federal infrastructure program.

9.4.3 Environmental Protection Agency (EPA) greenhouse gas regulation

During 2013, EPA will hopefully pursue its statutory and moral obligation to develop regulations to limit greenhouse gas production. The decentralized structure of having each state develop its own approach to conform to uniform outcome standards is a real opportunity for local creativity. EPA could insist upon use of accessibility-based evaluation techniques. In the past, EPA has tended to emphasize "demand restraint", which has anti-economy and anti-equity implications by damaging accessibility. By using accessibility metrics, EPA can shift the focus from demand restraint to supply restructuring, with the maintenance and improvement of accessibility while reducing greenhouse gas generation as the key evaluation criteria. The statutory requirement that state transportation plans must conform with State Implementation Plans pursuant to EPA Clean Air Act rulings, or forfeit 10 per cent of their road funds, provides substantial leverage to insist that state transportation investments support sustainable outcomes, and can help break the constraints of the current process.

It is worth considering reorganizing the metropolitan transportation system in a manner similar to the historic electric or telephone utilities, as regulated multi-modal monopolies with the right to charge access fees, and the obligation to meet district-wide service obligations based upon uniform and public standards, and subjected to public oversight. Such an entity would certainly raise the gasoline tax by one cent per year, rather than reaching a crisis point, as is the case with most road and transit agencies. It is interesting to note that there is public outrage when electric power outages (which are infrequent) occur, yet there is silence over transportation issues even though the system breaks down twice per day, fails to maintain or provide assets, doesn't provide uniform standards, and uses opaque evaluation criteria for deciding on system expansion. Developing a conceptual model for a Singapore-style system, but managed by a public utility, with transparent standards, subject to public review, could offer an institutional alternative to shift towards the pursuit of improved accessibility as the core mission.

9.5 Summary

Given the current politically difficult gridlock, it is important not to waste political capital on initiatives that are "too small to matter", or violate the win–win–win test. Any initiative large enough to be successful will face well-financed opposition from at least the petroleum companies – a major political challenge. As long as most federal money goes directly to highway agencies, it is unlikely that transit will get stable funding. Institutional change is an important component of success. For example, to encourage innovation at the state and local level, federal funds might flow to governors and MPOs.

Accessibility funding possibilities should be considered from the perspective of the Brundtland Commission and Rio de Janeiro conference sustainability principles, with explicit advocacy for win–win–win strategies from the perspective of the economy, environment, and equity. To deal with the substantial financing challenges of improving accessibility, while significantly reducing greenhouse gas generation, the economic imperative is that the revenue streams should be adequate to the challenge; the equity imperative is that accessibility for the less affluent must improve; and the environmental imperative is that greenhouse gas generation and petroleum consumption must substantially decrease.

These observations are heavily rooted in US practice and possibilities but are, I suspect, not so different from European or developing world experience. The need to stimulate the economy is unfortunately worldwide. The European Union and World Bank relationship to national governments is somewhat similar to that of the US federal government *vis-à-vis* states and cities. These institutions are in a position to exert benign influence, but the need for pioneer cities and regions is still similar. These ideas are intended to stimulate creative action at all levels.

Endnote

As a lifetime practitioner in public works and transportation, these observations are offered as a contribution to the new discussion of policy research from the perspective of five decades of observation of the frequent dichotomy between policy, as discussed in the research community, and periodically articulated in legislation and regulation, and practice in the institutional context of actual decision-making.

As Transportation Advisor to the Mayor of Boston from 1971–74, and Secretary of Transportation of Massachusetts from 1975–78, 1983–86, and 1987–90, I was directly engaged in policy formulation and transportation legislation at the city, state, and national level, as well as implementation at the city and state level.

As an active participant in national associations of transportation and public works practitioners, I had an opportunity to gain insight into both common and diverging practice among states. From 1992–96 I participated in a review of the practice in metropolitan transportation planning conducted by the Federal Department of Transportation, to observe the implementation of the 1991 legislative reforms known as ISTEA, at the working level. More recently, from 2000 to 2012, I have participated directly in the transportation planning process in the Boston area, and as a member of the governor's transition team on the ongoing process of transportation organizational restructuring in Massachusetts, and efforts to deal with transportation financing inadequacy that has persisted for over a decade. These two chapters reference the research efforts reported in prior chapters, but primarily report observations on policy implementation and institutional issues based on first-hand observation.

During the period from 1991 to the present at MIT, I have had an opportunity to advise and supervise many talented students working on their Master's theses and PhD dissertations, and many of the concepts referenced here are significantly related to their work. Those most clearly discussed in these chapters include issues of:

- the concept of self-selection as dealt with particularly by David Block-Schachter (PhD dissertation, 2012);
- changes in societal values over time (Jinhua Zhao, PhD dissertation, 2010);
- the reduced level of local tax contribution in "devolved" decision making (Giorgia Favero, 2006);
- applying the Baumol effect to public transit (Hazem Zureiqat; MST thesis, 2008);
- externalities in public transportation (Justin Antos, MCP thesis, 2007);
- the need to strengthen priority of maintenance of existing roads and transit, rather than focus primarily on new roadways (Andrew Lukmann, 2009);
- accessibility theory applied to transit (Caroline Ducas, MST thesis, 2011);
- agency culture undercutting structural policy and recognition of system dynamics to "nudge" policy (Vig Krishnamurthy, MST/MCP thesis, 2012).

Inevitably, my thinking has been influenced by the general literature of major authors, including especially Paul Samuelson, William Vickrey, William Baumol, Paul Krugman, Anthony Venables, Daniel Graham, Edward Glaeser, and Alan Altshuler. I am also indebted to my colleague Mikel Murga for his work on quantifying the savings in auto expenditures attributable to public transit in Boston and Bilbao, and for the helpful review and comments of David Block-Schachter, Vig Krishnamurthy, Mikel Murga, Lane Neumann, and Professor Nigel Wilson. Of course, the responsibility for the chapters is entirely my own.

Notes

1 Vickrey, W. (1994) *Public Economics: Selected Papers by William Vickrey*, Cambridge University Press.
2 McFadden, D. (2007) "The behavioral science of transportation", *Transport Policy* 14(4): 269–74. McFadden actually writes about economic agoraphobia in the private sector context. This reference explains the observations to public sector dynamics.
3 Zettel, R. and Carll, R. (1964) "The basic theory of efficiency tolls: the tolled, the tolled off, and the un-tolled", *Highway Research Record* 47, National Research Council.
4 Metz, D. (2008) "The myth of travel time savings", *Transport Reviews*, 28(3): 321–336.
5 Bradley, Ridge and Walker (2011) *Road to Recovery: Transforming America's Transportation*, Carnegie Endowment for International Peace.

6   Proposition 13, officially named the People's Initiative to Limit Property Taxation, is a 1978 amendment to the Constitution of California that limits the tax rate for real estate.
7   According to Wikipedia: "All politics is local" was used by Washington AP bureau chief Byron Price in 1932. Tip O'Neill first used the term in 1935, when he entered politics.

Chapter 10

Technology and information technology

Living with and paying for sustainable access

Robert E. Paaswell

10.1 Introduction: the technological evolution of urban access in the twenty-first century

How will modern information technology (IT) impact urban access? Cities are now in the very early stages of an IT revolution, whose ramifications will transform the spatial relations between mobility and co-location. In so doing they will reshape the meaning of urban access and the financing of this access. In this chapter the implications of this profound change for urban access are explored.

The IT revolution is already having far reaching impacts on every aspect of life, including urban spatial form. Fundamentally, urban transport is a technologically determined service. The modern industrial city was shaped first by rail and then by the advent of mass production of the automobile. The importance of IT to the quality of urban access is likely to have at least four dimensions:

- enhance the productivity of transport planners and providers;
- ease the matching between providers and users;
- change the concept of travel time from something to be minimized to something that can be productive;
- and radically increase the potential for sophisticated fares and other revenue sources that better reflect the costs and benefits of travel to users and providers.

It is likely that the IT revolution will have a similar impact on urban form as rail and the automobile in the twentieth century. Living PlanIt in Portugal, new smart cities in China and "wired" Stockholm are all examples of this twenty-first century shift in the access paradigm. Investments in urban transport since the mid-twentieth century have been about expanding physical capacity – infrastructure and rolling stock. Gradually, IT services will become the third area of significant investment. The availability of smartphones and tablets has also created a cultural shift in how users see and achieve their daily activities. Much of this shift is now generational

– age dependent – and is having an emerging, but powerful influence on how transport is supplied, how our urban areas look and function – and how access is financed.

10.2 Urban access and urban mobility: some perspective

By 1970 car ownership in the US was approaching one car per household, twice that of the UK, transit ridership was on the decline, and suburbs were growing rapidly.[1] Yet a large part of the population was left behind, described as the transportation disadvantaged. These were people living in low-income households, often in minority populations. Their car ownership rate was low – one for four households – and they often had to rely on an increasingly diminished public transit system. In the late 1960s urban riots in the US called attention to the fact that while unemployment among these disadvantaged groups was high, getting to a job, and holding a job was made even more difficult by the absence of a car, or by unreliable and insensitive user public transportation.[2] The net impact of this automobile-based spatial expansion of US metropolitan areas was to exacerbate patterns of residential segregation and cause major urban population groups, namely those with lower incomes, to lose significant transport access to employment and educational opportunities. Observers at that time termed this "spatial mismatch".[3] It was not until the last third of the twentieth century that urban thinkers recognized that the changes brought about by the automobile – especially suburbanization and stark separations of workplace from home – impacted hard on many segments of the population. It fell to public transportation to make up the gap between the disproportionate accessibility afforded to the more affluent and inadequate accessibility of these other groups. The importance of public transport for sustaining urban access has been actively recognized by the EU. In Europe, as in the US, the costs of maintaining public transport have become high, resulting in new approaches to provide supply – mainly involving the private sector. But perhaps the most dramatic answers to urban access have been in China, which has gone from a mainly bicycle society until as late as 1990 to an auto centered society and now is investing – annually – billions in rail and modern bus transit.

But transit alone – often viewed as the "poor person's" choice of travel – given its neglected state by the end of the 1960s did little to close the mobility and accessibility gaps between the transportation disadvantaged and the more affluent in the US. The gap only began to close as the result of federal legislation passed between 1970 and 2000 that spurred changes in the way transit services were delivered. Two landmark pieces of US Federal Legislation, Section 504 of the Rehabilitation Act of 1973 and the Americans with Disabilities Act (ADA) of 1990, were especially important. Both of these acts affirmed that all residents have the right of access to

public facilities, including public transportation and were aimed at addressing the mobility gaps based upon the assumption that access was a
fundamental right. These acts required public transit systems to spend a
portion of their operating budget on serving these disadvantaged populations. The compliance requirements of these acts sparked a technological
race to put wheel chair lifts on buses and develop cost effective, on demand
para-transit[4] for those unable to avail themselves of the regular services.
Such additions made it possible for many physically disadvantaged people
to continue to stay in the labor force. However, such advances did little for
the economically disadvantaged who increasingly found that affordable
housing was moving farther and farther away from available work, where
access subsequently declined. The gentrification process of inner cities has
exacerbated this development and made it more paradoxical. As high
income people move (back) to city centers and their easy access to all kinds
of services, the very persons supposed to provide these often low wage services are pushed out to the suburbs.

Technology to address the highway congestion problems faced by those
able to travel to work also began to develop in the form of intelligent transportation systems (ITS). The sustained concentration of employment in
both city centers and suburban rings created unprecedented traffic congestion causing transportation officials to seek technological solutions to
reduce the costs caused by congestion. Computer controlled traffic systems;
simple combinations of mechanical sensors and large computers became the
first line of defense in traffic management. But bigger changes occurred in
the 1990s with the first phases of ITS. Using real time information, ITS
provided the transportation world with variable message signs, safety warn-
ings, traffic control, new methods of toll and fare collection and new
approaches tohighway construction.

10.3 The IT revolution

The impact of contemporary IT technologies only started to become manifest in the context of urban travel quite recently. By 2000 computer and
sensor technology had become sufficiently miniaturized and devices
containing computers and sensors could be placed almost anywhere,
collecting, processing and transmiting information to some central control.
The transmission could be by cable, fiber optics, radio or satellite. The
result has been that desired information of traffic counts, people at a bus
stop, location of a vehicle, weather and extreme system behavior could all
be collected, analyzed and acted on in real time. The inexpensive collection
and processing of large amounts of data and the transmission of such data
to a central place is at the heart of the transport revolution fosterd by IT.

We are only at the very beginning of understanding how this new technology is leading to the invention and development of new tools, used by

transportation managers and users alike, and how these are reshaping urban access and urban spatial form.

Among these tools are:

- The internet – the worldwide web has become our instantaneous first source for information, from "where am I?", to "what jobs are available in my field – and where?", to general information of all sorts. It is available in remote locations, bringing urban access to rural areas. In many circumstances the internet is also available to low-income populations at local libraries. And this so very important source of information, once the tool of sophisticated computer users, is now used in greater proportion by those with access to smartphones.
- The cloud – large scale remote servers that can contain huge data files for quick retrieval from computers or smart devices.
- Ubiquitous geographic positioning systems (GPS) – the basis for location information. The almost universal ownership of GPS through smart devices enables personal travel decisions to be made instantaneously.
- Information displays – interactive kiosks (with computers and touch screens) in public spaces that provide information about the city, neighborhood or particular attraction. These are essentially public smartphones that provide answers to urban spatial questions.
- Smart buses and railcars (the norm) – new transit vehicles are more about computers than mechanical devices, easing operations and improving operational and maintenance efficiencies. They allow for more flexible routing and timing and better integration in to regional transportation networks.
- Smart cars and highways – the auto industry isn't asleep. Soon cars will be automatically guided, and highways, with embedded sensors, will allow them to operate safely, while increasing highway capacity. Demonstrations of this technology are occurring currently.[5]
- Smartphones – have more advanced computing capability and connectivity than a normal mobile phone, which makes it easier to access real time information in the palm of your hands. Of importance to urban access, smartphones have GPS and access to the internet. A user can find out what is happening and where, how to get there – with prices and schedules, and through social networks who to go with.
- Tablets – digital notebooks that are smaller and lighter than laptops. With huge amounts of storage capacity they provide mobile computing and internet connectivity capabilities to users.
- Mobile apps – help smartphone and tablet users access and sort through information in a faster, more seamless manner on topic specific issues than normal web searches on smartphones. Once downloaded and installed some apps do not even require internet access to function.

They help users with various parts of their daily routine and leisure ideas (and whims).

- Intelligent cities – eGov platforms provide citizens with access to government services 24-hours a day. They also monitor and evaluate the provision of online information and services.
- Smart cities – modern information and communication technologies (ICT) monitor city systems and collect data in uniform platforms. The systems implemented and data collected are used to optimize resources by decreasing functional overlap and duplication of inconsistent data. Smart systems provide cities with new information to help improve inter-agency collaboration, city life, social infrastructure, sustainable economic development, and civic participation.

The march of technological innovation was not spurred by concerns about gaps in urban access; rather, the advances provided by IT and ubiquitous computers stimulated transportation engineers to try to improve traffic flow and highway safety.

10.3.1 A note on logistics – the other half of the accessibility equation

Much of the literature on accessibility[6] addresses personal travel. Yet moving goods and supplying enterprises keep urban areas alive. While we are now facing a paradigm change in personal transportation of the use of real time information to make travel and activity decisions, the groundwork for such decision making was made two decades ago in the logistics industry. The technology was satellite-based GPS location devices and the ability to transmit bar code scans in real time. The problem of reducing the complexities involved in moving goods – muti modally – from supplier to buyer had to be reduced. Today's logistics has integrated the supplier and transportation chain into an information chain, reducing the costs of moving goods while increasing speed and reliability. Jobs depend on enterprises; which in turn depend on supplies. The supply chain depends on efficiencies – time in every sense is money and opportunity. Global freight movers (such as UPS, FedEx and DHL) have already understood the power of real time information and the translation of that information to useable tools, for example, tracking and distribution. The use of GPS, readable bar codes and satellite transfers of information dramatically changed logistics. In turn, these developments in logistics together with the sale of goods on the internet has transformed the way people shop, how they pay for their goods, and how they value the reliability of delivery that these new logistics bring. It is still too early to comprehend the full implications of this change for the spatial shape of urban areas. But one aspect of urban access, finding lower cost goods, has already resulted from this logistics shift; the creation of "big box stores" in Europe, Asia and the US which has changed how and where many thrifty households shop.

Underlying the quality of service (continual and comprehensive package tracking from order to delivery) has been the role of GPS, a technology developed through the government sponsored space exploration programs. GPS provides instantaneous positioning of anything – package, person, bus – with a tracking device. In fact, the technological advances of logistics have been a key aspect of the success of globalization, and the emergence of strong markets in Asia and Latin America. And, of course, the shifting of markets has had an equally strong role in the shifting of job locations. The revolution in technology-dependent logistics, integrating production and consumption, has shown the depth of IT applications.

10.3.2 Back to personal access and technology

There are at least four broad ways information technology can be applied to improve urban access. First, IT has a huge potential for enhancing transport productivity through its adoption on buses, railcars, cars, highways and for traffic control. These developments all result in improved productivity or reduce costs. Integrated networks: smart IT infrastructure permits real time control of an integrated transportation system, improving reliability and timetabling, scheduling of vehicles appropriate to the demand, improved safety and fewer delays.

Second, IT technology has the potential to change the very concept of travel. Transport engineers and economists start their analysis on the assumption that travel time should be reduced. However, the ubiquitous use of IT by travelers blurs the distinction between travel and work or travel and leisure. Internet access on commuter trains allows employers to view travel time as work time. The implication is that investments in transport should be aimed not only – or perhaps not even primarily – at reducing travel time but at impoving travel quality.

Third, IT will provide users, through a smart device, with information about system characteristics and enable them to make appropriate decisions about choice of mode, times of departure and arrival (critical to workers), necessity and convenience of transfers, weather conditions and prices and payment modes. All of these have the potential to lower both time and money costs for travelers. It is quite likely that this matching between provider and traveler will stimulate new forms of provisions such as non-route, flexible, scheduled bus services. This could be an advanced adaptation of the mini-bus industry now prevalent in third world cities.

Perhaps a combination of smart vehicles and smart users will give momentum to a change in the nature of transport vehicles. New personal vehicles – self propelled and automatically guided are already in production. Transit companies will look at the dynamics of a more variable demand and will develop more diverse fleets, many with smaller buses – again with full IT capabilities – serving a daily route schedule that meets a diversity of customers and a range of routes. Future cities could have fewer long distance fixed bus routes and more dynamic routes responsive to a more dynamic demand.

Fourth, and perhaps most important, IT opens up the potential for much more sophisticated ideas about fares and revenue-raising. Revenues have so far essentially been mode-based. Mass transit travelers are supposed to pay for mass transit and car owners are supposed to pay for car travel. Yet, it is obvious that mass transit benefits car travelers through reduced congestion. Fares moreover most often do not reflect the cost of peak capacity. IT opens up possibilities to design fares that reflect both these interdependencies and variations across the day. After all, technology has already eased the process for collecting and determining fares. And the modes of fare collection (smartphone codes combined with credit cards or other payments) also suggest new revenue generating transport partners.

The successes of GPS and logistics was immediately noticed by highway and transit providers who realised such applications could enable them to improve their service to their customers. These new technologies create the potential to ease the flow of traffic on existing infrastructure. Computers in cars can obtain GPS data on road conditions, information about restaurants and the ability to make reservations, location of parking and the ability to reserve a spot, traffic and weather information, and of course social network capability to stay in contact with friends.

Public transport for the most part lags behind in the adoption of these new technologies. However, there has been some progress. Public transportation systems in cities such as Shanghai, Hong Kong, Paris, London, Madrid and New York are adding new technologies to demonstrate that public transport can meet their customers' combined travel and activity needs. Joshua Robin, the technology chief for the Massachusetts Bay Transport Authority (MBTA) (Boston, US), put it most succinctly,

> The MBTA has been a leader in embracing the mobile phone as the best way to connect with customers. Over the last few years, our work on Open Data, Mobile Apps, and now with Mobile Ticketing has really been groundbreaking. We want to give customers the ability to do as much as possible from the phone in the palm of their hand.[7]

10.4 Technology and cost savings

How has technology improved transport system performance and reduced costs to the user?

From the beginning, technology has been used to improve vehicle speeds and reduce travel times. This, in fact has been the overwhelming approach since the mid 1800s; mechanical systems were used to improve speeds of street-cars, then the auto, and urban rail. Improvements in speed have resulted in dramatic changes in land use, not always to the benefit of the lower income or less skilled workers.

Technology has been used to improve traffic flow, again reducing travel times or improving reliability. Computerized signal systems have been used since the mid-twentieth century primarily to move auto traffic, but more recently to provide priority at signals for buses. Computerized traffic systems coupled with exclusive rights of way have led to the development of Bus Rapid Transit (BRT) systems, now operating in dozens of cities around the world, particularly in Latin America. The 30-year-old Curitiba Bus system provides transit for 70 per cent of local travelers, avoiding congestion and paying only a small proportion of their income for travel. The 7-year-old Mexico City BRT system, currently constructing the fourth of the planned 10 lines, has been financed phase by phase by a combination of public private partnerships and a US$2.4 million carbon reduction structure that sells carbon reduction credits on the international market.[8]

However, and perhaps of greatest importance, the integration of real time IT with existing and emerging technologies will have a much more profound influence on urban access by giving users the same information as system operators.

Primary attributes users need to satisfy or improve their own access to employment and access to urban activities:

- Full access to transportation system characteristics – schedules including departure and arrival times, reliability of the schedule and vehicle location.
- Knowledge of how to access and use the transportation system from any given location.
- Knowledge of payment methods and amounts, ease of paying fares and simplicity of use.
- Knowledge of system integration – transfers within and between modes, integration with taxis.
- Personal security in system use.
- Knowledge of the job market – locations and skills required.
- Knowledge of information networks – internet and social networks.
- The ability to understand the information on access regardless of the first language of the user.

The list above goes from the traditional – "Does the bus to my job come to the stop near my house?" to the IT modern: "How can I learn about job opportunities from information on employers posted on the internet and shared on Facebook?" Real time information places workers and job seekers in a much better position concerning employment than just a decade ago, but since this information is universally shared it also increases the competition for available jobs.

10.5 Applications and the networked city

While many IT developments have emerged from space and defense programs, entrepreneurs have been quick to adopt them to meet transportation needs. The applications can be thought of as single ones, such as a GPS unit in a car or telephone, or as part of a network, that locates all of the GPS information and speeds of vehicles to produce traffic maps. In fact, the power of IT and emerging technologies lies in the fact that systems can be merged forming networks to provide the user with individualized information concerning a specific trip, travel plans or location.

Networks are simply the connections among various information providers across users. Some examples of city networks are:

- Transportation networks – the roads in a community or the collection of transit routes.
- Energy networks – the electric grid, bringing power to home from far away.
- Water network – supplying water to houses and businesses from diverse sources.
- Communication networks – wiring and antennae that connect and transmit telecommunication and information communication technologies across city, state and national boundaries.

For modern technology, networks gain importance because they provide integration of information from almost unlimited diverse sources. The limiting factors of IT networks are the power of the devices, which receive the information and restrict the flow of information (bandwidth) from the source to the user. Smart cities depend on these networks to operate at efficiencies unheard of a decade ago. Stockholm – a historic city – has become a smart city by investing in a network that connects homes, businesses and government entities. The network does simple things like control traffic, yet provides residents with rapid access to medical advice or to get permits on their home computer. Because the quantities of information being stored, the programs and algorithms needed to have access to this data are becoming more complicated. While the user needs only a tiny fraction of this information and processing ability, IT has gone to the "cloud". The cloud is simply a large server bank dedicated to specific functions (city data, once stored in various department computers, is now in more accessible formats) and available to specific user groups. This, in fact, is the heart of new urban IT development and speeding access to information for urban residents. As cities become more networked, citizens gain more virtual rather than physical access, whereas before they were limited to simply physical access.

10.6 The paradigm shift – the shift to the user

Ease of and ability to gain access to important information has shifted to the user. Job availability and working conditions, available transportation and its cost, housing location, availability and prices, neighborhood characteristics – including ethnicity, and quality of life factors – schools, religious facilities, shops, recreation facilities – are all available with up–to-the-minute detail. Now through innovations in ICT networks in the form of smart devices loaded with mobile apps, network and information access is more dynamic than ever. By consulting their smart devices users can now make more informed travel decisions. Some apps allow users to add real time information that helps other users gain information and make informed decisions.

Smart devices have shifted the paradigm in three very important ways:

- First, they provide the user with real time and updated information. One of the greatest uses is location information – finding one's way. Three quarters of smartphone users access real time location information.[9] In many cities bus riders can find both the location of their bus and the time to arrival at their stop.
- Second, they allow the user to take part in social networks – like Facebook, LinkedIn and Twitter. These networks allow the user to connect with friends, family, and colleagues in real time from anywhere. The shared information can be used to schedule meeting times and locations based on information gained on the internet. For urban access, especially for employment conditions and opportunities, social networks are becoming the "go to" places for information. The old paradigm of researching an employment opportunity through employer provided information (website, printed material, interviews) has been replaced by a new paradigm of using social networks to learn about individual experiences with the employer, from general working conditions to the names of those who would be good or bad bosses.
- Third, they blur the distinction between work, home and leisure. Travel time can be quality time and not only a cost!

Smart devices are rapidly becoming ubiquitous. China is the greatest user and India a close second, with both having more than a billion mobile units. In the US there are more than 350 million mobile units, of which more than half are smartphones.[10] And these phones are used in a variety of ways, to:

- access the internet – more than 50 per cent of users in the US access the internet through their smartphones which are always on, rather than with their laptops or desktops;
- obtain general information – about products, pre-purchase, or locations of specific activities, or even phone numbers;
- purchase products;
- carry out banking. In many EU countries, purchases, no matter how small are carried out by phone. The concept of the mobile wallet is gaining momentum, with players like Google and Citibank leading the way. Going to the bank, once a trip by walking, transit, bike or car is now done from anywhere by phone;
- read and listen to music;
- check transit and train schedules, job openings, the carbon footprint of neighborhoods, and even check in for flights.

Tablets are replacing printed texts (for example operational manuals) to give users up-to-the-minute versions of required data. The author and his colleagues[11] are working with a major transit company to move all of their operating manuals to smart devices and to develop new apps to enable managers and workers to gain instant access to appropriate procedures. By the development of such mobile apps, transit company executives can have the same information simultaneously as managers and workers, making critical decision-making more efficient. nearly three quarters of companies worldwide have created or are looking to create mobile apps to add to their business toolkits; and three quarters of these are seeing increased worker productivity as a result.[12] In the US alone, since the onset of the app market in 2007 about 500,000 "app economy" jobs have been created.[13]

10.7 Who has Smartphones?

Given this paradigm shift, both providers (transportation, employers and enterprises) and users now demand access to real time network information. However, not everyone owns a smartphone or tablet and the ownership in the US varies by age and income (see Figure 10.1). In the US more than 50 per cent of those under the age of 45 have a smartphone, with a 66 per cent penetration in the 25–34 age group. For those over 65, fewer than 2 per cent have smartphones. The data is similar for the other countries shown in Figure 10.1. Finally smartphone users are primarily urban dwellers, with those in the suburbs following while penetration remains low in rural areas.

By income, in the US 75 per cent of those earning more than US$100,000 and 50 per cent of those earning US$35,000–$50,000 have smartphones. Even lower down the income scale, penetration remains high as 31 per cent of those earning less than US$15,000 have one, which illustrates how important having access to information has become.

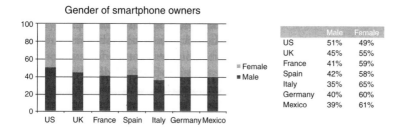

Gender of smartphone owners

	Male	Female
US	51%	49%
UK	45%	55%
France	41%	59%
Spain	42%	58%
Italy	35%	65%
Germany	40%	60%
Mexico	39%	61%

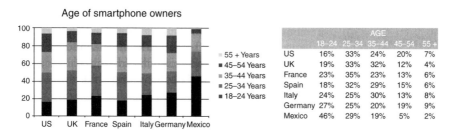

Age of smartphone owners

	AGE				
	18–24	25–34	35–44	45–54	55 +
US	16%	33%	24%	20%	7%
UK	19%	33%	32%	12%	4%
France	23%	35%	23%	13%	6%
Spain	18%	32%	29%	15%	6%
Italy	24%	25%	30%	13%	8%
Germany	27%	25%	20%	19%	9%
Mexico	46%	29%	19%	5%	2%

Figure 10.1 Who uses Smart phones?

10.8 The organizational challenge of technological change

The discussion thus far has treated the issue of technological change in isolation from the challenge of actually introducing change within the institutional structure in which transport is provided. Within the public transport industry, especially in the public sector, it is often difficult to introduce new technology because of fears on the part of line workers, represented by unions and often echoed by middle managers, that the change will threaten their livelihoods which are tied to job descriptions based on existing technologies. As a result many middle managers are instinctually averse to new technologies and become the greatest impediment to significant operating changes and efficiencies. They do this by slowing down efficiency improvements, allowing operating costs to escalate and service to decline. In the experience of the author this is a far more universal challenge than is commonly understood. The lesson here is clear, introducing new IT on the supply side requires bringing middle managers and unions into the discussion early in the change process. There are ways to incentivize cooperation. For example, there is evidence from many enterprises, that middle managers and line workers using smartphones are more productive and more creative; this is an incentive for technology training to gain employment access. In the twenty-first century, transportation is only part of the access variable. Information use is the other part.

Like the internet, smart phones, tablets and apps will not eliminate the need for business trips or other travel; they will simply become more focused and efficient. As more cities become more data driven and smart cities become the norm, vehicles (public and private transport) will need to include systems that monitor and collect performance data. Information is being generated rapidly and for urban access the true value of data is having more publicly-available open-sourced data. Open data can give citizens access to information that they would have otherwise had to access through travel. Additionally, open data is also critical to making "smart" cities smarter. It lets private industry create creative city solutions using public data. However, a challenge is that not all cities are comfortable sharing data. App developers in pioneering cities like San Francisco are showing other cities the benefits of open sourced data with apps like EcoFinder, Routesy and SFPark.org.

10.9 What have we learned?

As late as the 1980s, urban access was primarily about the ability to find meaningful employment and the journey to work. The mode to work – transport – had been the subject of voluminous studies of personal travel and costs, and economic affordability. Thus, by the end of the twentieth century underfunding or under provision of reliable transport such as improved roads and good public transport had increased the costs of access. Transport remains critical for access. Indeed, engineers and technologists have been making great strides to reduce those costs through improved technology. Thus computerized traffic control and signal prioritization, real time variable message signs – now available on car consoles – route guidance, automatic toll collection, and BRT and information technology on computer-driven rapid transit. All are an attempt to improve system throughput, reliability, and enable facility maintenance and efficiency. Benefits – reductions in user costs – outweigh the costs. But the issue for national and local governments is that the initial capital and levels of maintenance funding needed are not available. Eliasson[14] has given an extensive summary of methods to capture the costs, but concludes that the public sector in 2012 still lacks the will to make beneficiaries pay for improved access. The EU and its new demands on financing public transport puts greater weight on beneficiaries paying for access.

As noted, real time information on system characteristics and performance, processed to the needs of specific users, has changed how transport is provided, seen by the potential users and finally used. Looking at all the riders "plugged in" on the subway makes me realize:

- Rapidly changing technologies have made real time information about most urban activities available to more people.
- This real time information is available on smart devices to both provider and user.
- Smart devices also provide access to social networks, generating new communities of users and providers, who can discuss and make instantaneous decisions about the information directly through an app. These riders, plugged in, who once read well folded copies of *The NY Times* are now communicating with their networks about activities and schedules in their lives. And this is based upon information, not only about their activities, but about the transport connections (and costs) they must make to achieve them.
- So powerful is the availability of this information, that a new movement – smart cites and intelligent cities[15] has evolved with the intent of harnessing these new efficiencies to help residents in almost every aspect of the conduct of their daily lives.

It is clear that technological change has its own inertia, and mobility improvements come about through understanding the nature and power of such changes and adapting them to individual use. Two examples stand out:

- The Curitiba bus network. A simple solution evolved to overcome barriers preventing citizens in Curitiba from accessing their jobs. Linear bus lanes, with off-vehicle payment and organization of boarding and disembarking set a new standard for bus transport worldwide that became known as BRT. Signal prioritization enabled the buses to reach maximum speed between stops ensuring fast journeys. Newer BRT systems use GPS and other tracking systems to ensure smooth transfers. All use off-board payment to guarantee rapid boarding. System reliability and the high volumes of riders carried per day (2.2 million in Curitiba) stimulated planners to rethink land uses, engaging more of the underserved populations in greater access to work and social needs.
- Use of cell phones in Indian villages. "In Khairat, a village 45 miles outside Mumbai that is only accessible on foot or by motorcycle, buffalo farmer Mohan Zore makes around US$80 a month but figured he still needed a phone once his village got coverage. He doesn't have to walk into the market to find out the price of buffalo milk, he now just dials friends at the market from his phone".[16] The rapid growth of cell phone users among Southeast Asia's poorest shows the power of this almost ubiquitous technology to change personal opportunity and to save time spent on traveling, and its cost.

The following quotes from a World Bank Report demonstrate the extent of this impact:[17]

- "The number of mobile subscriptions in use worldwide, both pre-paid and post-paid, has grown from fewer than 1 billion in 2000 to over 6 billion now, of which nearly 5 billion are in developing countries".
- "More than 30 billion mobile applications, or 'apps', were downloaded in 2011 (worldwide)".
- "In Palestine, Souktel's JobMatch service is helping young people find jobs. College graduates using the service reported a reduction in the time spent looking for employment from an average of twelve weeks to one week or less, and an increase in wages of up to 50 per cent".

Technological change creates improvements through the use of the technology itself and through the personal, institutional and social changes that it stimulates. In this chapter we have seen urban access gradually change from being transport dependent to information dependent. We will see, below, how the use of this information, through smart devices, social networks and more responsive transport systems is having an impact on travel. The services we need for access, transportation, employment centers are becoming more dependent on information-based operations. The author is involved with a team helping to demonstrate how making available all system information on iPhones and iPads will lead to the NY MTA becoming more productive, efficient and customer responsive. With each technological development introduced by the MTA such as Metrocards, count down clocks, etc.) it has gained substantial riders.[18]

New IT systems are facilitating more sophisticated fare collection systems that bring more efficiencies and cost savings to users and providers. London's Oyster card system was set up in 2003 as a reusable card system that works on the bus, Tube, tram, DLR, London Overground and most National Rail services in London. In 2004 Seoul launched T-money, a smartcard that can be used to pay for bus, subway and some taxi fares. They are even accepted in other businesses. Both systems integrate multiple public transportation providers and offer reduced fares from the price of journeys paid for individually per trip or provider. However, whereas the London system is solely an account-linked payment service (ALPS), eight Korean banks have also given the Seoul system the ability to directly use their credit cards as T-Money.

Clearly, the improvement of one factor of access, reliability, has had a great impact on attracting system users. Such changes have already swept across European and Asian Transit systems – London, Hong Kong, Shanghai all come to mind. The impact of these technologies is to induce new riders, yet reduce the costs of attracting each rider. Technological changes are forcing transit systems to rethink capital plans. "Can we gain capacity without adding tracks and vehicles?"

One additional impact of information modernization is the creation of new jobs and the subsequent search for workers with new skills. Training for such skills can be done remotely on computers or even smartphones – making training a more democratic process. The transit industry in the US is coming to grips with the problem of identifying and gaining a future workforce cognizant of new and emerging technologies, while trying to address what to do with obsolescent skills with workforce retraining initiatives.

10.10 Paying for all of this

Embracing technology does not come free. In the long run new technology savings are apparent and provide new revenue generating financing opportunities. For instance, they will reduce operating costs and attract new riders that will increase fare revenues and economies of scale. They will also impact organizational structures in transit agencies; and changes in core business models can result in increased savings and revenues. New technologies can also bring about increased sustainability that in itself induces new savings. Technology will also give way to new payment tools, translating into increased sales and subsequently tax revenues from surrounding businesses that can go towards paying for new information infrastructure. New technology companies are very entrepreneurial and can bring new investments and cost-sharing opportunities to traditional transportation providers. For instance, in Madrid, telecom providers partnered with Metro Madrid to bring cell phone and WiFi access to transit riders. Metro Madrid paid only part of the infrastructure investments which allowed telecom providers to provide uninterrupted service to customers riding the metro. The London Underground is also experimenting with this.

On another front in many cities in developing countries, there is a burgeoning trend of carbon finance being used to fund public transportation development. Followed by the success of Mexico City to partially fund Metrobus in 2005 with carbon credits, 18 other transit agencies in developing countries are currently pursuing carbon finance structures to build BRT systems.[19] These new systems require less polluting buses to optimize carbon reduction returns. Investments in these new, more sustainable technologies will also translate into operating cost savings.

10.11 The bottom line

Who pays for the investment in transport infrastructure remains the key question. In Asia, the social benefits of providing improved access to increasingly mobile workers has led governments to eschew neoliberal policies and believe that the public should be the key provider of capital of the first instance. Certainly China has seen a correlation between public investment in infrastructure and robust economic growth. But this has not been the case in the West. The nature of the investment needed is made more complex by the personal use of information technology – where both public and private investments continue with great speed. The public is aware that this new duality – information and the sustained need for access and mobility are greatly intertwined – as they reach for their smart gadgets to gain information about a particular topic or to check on optimal travel options given their location and time. Yet they perceive transport investments as part of the old paradigm and it is difficult, politically, to generate informed discussion about the wider beneficiaries paying for such investments. This is the dilemma of providing transportation in the twenty-first century.

Acknowledgements

Claudia P. Huerta, MSUP, a brilliant urban planner, blogger and iPhone user provided valuable assistance in data collection and assessment, editorial comments and a unique generational perspective for this paper. Christian Wolmar, Måns Lönnroth and Elliott Sclar provided much guidance, focus and thought to the paper. I thank them one and all. I also thank the Volvo Research and Education Foundations for the opportunity to put these ideas to paper. Any errors of fact or thought – as always – remain the property of the author.

Notes

1   The white paper was published as R. Paaswell, "Problems of the Carless in the US and UK", *Transportation* 2(4): 1973.
2   J.L. Schofer and M. Wachs, "Job Accessibility For The Unemployed: An Analysis Of Public Transportation In Chicago", Chicago Committee for Economic and Cultural Development (March 1972).
3   John F. Kain, "Housing Segregation, Negro Employment, and Metropolitan Decentralization", in *Quarterly Journal of Economics*, May 1968, 82(2): 175–97.
4   The wide availability of computers made scheduling and managing complex paratransit services possible and accessible to a growing urban population – although at a significant price per trip.
5   This is occurring through a partnership of the University of Michigan and the USDOT.
6   See Rosario Macário, "Access as a Social Good and as an Economic Good", a paper prepared for the 2012 Volvo Bellagio Workshop for a comprehensive discussion of Accessibility and Access addressing personal movement.
7   Thetransitwire.com, 13 September, 2012.
8   Claudia Huerta, "Carbon Credits Give Metrobus a Competive Edge", Columbia University GSAPP, December 2011.
9   Pew Internet and American Life project: Smartphone Ownership 2012, www.pewinternet.org
10 Pew, Ibid.
11 From the University Transportation Research Center, and Silver Lining.
12 Symantec, "State of Mobility Survey," Global Findings 2012.
13 Dr Michael Mandel, "Where the Jobs are: The App Economy". Tech Net, February 2012: http://www.technet.org.

14 Jonas Elliason, "Opportunities for Transport Financing through new Technologies", a paper presented at the VREF Bellagio Workshop, May 2012.
15 A brilliant example can be seen on www.living-planit.com: a totally new city for 250,000 being constructed in Portugal – a sustainable city that "runs itself".
16 Eric Bellman, WSJ.com.
17 The World Bank, News and Views, "Information and Communications for Development 2012: Maximizing Mobile", July 2012.
18 The introduction of Metrocards – electronic payment using stored value, allowing ease of transfer, was followed by an increase of one million trips per day.
19 Huerta, Ibid.

Chapter 11

Conclusions

The end of the paradigm

Elliott D. Sclar and Måns Lönnroth

11.1 Introduction

The present urban transport paradigm is no longer working. Its distinguishing feature is the belief that urban access is enhanced through increased travel speed. This paradigm emerged as a result of a unique set of circumstances in North America and Western Europe in the decades after World War II. For at least the next half-century urban transport planners presumed that these circumstances were universal. However, as experience has shown the beneficial link between speed and access is only true sometimes and only in some places. It is not a universal truth.

The belief underlying the paradigm is that increased urban travel speed invariably translates into diminished travel time and that in turn is presumed to yield more quality time for the productive and cultural activities that make urban life desirable. In terms of travel mode this powerful paradigmatic link between speed and access was explicitly built on an urban vision in which the private automobile took precedence over public transport alternatives. Consistent with this paradigmatic belief and its attendant urban vision, the goal of transport infrastructure investments in the second half of the twentieth century focused on spatially transforming cities to accommodate the space consuming needs of cars. The essential urban transport story everywhere was about the design and redesign of new and existing urban street networks to accommodate the speed and parking needs of automobiles. The story also involved tearing up large segments of older cities for expansions of limited access highways and building newer cities around such ring and radial routes. In all these undertakings the goal remained the same: more capacity to accommodate the needs for moving expanding numbers of automobiles more quickly into, out of and around burgeoning metropolitan areas. It might all have started in North America and Western Europe but by the 1970s this paradigm and vision had become the standard for cities everywhere. Few questioned the wisdom of equating speed with urban access.

If measured only in terms of the sheer quantity of vehicles that now ply the streets and highways of the world's metropolises it would be reasonable to conclude that the paradigm and the ensuing policy implementation has been a huge success. In the most extreme case, the United States, the number of registered vehicles exceeds the population of licensed drivers. And yet despite this seeming plethora of vehicular mobility and an extensive network of freeways, toll ways, interfaced with modern traffic engineered city streets even more urban residents are finding it increasingly difficult to go anywhere. The paradox is of global proportions: at a time when the world's urban population seemingly has the greatest means of mobility in human history it is also facing a worsening situation with regard to its ability to access even the most mundane features of urban life. The casualty list is long. Even for those in the middle classes who own or have easy access to automobiles, the group for whom the paradigm and policy is supposed to work best, they find themselves spending large amount of time in ever longer queues of congested traffic. For this group at least travel remains doable if increasingly difficult. The vast majority of others are not as fortunate. These others include the urban working classes and the poor who comprise more than three-quarters of the world's urban population that cannot afford the costs of auto–based mobility, the large and growing population of the elderly, especially in the global north who are unable to drive because of infirmities, and the rising youthful population of the global south not yet able to drive because of either age, income or both.[1]

To fully appreciate the implications of this situation it is necessary to put these observations into a dynamic context. In 2010, according to the Population Reference Bureau, the world population was estimated at approximately 6.9 billion people.[2] In that year the United Nations estimated the world's urban population to be about 3.6 billion.[3] By 2050 when the Population Reference Bureau forecasts the global population to be approximately 9.5 billion,[4] the United Nations forecasts the urban population to be 6.3 billion.[5] Thus the urban population is more or less expected to double in absolute terms by 2050. The conclusion is simple: the present urban transport paradigm, born of a unique set of circumstances after World War II, will cease to be a driver of global human progress. Instead, if urban access is permitted to dissolve in a morass of immobility the productivity and cultural promises of urban life will decline and decline.

Public transport, which could provide some relief, does not exist in many places. Where it does exist given its present state, its help is most often limited. Only in a few cities is the public transport of a scale and a quality to provide a real alternative for a rich and varied urban life. The reasons for this state of affairs are many; public transport is often inadequate since it does not run frequently and/or reliably enough, or it is too expensive or it does not go where travelers wish to be. The present configuration of urban land use and transport is not up to the access challenges that twenty-first century urbanization is imposing. The old paradigm has to go.

What were the circumstances that shaped this paradigm? It evolved out of the condition of the cities of Western Europe and North America in the immediate aftermath of World War II. Oil was inexpensive; clean water was plentiful, and land around central cities was reasonably priced and under-utilized. Together these conditions provided fertile grounds for conceiving automobile-based mobility as the way to meet the challenge of accommo-dating urbanization. Those years were also a time when real household income was increasing in those cities. Hence increasing numbers of people saw themselves as belonging to a growing middle class. The automobile held out the promise of reliable door-to-door convenience that the bus or rail-based public transport could not provide. Wherever roads and high-ways were placed this expanded middle class could make a home for itself and enjoy the benefits of suburban life.

So suburban land development drove transport planning and transport planning assumed that the automobile was the future and mass transport the past. With the wisdom of hindsight it is reasonable to say that the para-digm as it took actual physical form became, de facto, a paradigm of and for urban sprawl. While the future is never clear, what is certain from past experience is that the model of the past half-century is wrong for a global future in which the urban population will double during the next forty years.

Developing a new paradigm has to start with the appreciation of how deeply embedded the present urban sprawl paradigm is in the policy and planning process. A good illustration of this deep embeddedness is found in the routine conceptualizations of cost–benefit analysis (CBA) when applied to urban transport. In the abstract CBA is a rather straightforward idea. It states that in making a major infrastructure investment decision both the long- and short-term costs and benefits of the alternatives should be weighed. The alternative in which the benefits exceed the costs the most should be pursued. In practice the outcome of this exercise depends entirely on which alternatives are presented and how their benefits and costs are first defined and then measured. In the case of transport infrastructure construction the paradigmatic assumption that speed equates to timesaving is a firm and unquestioned given. In practice this translates into a benefit cost calculus in which between 70 and 80 per cent of the calculated bene-fits are estimated as time saving valued at a monetary cost. This is true even as the CBA studies which government ministries require to help politically justify large and costly infrastructure projects become ever more method-ologically sophisticated. These studies estimate the discounted present monetized value of the time saved relative to the discounted present mone-tized project cost. If the value of the saved travel time plus other ancillary benefits exceeds costs, the project can proceed. However even within its own terms it is not clear that all timesavings are equal.

If 2 million drivers were projected to each save one minute a day and their time was valued at €100 per hour or €1.67 per minute the daily savings on 2 million minutes would equal €3.34 million per day, or, assuming a 240 day work year, €802 million per year on the infrastructure investment being evaluated. For simplicity sake let us assume no price inflation, a zero discount rate and a 25 year life span for the project, we have a project that on paper would yield a cumulative benefit to commuters in time saved equal to €20.0 billion. If that lifetime benefit exceeded the lifetime cost of the project it could be implemented. If an alternative project benefited 200,000 rail commuters, a tenth the number, but each saved 10 minutes the math on benefits would work out just the same. Assume further for simplicity's sake that the project costs were identical. Even though there is a substantial socially significant qualitative difference on a one-hour daily commute in which one minute is saved or one in which ten minutes are saved the former would be more politically appealing than the latter. In formal CBA terms all minutes are equal. Thus while the numeric result is identical, the reality is that functionally a single minute saving is meaningless to the traveler. By extension it is also functionally meaningless for the larger society. The savings for the smaller number of travelers would be meaningful individually and socially. Despite this, the political logic that flows from treating all minutes equally is such that given a choice between the two projects politicians tend to be drawn, like moths to a flame, to favor the first over the second. It is the powerful embedded nature of this type of thinking about speed and time that keeps societies on a path of constructing ever more urban mobility, when meaningful access is truly what is called for. While cost–benefit studies alone never close the deal on a project, the example nicely illustrates the type of conflation of paradigm, politics and planning methods that must be addressed if the path dependency along which urban transport planning is now proceeding is to be changed.

Perhaps more fundamentally, the data on travel time budgets that have been carefully measured for four decades or more demonstrate virtually no change in the time allocated to travel, about one hour per day. The implication of these travel time budgets for CBA is that more travel time functionally translates not into more time for other activities of daily living but more distant commutes for urban residents.

11.2 Turning the page on sprawl

Turning the page on the present sprawl paradigm requires turning the page on the analytic methodologies that sustain this paradigm. But criticizing the existing theory and methods is not enough. The critique by itself can never do more than damage its intellectual standing. Only a new paradigm – a new theory of urban access – can move society from the old and dysfunctional path to a new one. The new paradigm, if it is to take hold, must plausibly ameliorate the problems not addressed by the older one and hold out the promise of a better general all around outcome. Articulating parameters of, and demonstrating the potential for an improved approach is the more difficult part of the challenge. Although the task is a large one intellectually, it is both reasonable and possible to accomplish. The papers in this volume should be seen as the beginning of the dialogue out of which a new urban transport paradigm can emerge.

The new paradigm will need to foster cities that are socially inclusive, environmentally sustainable and efficient in the deployment of resources for mobility. With regard to the first, cities work best when everyone has sufficient access. In a world that needs to both mitigate the sources of climate change as well as adapt to climate change, creating urban access with a lower carbon footprint is a given. In addition cities, in physical terms, can no longer be voracious users of land and fresh water but must husband the natural resources. Urban access must address the need to conserve natural resources. In terms of an urban transport paradigm access, and not mobility, must be the policy target and will have to be achieved through the combination of a wise use of land and mobility. These will range from design density and walking through to bicycling, more and better public transport options, integrated urban freight and there will still be places where only the automobile is the solution.

The new paradigm will require new principles of governance as well as financing, since the current methods of governance and finance are reflective of and accommodate the existing paradigm. In terms of moving from the present to the future four themes emerged from the papers presented in this volume. Each will require much thought, dialogue and research if a new paradigmatic consensus is to emerge.

11.2.1 Measuring access and estimating its impact

The old management adage states that you can't manage what you can't measure. One of the most powerful and intellectually seductive features of mobility as a policy target is the ease with which it can be quantified. Mobility can be measured in units of passengers carried, distance covered, volume of goods hauled, units of energy expended, cost per unit of distance, etc. If urban access is to become the policy target, a number of complex questions arise: How should it be defined? How is it to be measured? How to value it? How is its cost to be estimated? The chapters in the volume by Fol and Gallez (Chapter 3) Macário (Chapter 4) demonstrate the dimensions of challenges in developing simple and yet meaningful measures of access.

Access has both a physical and a social dimension. The travel time between any two points via alternative travel modes can be measured. But this will not be enough. The friction of distance is but one qualitative aspect of access. Slum dwellers often live in walking distance of the central business district and in purely physical terms have easy time-based access to the urban core. But as Fol and Gallez make clear proximity in space is not the same thing as access in social terms. They argue that the social characteristics of space and of individuals, along with the provision of urban amenities in a given urban environment, are essential elements in the complex notion of urban access. Macário points out that there has been an overemphasis on the economic costs of access and not on the larger social utility. Put another way: one should think of access much as one thinks of water, power and sanitation as public utilities. One element of such thinking requires developing a paradigm that requires measuring and valuing access across all the residents and stakeholders of specific urban places. Such measurement and valuation is the starting point for understanding what is gained and lost in critical land use and transport policy and planning decisions.

11.2.2 The re-organization of urban transport

Macário raises the issue of thinking about all of the urban transport system as a single public utility regulated much as other natural monopoly types of public services are regulated. To the extent that access by all means (co-location and/or mobility via all modes) is the goal there needs to be a clear vision that treats urban transport in all forms as a complete system and organizes it accordingly. It is important to bear in mind that urban travel almost always involves walking plus travel that requires transferring between modes along the way. In the present paradigm, the different modes of urban transport are organized in separate silos, reflecting the silos of financial flows that define these modes, and the ways in which they govern their market through various combinations of public regulation, private cartels and competition for customers. The exact combination of these differs greatly from place to place but the elements are always the same. Achieving integration across silos in specific places will depend upon the initial conditions of these elements. New technologies such as transponders and smart cards open up the possibilities for thinking about integrative organization in new ways. Chapter 10 by Paaswell addresses the potential of new technologies to capture these advantages.

11.2.3 The financing of urban access

Organization is never separate from finance. The chapters by Eliasson (Chapter 5), Viegas (Chapter 6), and Salvucci (Chapter 9) all address various aspects of this question. Eliasson lays out the problems of time, place and service quality in creating a realistic pricing system for urban transport. Viegas takes the challenge to the next level in his discussion of the issues involved in creating what he calls solid and stable financing frameworks for urban mobility. Salvucci then points us to the difficulties of integrating new financial models into the political context of governance in which they must inevitably operate.

What these chapters make clear is that while the theoretical elements of how integrative financing are often quite clear cut, the complexities of practical applications also need to be addressed. Concepts that are theoretically clear are not necessarily administratively workable given the realities of culture and politics in different places. For a new paradigm to emerge this connection between theory and practice has to be clearly defined and articulated. What works in one place may not in another. There will need to be more than one model of finance. On the other hand the number need not be infinite. It would seem that three or four general templates might emerge within the context of the new paradigm.

11.2.4 The institutional design and governance of access

Historically land use and transport have been governed separately from one another. The typical form of this governance has been that land use is governed as a local matter and transport is either addressed regionally or nationally. In Chapter 8, Salvucci addresses the challenge of an institutional context that can integrate these two functionally connected yet administratively separated domains that govern access. There has been some integration of these in some places but the challenge of tying this to the goal of enhanced urban access has not yet been accomplished. In Chapter 7 of this volume, Vasconcellos, focusing on the challenge of formal and informal transport in low- and middle-income countries addresses this question in part through addressing the challenge of transforming the informal transport that is typically the dominant characteristic in these places into a more formal system of public transport.

11.3 Towards a new paradigm

Shifting from a paradigm rooted in mobility maximization to one rooted in socially inclusive access has to expand the range of possible courses of action. Mobility is only one way to enhance access. The four themes above illustrate important dimensions that come into play as we redefine the policy goal away from an exclusive focus on mobility to a broader social focus on access. Dimensions beyond these may emerge, as the effort proceeds, but these suggest the direction in which we will be moving as we go from a static and mechanistic view of mobility to a dynamic and interactive understanding of the contribution of access to the quality of urban life.

Using the perspective of cost–benefit analysis once more as an illustration, one could say that analytic attention should shift from an assessment of mobility options assuming that all else remains constant to dynamically understanding, assessing and ultimately managing the processes through which different access options are generated and the ways that they change the possibilities for mobility and land use. Such a shift of focus invariably broadens options for alternative courses of action. Once that occurs, it is the connections among organizations, finance and governance that increasingly become the central concern for analysis and policy rather than the individual elements in isolation from one another. With that, new possibilities for the academic study of urban transport expand beyond the domains that traditionally dominated, transport planning and transport economics, to a wider group of social scientists including urban sociologists, urban historians, urban political scientists and public administration and management scholars. This will be reflective of the broader and deeper understanding of the challenges of creating environmentally and socially equitable urban access that a doubling of the world's urban population urgently requires.

Notes

1   To mitigate these economic barriers increasing numbers of urban residents are turning to motorized two wheel modes (motorcycles and motorbikes). But this is at best a compromise with a bad situation and not a substantial improvement in the condition of urban life.
2   www.prb.org/pdf10/10wpds_eng.pdf (accessed 20 July 2013).
3   *World Urbanization Prospects, the 2011 Revision*, http://esa.un.org/unup/ (accessed 20 July 2013).
4   www.prb.org/pdf10/10wpds_eng.pdf (accessed 20 July 2013).
5   *World Urbanization Prospects, the 2011 Revision*, http://esa.un.org/unup/ (accessed 20 July 2013).

Index